About Island Press

Island Press is the only nonprofit organization in the United States whose principal purpose is the publication of books on environmental issues and natural resource management. We provide solutions-oriented information to professionals, public officials, business and community leaders, and concerned citizens who are shaping responses to environmental problems.

In 2000, Island Press celebrates its sixteenth anniversary as the leading provider of timely and practical books that take a multidisciplinary approach to critical environmental concerns. Our growing list of titles reflects our commitment to bringing the best of an expanding body of literature to the environmental community throughout North America and the world.

Support for Island Press is provided by The Jenifer Altman Foundation, The Bullitt Foundation, The Mary Flagler Cary Charitable Trust, The Nathan Cummings Foundation, The Geraldine R. Dodge Foundation, The Charles Engelhard Foundation, The Ford Foundation, The German Marshall Fund of the United States, The George Gund Foundation, The Vira I. Heinz Endowment, The William and Flora Hewlett Foundation, The W. Alton Jones Foundation, The John D. and Catherine T. MacArthur Foundation, The Andrew W. Mellon Foundation, The Charles Stewart Mott Foundation, The Curtis and Edith Munson Foundation, The National Fish and Wildlife Foundation, The New-Land Foundation, The Oak Foundation, The Overbrook Foundation, The David and Lucile Packard Foundation, The Pew Charitable Trusts, The Rockefeller Brothers Fund, Rockefeller Financial Services, The Winslow Foundation, and individual donors.

PARTNERSHIPS
IN COMMUNITIES

PARTNERSHIPS IN COMMUNITIES

REWEAVING THE FABRIC OF RURAL AMERICA

JEAN RICHARDSON

ISLAND PRESS

Washington, D.C. • Covelo, California

Library of Congress Cataloging-in-Publication Data
Richardson, Jean 1943–
   Partnerships in communities : reweaving the fabric of rural
America / Jean Richardson.
      p.   cm.
Includes bibliographical references and index.
   ISBN 1–55963–736–6 (acid-free)
   1. Rural development—United States.   2. Community
development—United States.   I. Title.
HN46.C6 R53   2000
307.1'412'0973—dc21   00–008286
      .   CIP

Printed on recycled, acid-free paper

Printed in Canada
10 9 8 7 6 5 4 3 2 1

To the memory of my twin brother,
Philip Richardson (1943–1997) of Northumberland, England,
who, throughout his life, served his rural community well
and who was always ready to help anyone in need.

Contents

Foreword

The reality of rural America is too often shrouded in popular myth. On one hand, rural people are seen as self-sufficient and hardworking, competent, family-centered, patriotic, moral, and quintessentially American. Rural and small-town life in this view is presented as idyllic, simple, elemental, grounded, and wholesome. A counterview is emerging as well: one that sees rural America as peopled by paranoid, xenophobic, depraved, backwoods gun enthusiasts ready to commit mayhem and havoc against anyone unlike them and against the very institutions of wider society and culture. We are left to ponder a landscape peopled by John Boy Walton and sheriff Andy of *Mayberry R.F.D.* on the one hand and the militias and mountain men of *Deliverance* on the other.

Both myths are distortions, of course, and mask the reality that rural America is diverse, changing, multifaceted, and complex. There is nothing "simple" about the purported simplicity of rural life in contemporary America.

The basic facts about rural America suggest substantial reason to be concerned for the future of rural people and rural places in this country. Rural people are far more likely to be poor, less educated, and less serviced by government and private organizations than are their urban or suburban counterparts. They have higher rates of illiteracy, are more likely to live in poor-quality housing, have less access to decent educational, social, nutritional, and health services, and have an ever-narrowing range of economic opportunities compared to other Americans. In other words, the real rural America is one facing a multitude of challenges, not the least of which is indifference from the rest of the country. Freed of our myths, this is the rural America that emerges from the vast countryside of the nation.

How best to respond? There is no single or simple answer to this question. Rural areas require committed, persistent, and sustained investment. Our national attention span seems to militate against a thorough, long-term strategy of rural development. But chronic problems will not be alleviated overnight, and we seem indifferent at best to the problems and issues of rural areas and small towns. Lucky are those communities that have come to realize this and now depend less on others and more on themselves. The stories of rural development success in the United States are, in fact, growing, and common to almost all of these are the traits and characteristics of local initiative, local leadership, local investment, and local will and vision. The EPIC (Environmental Programs/Partnerships in Communities) project of Vermont, under the leadership of Jean Richardson, is one example of this model and constitutes a genuine prototype of what we mean when we use the phrase "sustainable rural development."

This is a story with themes and lessons that resonate throughout the world. It is not that a specific EPIC project can or should be replicated elsewhere. Rather, it is that the principles and approaches of EPIC—humility; respect; decency; an appreciation for scale; neighborliness; a focus upon local people; the empowerment and inclusion of women, the young, and the elderly; and a wedding between civic culture and environmental stewardship—that travel well and have wide applicability. These principles are confirmed by the case studies and stories from across the United States that Jean Richardson has included in this timely book. It captures stories that are wholly local and universal at one and the same time. It should be read by those intent on learning which approaches might work in small towns and rural areas throughout America.

This would not be an honest foreword to an important book if I did not tell you that I have known and admired Jean Richardson for better than twenty years as a person brimming with ideas and with the energy and passion to make a difference. *Partnerships in Communities: Reweaving the Fabric of Rural America,* provides much to consider within its pages. Take your time with it, puzzle through its many insights, consider what has worked and what has not, and then, get on with it!

MARK B. LAPPING
Provost and Vice President for Academic Affairs
University of Southern Maine

Preface

Most of the United States is *rural*. This is the working landscape that provides us with food and natural resources for both consumption and conservation. Few Americans live permanently in rural areas. Ours is an urban society, and despite the fact that the concept of rurality defies precise definition, the complex task of understanding rural America is of great importance for us all, for today and for future generations. Although there is much evidence that all is not well in our rural regions—the urban hinterlands—there are many rural communities that have shown a remarkable renaissance in the last few years. These communities, which are actively addressing the changes in land use and society around them, give us hope for the future. I try to capture in this book some of those stories—stories of trial and error. Much of the information, ideas, lessons learned, and mistakes made that are discussed in this book have been derived from internal reports, unpublished research and activities, and interviews and experience and then set in the context of literature (both scholarly and popular) from a wide diversity of disciplines.

I seek to provide an integrated and relatively comprehensive overview of sustainable rural community development and some detailed case studies. I also include assessments of community-based rural development projects, which convey a more thorough, in-depth understanding of what is *really* taking place in rural America, where people struggle to earn adequate livelihoods while at the same time maintaining viable communities and protecting the environment.

These examples are templates that can be transferred, at least in part, from one community to another, or from one region to another. I have been highly selective in presenting case studies, providing a few in detail as well as the opinions asnd experiences of individuals involved in community-based rural development projects in their own words. The context for this work includes concepts and data from the biological and social sciences, law and planning, history and human behavior, agriculture, and economics.

Trained in the sciences and also in law, I am an interdisciplinary thinker. I live and have been active in rural areas in various parts of the world for well over a half a century. As a biogeographer, I see the world as communities of plants and animals living on amazing substrates of soils and bedrock geology. As a person trained in law, I see the statutory and regulatory system of rules that we use at many levels to constrain personal action, modify property rights, and control use of natural resources. As a sheep farmer, I have learned to apply ecology to farming. As a professor and a mother, I was disappointed to find how little was taught in elementary and high schools about agriculture and rural life. I also learned that, with the exception of a few notable faculty members, land grant universities do not typically work with communities in ways that are empowering to community members.

It took time and a lot of firsthand experience to realize that sustainable rural community development takes place only after we stop handling each crisis separately and instead try to understand more about the whole of the community as a system within broader interconnected contexts. Such development means that we need to spend more time working on goals common to many community members.

In 1989, as a professor of environmental studies at the University of Vermont, I asked the W.K. Kellogg Foundation to help rural Vermont develop a more comprehensive, and potentially more sustainable, integrated approach to rural development. After I persuaded the Kellogg Board that Vermont has many problems common to other parts of rural America, it provided generous assistance for this effort. (Although the project was funded for only three short years, we have been able to stretch the funding to the present.) Thus, from 1992 until now, I have directed a project called EPIC (Environmental Programs/Partnerships in Communities) to work with rural communities to achieve sustainable rural development. One outcome of this work was an enormous amount of carefully collected data, information, and project activities, which I have added to the experiences I've accumulated over the last several decades.

Scope of This Book

Innovation and the EPIC model of rural development form a theme in this book and are introduced in Chapter Two. This is not to suggest that there is one perfect rural development model that will provide simple-to-transfer, do-it-yourself sets of ideas that will solve all rural development problems. Each region of North America has its own distinctive culture, and the model presented here must be adapted locally to craft distinctive, community-based, regional models.

Chapter Three discusses assessment and evaluation methods as learning tools fundamental to sustainable rural development and to the necessary sharing of lessons learned, so that communities do not spend time and money re-inventing the wheel or making the same mistakes again. Various approaches to community leadership development are presented in Chapter Four, including programs for community leadership, forestry leadership, urban stewardship, youth in leadership, and conservation leadership. Chapter Five provides examples of seed grants, rural marketing, and entrepreneurship.

Chapter Six addresses the spread of innovation in rural agricultural communities, with special reference to intensive grazing as one in-depth example, and provides an analysis of the changing agricultural, ecological, and social fabric, presenting a new way to view the land and its resources. The significant role that the media, publications, and celebrations can play in maximizing community successes are discussed in Chapter Seven. Chapter Eight presents several integrated projects in rural towns across America that shed light on what made community renaissance in the late 1990s work in some situations and not in others. Chapter Nine addresses transferability of ideas and lessons learned and reassesses key principles of sustainable rural community development.

Three appendices provide sample templates for community use or educational purposes, organizational resources, and names of potential funding sources.

The goal of this book is not to describe and list all the problems in rural America but rather to identify successful activities, models, programs, projects, and the like from specific towns and villages across America, and to evaluate and share lessons learned in the hope that many other communities can benefit by adapting some of these activities to the needs of their own local, rural communities. The case studies permit an in-depth understanding of key principles of rural community development and how they can be applied by others.

For example, a small group of women in the rural town of Fairfield, Vermont, faced with the prospect of the old village school being turned into a business that would occupy the only open public space in the village center, instead established a community center that offers a variety of programs and even boasts its own health clinic. The rural village and adjacent communities have quietly been transformed, and since then many citizens, especially women, youth, and seniors, have stepped forward to become leaders in their communities.

As in the community of Fairfield, rural citizens across the United States are learning to actively work to revitalize their own communities and to develop a sustainable way of life for themselves and for future generations. Lessons from the EPIC experience and similar programs in communities across the United States are the focus of this book and are presented in the context of the social, cultural, economic, and environmental conditions dominating rural America today.

My hope is that this book will be useful to community leaders and others who work in rural development, including those who teach and research these subjects. I look forward to hearing from those of you living and working in rural communities, and I thank everyone who has participated in EPIC. I hope that this book will inspire you in your endeavors on behalf of rural communities. Read on!

JEAN RICHARDSON
North Ferrisburgh, Vermont
October 1999

Acknowledgments

The author gratefully acknowledges the following people: The over 1,000 citizens in the state of Vermont, in other parts of New England, and in New York State who took an active part in the original EPIC project, and all those who have been involved in follow-up discussions to help us all learn lessons that we can share with others in rural America; and the EPIC team leaders and staff from the university and the community who worked with the collaborative EPIC team at some point during the five-year period from 1992 to 1997. These include Susan Bean, Susan Clark, Jane Difley, Peg Elmer, Sarah Flack, Lois Frey, Dave Hoke, Chester Liebs, Lisa McCrory, Bill Murphy, Christine Negra, Colette Paul, Virgina Rasch, Carl Reidel, Ron Savitt, Abdon Schmidt, Fred Schmidt, Joshua Silman, Kristin Sonnerup, Barry Stryker, Pauline Sullivan, Ashley Weld, Jon Winsten, Michelle Witten, Ivy Zeller, community organizations such as the Vermont Natural Resources Council (VNRC), the Vermont Land Trust, and Deb Brighton (for her external evaluation work).

Lois Frey, a dedicated extension specialist, deserves special mention for her leadership work and for her assistance with evaluation. Chapter Four includes her research findings and outreach work, and Appendix A1 contains her foundation template materials on forestry leadership. Lois also reviewed and commented on parts of this draft manuscript. In Chapter Five, the rural entrepreneurship section draws on the research and outreach work of Ron Savitt, School of Business, and Pauline Sullivan, Department of Community Development and Applied Economics, University of Vermont. Chapter Six draws on the collaborative research of Bill Murphy, Department of Plant and Soil Science, University of Vermont; on the early innovative ideas on pasture management of Doug Flack, farmer-ecologist; and especially on the generosity of the following farm families whose farms became demonstration farms for other farmers, and from whom the author learned much about farm life and rural communities: Barbara and Richard Albertini; Alice and Larry Allen; Tim Barrows; Bud and Carol Barup; Geoffrey Bentley; Scott Birch; Sonny and Carolyn Boomhower; Tom and Ann Brazier; Andy Brouillette; Mark Brouillette; Sarah and Ed Burger; Mark and Karen Burrill; John Butler; Emily Carlson and Richard Norris; David and Melanie Carmichael; Jon and Tammy Carpenter; Rupert Chamberlain; Ed and Celine Champine; Ben Churchill; John and Judy Clark; Patrick Cochran; Gerry Coleman; Robert and Georgia Compagna; Everett, Linda, and Connie Corey; Barbara and Bill Corwin; Luc and Amy Dandurand; Gary Davis; Paul Delabruere; Richard Delfavero; Neal Doane; Carol Dunsmore; Mike Eastman; Zylpha and Randall Eastman; Jerry Elzinga; Nancy Everhart and Peter Young; Sharon Faylor; Marc Esterbrook; Bob Fitzsimmons; John Ferland; Craig and Theresa Fisk; Peter Flint; Henry, Sally, and Travis Forgues; Catlin Fox and Annie Claghorn; Seth Gardner and Michelle Biron; Paul Gingue; Dennis Guillemette; Mike and Tammy Hanson; Pat Hayes; Jon and Kim Hescock; Peggy Hews and Larry Scott; Ron and Robin Hibbard; Allen Hitchcock; Larry Holmes; Brian and Vicki Houghton; David Howrigan; Steven and Trudy Hurd; Vernon Hurd; Frank Hutchins; Robin Jackman; David Jackson; Ron Jerry; Steve Jones; Steve Judge and Heath Noble; Philip and Christine Kaiser; Ed Kearney; Charlie Keeler; Larry Kempton; Jack and Ann Lazor; Bob Light; Norman Lusier; David and Barb Machell; Fred Magdoff; Ed and Carol Mahoney; Marjorie Major; Chris Marcotte; James Maroner and Suki Fredricks; Don Maynard and Doug Watkin; Edward Melby; Art Menut; Marcel Moreau; Ron Paradis; John Pease; Wayne Pecor; Russ Persons; Caleb Pitkin; Dave Pullman; Janine Putman; Frank and Pam Riley; John Roberts; Ken and Beverly Robinson; Charlie and Dave Rooney; Pete and Marcia Roorda; Mark and Sarah Russell; Jon and Beverly Rutter; Paul Seiler; David Shepherd; Ruth Shepherd and Ken Polman; Jeff Sibley; Brian and Kathy Somers; Hubert Spaulding; Linda Stanley; Susan and Gary Storrs; Ronnie Sweet; Joe Tisbert; Bob Titus; Bill and Beth Treadwell; Chris Wagner and John Jeleniewski; Alex Webb; Dan Wentworth; Owen Whitcomb; Marian White; Ted Yandow; Carole and Tom Younkman.

Photo credits: Genevieve Russell, of Charlottesville, Virginia: Photos

1.7, 1.8, 2.2, and 6.5. Carl Reidel of North Ferrisburgh, Vermont: Photos 1.9, 1.10, 1.11, 1.12, 4.1, 4.2, 4.3, 5.1, 5.2, 7.4, and 7.5. The W.K. Kellogg Foundation, Battle Creek, Michigan: Photo 1.8. *The St. Albans Messenger,* St. Albans, Vermont: Photo 8.3.

Susan Clark, graduate student (1992–96) and coordinator of EPIC seed grants, played a key leadership role in managing and evaluating the seed grants, in media coverage, and in organizing celebrations (Susan is famous for her celebrations!) discussed in Chapters Five and Seven. A special word of thanks to Emerson Lynn, editor of the *The St. Albans Messenger,* who made sure that the good news stories were well covered in his paper for all to see and learn.

I lived for many years in the town of Fairfield, population about 1,600, one of the case-study towns discussed in Chapter Eight. She gratefully acknowledges the citizenry of that town who, over the years since 1972, have taught her so much and shared with her so many aspects of their lives. A special word of thanks to Francis Howrigan, town father with a heart of gold.

A word of thanks to those who caught our EPIC ideas and made them their own, thereby strengthening the rural fabric by spreading the findings, concepts applied, and lessons learned by publishing our work, sometimes without our knowing about it, and in many cases institutionalizing EPIC ideas.

Thanks to Gary King, retired program officer at the W.K. Kellogg Foundation, for believing in me and my EPIC idea in the first place. And a very special word of thanks to Tom Thorburn, program officer at the W.K. Kellogg Foundation, for his professional support, ideas shared, advice freely given, and very helpful comments on drafts of the manuscript. Regular discussions with the program officers at the Foundation proved invaluable. Tom Thorburn not only has experience in the field as a former extension agent but also oversees a large number of rural development and agricultural grants in the United States and overseas. He was thus able to draw on his vast knowledge, recalling success and failures. Discussions by telephone were very helpful. This ongoing assessment benefited everyone involved in the rural development initiative, both in the rural communities and in the participating institutions, and was crucial to our developing EPIC's Key Principles of Sustainable Rural Development.

The EPIC project, including this book, was supported by a generous grant from the W.K. Kellogg Foundation, which allowed us to receive

xxii | Acknowledgments

support from the University of Vermont and other grants from the Schumann Foundation, The Friendship Fund, Vermont Land Trust, Vermont citizens, and citizens in other states, towns, and municipalities.

If I have omitted anyone, I apologize. Please let me know so that I can correct my error in a future edition.

Chapter One

The Threadbare Fabric
of Rural America

Beyond megalopolis and the cities where most Americans live, and beyond the Interstate ribbons of development that link the nation's coasts and join us to Mexico and Canada, are vast stretches of rural areas. Here are varied physical resources and socioeconomic character- istics, fewer people, low or declining populations, relatively low aver- age incomes (linked primarily with agricultural and extractive industry sector jobs), a shortage of alternative jobs, little or no public trans- portation, stores closing on Main Street, and poorer provisions of serv- ices and facilities than in urban areas. The patterns of rural settlement are low density and small scale.

There are many different perspectives on rural areas. Some view these expansive and sometimes isolated rural tracts as "problem areas" in need of "rural development," while others see them as relatively unspoiled recreation areas for the weekend or longer vacations. Others see rural America as a "reservoir" of land for conservation of ecosys- tems for future generations or for future development as hazardous waste repositories, prisons and military bases, and other needs yet to be articulated by sophisticates within the Beltway in Washington, D.C. Regardless of perspective, however, most (at least 83 percent) of the United States' land mass is classified as rural, devoted to farming, forestry, mining, or recreation, with related rural service centers (towns) and many "unproductive" and protected land areas in public owner- ship or control.

These rural regions have rarely experienced long periods of stability. The dynamic nature of American society, with its distinctive property

1

ownership patterns, combined with a principally market-driven economy, provides challenges and opportunities for rural regions and their communities. From a pragmatic perspective, however, since we are all dependent on rural America for our food and fiber, sustainable rural development must be a high national priority for both urban and rural citizens. Because a buoyant rural economy requires vibrant rural communities with strong links to urban regions, it is necessary to gain a clearer understanding of some of the realities of life in rural areas and to consider the diverse opportunities communities have for strengthening the rural fabric.

From Closed School to Busy Rural Community Center

The rural township of Fairfield in northern Vermont provides an example of a community with several problems typical of rural areas and the way in which local citizens can determine how to reinvigorate their community. Fairfield has a total population of about 1,600 people and includes the two unincorporated villages of East Fairfield and Fairfield Center. Most of the land in Fairfield is open pasture for the town's eighty small dairy farms and one sheep farm, and the rest is forest or swamp, with a few small streams and plenty of rock. Despite the farms, at least 60 percent of all the employed people in Fairfield work outside the rural town in one of the major or minor service centers twenty to sixty miles away, and most mothers with small children have to work outside the home, usually outside the rural village. Students must travel to other towns to attend high school. The annual Town Meeting is held in the elementary school located in Fairfield Center (Photo 1.1).

The town, first settled by Europeans in 1788, has a long history. It was and still is predominantly an agricultural town. There had once been fifteen small schools scattered across town, including the one in the village of East Fairfield (Photo 1.2). By the early 1990s East Fairfield no longer had a railroad going through town, and there had been little business growth for many years. The station buildings had been removed in the 1960s (Photo 1.3). The village buildings mostly looked run down, in need of more than paint. With the closure of the elementary school in East Fairfield in the 1980s (part of school consolidation), the village had become little more than a bedroom community. The village today does not look like one of the perfect, quintessential New England towns, and few tourists have East Fairfield on their scheduled routes. There are no craft shops, ATM machines, banks, or hotels, and

Photo 1.1. Sometimes it takes no more than a local person deciding to improve the entrance to the town to start people thinking differently about their town. This locally made sign engendered a sense of pride in the community and the school.

Photo 1.2. East Fairfield School in 1921. Town history is often a useful foundation for discussions about the direction of change and development for a community.

Photo 1.3. East Fairfield railroad station about 1910; it was closed and removed in 1961. The railroad shut down in the 1980s, replaced by increased truck traffic on roads.

the nearest coffee shop is Chester's Bakery, a new bakery-cafe in a renovated post office, five miles away.

The need for women to take on more leadership roles in rural communities is a critical factor in rural development. In the early 1970s, Michele Bessett moved from New York City to East Fairfield. She married and raised her son there, going on to become a business entrepreneur with a food store and cafe in the regional service center of St. Albans, about twenty miles away. Michele noticed that it was increasingly stressful for many in town to have to travel to the service center to go to the doctor, find a wider range of shops, transport children to school and youth activities, and so on. When rumors surfaced that the town was planning to sell the old elementary school buildings and grounds to be converted into a business, Michele and several of the town families realized that they would have to act quickly to preserve the village green and centrally located public space at the old school. A group of (mostly) women came together to determine how to keep the land open and make it useful to the public. They were not opposed to a business in town, just to one in that location, because it had always been public space since the founding of the town in the eighteenth century. Most of the women had never taken a public leadership role, and they were very nervous about how to persuade the town fathers, a three-person, all-male board of Selectmen, that they should give the building to *them*, a local community group, rather than to a private business.

As chance would have it, an article appeared in the local daily newspaper in 1992 describing the availability of small seed grants for support of community-based ideas. Michele was designated by other community members to call the university office to find out how to get a small community grant from the recently formed, community-driven, rural development project that I was directing. I explained that she needed to involve community people of all ages and their many diverse perspectives so that they could determine collaboratively what common purpose they might have for such a building. There were many subsequent conversations between the Fairfield community members and my assistant and me. Visits were made to the town to facilitate the community's conversations (goal-setting process) as the ideas developed and the group struggled to gain the confidence to provide the town leadership with a clear vision of the planned use for the old school. As a newly established board (many of whose members had never served on any board, let alone set up a formal organization), the issues of laws and state permits, and the concepts of *Robert's Rules of Order* to run efficient meetings were all quite alien to them. The Chair believed that she "had to let people talk as needed."

The building, replacing an older school on the same site, had served as a school until the 1980s. The community went to work with building renovation (Photo 1.4). Today the old school is a thriving community center where none had existed before. It serves not only the immediate village area but also the rest of the town and neighboring communities. It is a model for other towns of "cradle to grave" services and volunteer efforts. The Center houses a full rural health clinic, a satellite center of the local hospital, the town's Senior Citizen Program, Meals on Wheels for "shut ins," after-school and summer programs for children, adult basic education classes, and several other programs. One group built an ice-skating rink on the basketball court to provide year-round use and to attract children to play in the community with their families close at hand rather than be driven into the city or to a distant shopping mall for entertainment. Each of these diverse programs is run by small groups of volunteers, some of whom were able to receive small seed grants to get their ideas off the ground. Today, all activities are coordinated by a full-time local staff person. Groups of volunteers meet at the Center to make and wrap gifts for the poor and needy, or simply to meet and chat about nothing in particular.

An early hurdle was that the school (located at the other end of

Photo 1.4. East Fairfield School in 1996 with a group of volunteers who had helped turn it into a community center and rural health clinic.

town) was slow to work with the center, but recently there has been good collaboration and joint projects. The Center is not perfect, of course. It still struggles to keep enough money to run it and it has a debt to pay off soon. Nonetheless, it has reinvigorated the town and region, has inspired seniors, women, and youth to be active in their local community, and is a state model.

Seven years after the first $2,000 seed grant, the East Fairfield Community Center can look back and realize that it was not the grant alone that helped the initial group, but rather it was the affirmation that someone outside the town had confidence in their abilities to make their ideas work. The community and individuals say that they feel less isolated today and that "there is a sense of a reinvigorated town connected with other towns and the region more broadly." During this period the same rural development project was also able to act as a catalyst leading to an increase in numbers of farmers placing their farms in land trusts in order to ensure viable farms into the future. The rural development project was also able to encourage and reward projects to conserve barns (Photo 1.5), improve pastures, and build better urban rural connections through farm bed and breakfasts. The cluster of grants and other activities in and around Fairfield has meant that the East Fairfield Community Center is not merely an isolated place for the location of a

Photo 1.5. Preserving historic barns is critically important in many parts of the country. Those farming at the economic margins are unlikely to be able to afford to repair or renovate buildings such as the farm shown here. A wealthier farmer purchasing such a set of farm buildings might even replace the whole historical unit with more convenient modern structures.

series of programs but is part of a quietly comprehensive approach to community-based rural development.

Fairfield (in upland Vermont) is likely not as isolated as other rural areas in America, and the mechanisms used to identify and address local problems in Fairfield may be quite different in Alabama or Colorado or Nebraska. In some rural communities, the church may be central, in others the farm cooperatives may be key, and in Leeds, North Dakota, a new pasta factory, which adds local value to the Durum wheat crop, may be key to a regional rural renaissance. But in all regions, small seed grants and leadership development are likely to be important (Photo 1.6).

So, What Is *Rural?*

In meeting the challenges and opportunities in rural America, it is necessary to not only better understand what it is really like for those who live there, and for those who visit, but also to look at some of the data

Photo 1.6. Ongoing local leadership education is key to the success and sustainability of rural development projects.

and definitions of what constitutes "rural." To understand rural America in all its complexities, we must address as well the real impact of rural areas on urban America. This deeper comprehension of "rural" requires that we understand and use more than one perspective.

Our Preferred Vision

Surveys and research (such as Lapping 1997) still clearly demonstrate that, despite news of drought and failed crops in the Heartland and despite out-migration swelling urban populations, Americans still firmly believe in the agrarian myth of pastoral landscapes peopled with friendly rural people living wonderful lives based on solid family values. In this vision, urban is seen as quite separate from rural—and we tend to like it that way.

This tendency to generalize about urban and rural as though they are separate and distinct from each other can be misleading at this stage in American history. Certainly there are criteria that we all intuitively use when we talk about urban or rural. These provide core characteristics that help us define these regions. Given that most of us live and work in one location, we rely on the various forms of media for accurate information. This probably means that for the predominantly urban population (80 percent of all Americans live in urban areas), this will be an urban perspective. We hear urban stories about the homeless, drug addicts, declining industry, deteriorating neighborhoods, crime, violent death, political scandal, and general mayhem. In contrast, stories about small towns such as East Fairfield are not common except in local papers or on local television. Further, when rural and small town stories reach the national media, many journalists choose to glorify the apparently low-key, gentle life of the rural person and extol the beauty of the landscape. Stories about the town of Fairfield that have appeared in *Vermont Life* magazine present another view of the same town. The magazine, seeking to assuage our romantic need for nostalgia, shows the fall leaf colors to entice "leaf peeper" tourists, vital for the new economy, and shows springtime photographs of locals gathering maple sap with horse-drawn sleds to make maple syrup. And in the nation's capital one of the Vermont senators offers ten gallons of Vermont Grade Fancy Maple Syrup to any senator who believes that their home state has better fall colors than Vermont. Thus we feed our preferred vision of the pastoral landscapes that we hope are still "out there." This is clearly seen in the magazines published by rural states seeking tourist dollars, such as *Arizona Highways* and *Vermont Life*—nostalgic images increasingly at odds with rural reality. Landscapes are portrayed as backdrops against which the bucolic rural natives play out their lives. Americans want to believe that these portrayals are reality. Hardworking urbanites and suburbanites, spending countless hours in air-polluted traffic jams and stressful jobs, profess a need to believe that small-town America and the rural Heartland are alive and well; that Virginia is for Lovers, and that, as some T-shirts claim, "if you say your prayers, eat all your spinach, when you die you will go to Vermont."

It is reasonable to assume that some Americans feel drawn to rural regions for leisure activities or as a place to live because of the lower population densities, open spaces, and the possibility of a community of which they could be part. Conversely, many rural residents move to urban areas seeking such things as employment, further education, and higher wages. Urban America, with its serious problems, seems to be taken more seriously by politicians than rural America. Certainly urban problems directly affect far more people in glaringly obvious ways to anyone reading a paper or watching television news. Thus, for some, it seems more logical for the nation to concentrate on resolving urban problems rather than to acknowledge and attempt to understand the nature of the decline in some rural regions and the complex changes taking place in all rural regions. Problems in rural areas, such as under-employment, declining agriculture and forest industries, and a low standard of living, are, of course, intricately connected with the trends and changes in urban environments. One feeds the other. Indeed, to separate problems of "urban" from the perceived or preferred vision of "rural" is to do a disservice to the complexity and diversity of rural America.

The Statistical Definition of Rural

If the preferred vision of rural America is a tad misleading, surely the U.S. Census Bureau can provide crisp and clear data. The United States is a nation that loves statistics, but even the Census Bureau finds that it is not simple to precisely define "rural." The Census provides us with what is, in essence, a default definition: those areas and populations not classified as urban. So, what is urban? It is defined in the 1990 Census as "all territory, populations and housing units in urbanized areas, and in places of 2,500 or more persons outside urban areas." To be more specific, the Census adds the following urban definition: "Places of 2,500 or more persons incorporated as cities, villages, boroughs (except in Alaska and New York) and towns (except in the six New England states, New York, and Wisconsin), but excluding the rural portions of 'extended cities.'" The Census clarifies the definition of the word "rural" to include not only those places of fewer than 2,500 people, but also "rural areas outside incorporated and census-designated places," and, further, that rural also includes rural portions of "extended cities." Many who live in rural America are, in effect, living in what may be more accurately described as the urban hinterland.

The U.S. Office of Management and Budget uses metropolitan statistical areas (MSAs). An MSA includes one city with 50,000 inhabitants or an urbanized area of at least 50,000 and a total metropolitan population of 100,000 (but 75,000 in New England). (Further definitions can be found in the glossary.) These MSAs are measured in part on commuting patterns between counties and thus are not of standard geographical size.

Economic activity does not necessarily clarify the further definition of rural at this time. Agriculture, a significant industry in rural America, directly employs only about 2 percent of the U.S. population, and yet 21 percent of America's population is described as living in areas statistically defined as rural. So there is a lot more to "rural" than agriculture alone. Furthermore, with consolidation of services, the typical rural resident is probably linked to an urban center for medical care, school, banking, and related activities, albeit at a distance.

Rural Characteristics

The various statistical definitions of urban, even with their regional variations in application, leave us with a lack of clarity regarding the meaning of "rural" that is lacking clarity of definition. The statistical classification is, of course, helpful where a community needs to show that it lies inside or outside the statistically determined area in order to qualify for federal programs and grants for economic development; but the "rurality" of a region is more complex than numbers alone. The traveler driving through a region, for example, may see what appears to be rural countryside, with active farms, open land, and small scattered settlements, but which may be classified by the government as urban. The term "countryside" does provide us with a word that is more descriptive of some rural regions than numbers alone, but there is more to rural America than the countryside concept evokes. There are in fact wilderness and forested areas with very low population densities that have many rural characteristics.

In an effort to clarify the question of what is considered rural, I propose the following:

- Agriculture and forestry, at large and small scales, are important industries. Although they may be declining, they still are believed, *especially by local people,* to be important industries worth saving.
- The landscape is still primarily open. It can be a working landscape of farms and forest, or large areas of forest or other vegetated regions, with scattered settlements.
- Communities—settlements of several houses where people live—are scattered with relatively low densities of population over a large area, with open land between. This includes towns and villages under 2,500 in a statistical sense, but also includes those "urban" settlements in rural areas that serve the larger rural region. Such service-center towns have rural as well as urban functions.
- The region may have characteristics of both rural and urban areas— an urban fringe—where rural characteristics predominate, *especially in the perception of local residents.*
- The local resident population believes that the mix of land uses where they live feels "rural" to them.

Indices of Rurality

In many ways, it would be useful to develop more detailed definitions of "rural" in modern-day America. Some rural regions are far more isolated than others. Some have more agricultural land use, some more forestry or mining, while other regions are valued almost purely for their recreational uses or wilderness characteristics. Some regions are, in reality, simply urban fringes.

To address the need for not one but a range of approaches to rural development in Britain, an index of rurality was devised. Using sixteen different variables, including population pressure and degree of urban dominance, Cloke (1977) provides some useful regional maps. These variables were statistically derived from data on changes in population numbers and densities over several decades, as well as on journey to work, commuting distances, and other related socioeconomic data. From Cloke's work three rural types were identified: extreme rural areas where urban influences were slight except for the temporary impact of summer tourism and short-stay recreation; intermediate rural areas, typically farming areas, with a relative balance of rural and urban influences; and rural areas where urban influences dominate. In these latter communities, there may be a superficial appearance of unaltered countryside, but in reality they are dominated socially and economically by urban values.

Such indices of rurality have not been developed to date in the United States, and it is not the intention of this book to provide them. There is, however, a useful reference to be found in Tom Daniel's book, *When City and Country Collide* (1999), in which detailed data are presented about the urban–rural fringe, and an application of some of the concepts of rurality are addressed by Mark Lapping (1997) in his discussion of the Amish.

The concept of varying degrees of rurality, using environmental, social, and economic characteristics, is useful to keep in mind as the discussions in this book unfold, because it forces us to remember the importance of the degree of dominance of urban influence in the evolving rural landscape. Obviously, the manicured landscapes of rural Britain that Cloke researched contrast with the diverse American landscapes of benign neglect. However, the concept of examining the relationship between urban and rural regions, a relationship that is transitional in time and space, is important when determining the best means of moving us toward more sustainable rural communities. Such thinking can help avoid the mistake of assuming a complete and clear separation between urban and rural.

The Linkages between Rural and Urban Areas

The dichotomy between rural and urban America is not clear, either statistically or in the traditional economic sense. Many "urban" people, with "urban" jobs and lifestyles, live in "rural" America. Today, rural areas are often clearly linked with urban areas.

If the official statistical definitions of "rural" and "urban" are somewhat arbitrary, then certainly the lines between rural, urban, suburban, and other such governmental/geographical notations become blurred, both literally and metaphorically. Perception, lifestyles, sense of place, and other criteria not easily quantified must be considered to create more accurate characterizations of urban or rural. Additionally, people moving to and living in rural areas today function in what may be described as urban ways: flying to the city for meetings but having an office at home, commuting via modem, running the farm through complex computerized systems, and marketing globally via the World Wide Web.

> We use the word "rural" here broadly applied to all those areas not classified by the U.S. Census as urban and to those areas that have rural characteristics. Rural may also be a state of mind.

Given the fact that the definitions of rural and urban do not provide clear lines of separation, some attention must be paid to the boundaries between them. The demarcation is a zone where conflict and tension over land use and lifestyles often exists, disturbing or changing communities. Urban sprawl is perceived by many as a frustrating encroachment of urban growth into rural areas. The tension is exacerbated by the fact that growing towns are often located on the best soils, in river valleys, in wetland zones, or at a confluence of rivers, where the soil is good for agriculture as well as for septic systems and construction.

In context, a more ecological perspective could prevail. For example, the ecological perspective of this "development" boundary zone is analogous to the ecotone, a transitional zone that lies between two ecological communities such as forest and grassland. In this diffuse ecotone, there are elements of plant and animal species typical of both forest and grassland communities. There is often considerable complexity in this boundary zone, and the ability to manage it carefully has become a significant aspect of effective wildlife and ecosystem management. These edge areas, with adaptable species of plants and animals, are of considerable ecological significance in many ways, including species diversity. Management is difficult and is based on many criteria, including carrying capacity. Similarly, these ecotones between rural and urban are often neither town nor city. In many areas of the nation they are typically under unincorporated township/city jurisdiction. These are lands that can be annexed by cities when the suburban tax base becomes attractive. We use the word "rural" here broadly applied to all those areas not classified by the U.S. Census as urban and to those areas that have rural characteristics. Rural may also be a state of mind.

Within the vast and varied rural landscapes exist communities, and it is these communities and the people who live in them that are the focus of this book. Attention is also given to the urban-rural margins and to the linkages between these two subsets of America, urban and rural.

Threadbare Fabric

If rural America is not simple to define, it is also not static when measured by economic, ecological, or social criteria. Understanding the changing nature of rural regions and the many challenges that face rural America is vitally important if we are to be able to provide for future generations. The present transition in rural America from an economy based primarily on the land and its natural resources to one of increased diversity of economic linkages and social constructs is a major one. This is certainly not the first, and probably not the last, major transition to take place in rural areas since farming communities were first established in what became known as the United States. But that does not make it any easier for the people who live and work there. The newer industries, including service sector jobs, have benefited some rural areas. However, the combination of international competition and negative economic stresses (social costs such as air and water pollution) still result in low wages, low standards of living, isolation, and severe stress on many rural families.

Just four decades ago, 15 percent of all Americans and 40 percent of all rural Americans lived on farms, and agriculture engaged roughly one-third of the rural work force. Today only about 2 percent of all Americans live and work on farms. This dramatic decline reflects our ability to produce more food and fiber with fewer people (Figures 1.1 and 1.2) and the desire of rural people to seek a more urban lifestyle. The result of these trends has placed considerable stress on the remaining rural communities.

National trends that also contribute to the rural community crisis include decreased federal financial support for rural communities, including support for rural economic development, farming, small rural businesses, and the like. This includes is a 66-percent reduction in direct spending since 1980 and a 41-percent reduction in loan guarantees dur-

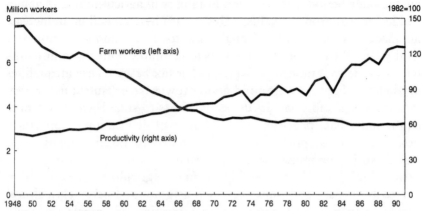

Figure 1.1. Farming's "double-edged sword": increases in productivity mean fewer workers are needed. (Source: USDA, Economic Research Service, 1995, p. 4.)

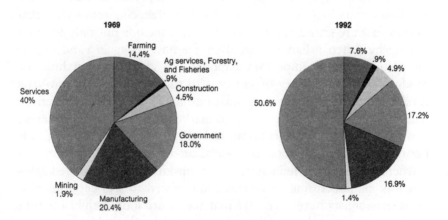

Figure 1.2. Services and manufacturing together employ more than two out of three rural workers. (Source: USDA, Economic Research Service, 1995, p. 5.)

ing the same period, coupled with instability in agricultural land values and lower real property values. This in turn has resulted in an increasing inequity in the ability of small rural towns to fund education at a level where their children can compete favorably with those in towns with schools well funded by larger, richer tax bases. These inequalities in education between richer and poorer towns have resulted in lawsuits in some states and clear directives by courts to state legislatures mandating immediate provision of equal access to educational opportunities. These access problems are not limited to racial inequities but include socioeconomic imbalances as well.

Rural job losses have been highest in the agricultural sectors and in related businesses and industries such as grain and other agricultural supply companies, meat processing, construction, and repair. Declining jobs and income in natural-resource–based industries upon which many rural areas depend have forced workers in those industries to find new ways to make a living. In Oregon, for example, the timber industry contributes only 3 percent to the state's economy, whereas 20 years ago it was the leading contributor.

Often, new ways of making a living are found only in a city. A business can remain in a rural area only if it has direct connections to urban centers that are critical to its growth. These include not only telecommuting by (often urban-educated) people now living in rural regions but also the vitally important national and global market links for products and for delivery of services. To succeed, low-skill, low-wage rural manufacturing industries must find a way to compete effectively with foreign competitors in a global marketplace. In many rural areas, new jobs are projected to continue to be in the service sector (i.e., waitpersons, salespersons, food preparers, attendants, childcare workers, teacher's aides, hotel managers) or in unskilled or semiskilled labor (such as manufacturing or construction related to service industries). Some economists have even said that the future looks bright for rural residents who want low-paying jobs—or, as some bumper stickers say: "You just don't understand the quality of our poverty in West Virginia," or "Moonlight in Vermont or Starve." Another bumper sticker asks that you "Don't Criticize Farmers with Your Mouth Full." But these are not very funny for those who seek their living in rural regions. The bumper stickers reflect not only frustration with forced transformation into service-sector economies' low-paying jobs but also the often-seasonal nature of these newer jobs and most importantly the limited understanding of farming as a business and a way of life. It is also important to note that while some rural areas have been able to develop new jobs in the service sector and manufacturing in particular, there are still large pockets of persistent rural poverty, especially in the Southeast, Southwest, and Appalachia.

In 1990, fifty-eight percent of U.S. farm-operator households received wages and salaries (averaging $30,000 per reporting household) from off-farm employment. For example, one or more household members might work at a manufacturing plant, a telemarketing office, or in retail trade (USDA 1995). Therefore, even for the remaining households, the nonfarm rural economy is an essential source of employment and income.

Although there is a higher *diversity* of rural economic activity than in the recent past, and greater connections economically between rural and urban areas, there is also considerable isolation and community fragmentation at many levels in rural areas. This concept will be examined (in several chapters) from diverse perspectives. Television, telephones, and the Internet, combined with the Interstate road system, have effectively reduced some of the obvious physical isolation and have also reduced many of the cultural differences between and within regions. This cultural gap was further reduced in the late 1980s and early 1990s by an increase in the migration of urban populations into some rural areas in the United States (Figure 1.3). This new migration is not the same as the back-to-the-land movement of the 1970s, which was partially a reaction to the Vietnam War and the "freedoms" desired by American society in the 1960s. There are certainly some new rural dwellers of the last decade who are homesteading, especially in the Northwest, Alaska, and the Southwest, with pockets elsewhere, including the upland regions of the East and New England. But at the same time there are new types of rural migrations, such as retirement populations moving to Florida, the West, and the Southwest—indeed so many retirees have moved that many of the areas settled by retired Americans are no longer rural, but relatively urban, with complex social service needs. Other recent immigrants are actually living urban lifestyles in rural landscapes, commuting by modem rather than by car. Migrations to rural areas are thus far more complex than they were two decades ago. The ability to work from home with computer and Internet links and the general national prosperity of recent years have increased migration to rural areas, as urban and suburban life has become more violent and unpredictable, especially for families with young children.

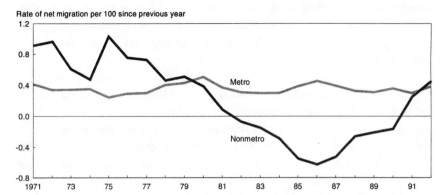

Rate of net migration per 100 since previous year

Figure 1.3. After attracting new residents in the 1970s, nonmetro areas reverted to their long-term trend of out-migration in the 1980s. So far in the 1990s rural areas have seen population gains through in-migration. (Source: USDA, Economic Research Service, 1995, p. 7.)

If rural America is to become a place where people of diverse socioeconomic and cultural groups can afford to live in safe housing and where they can keep their families together, it must be a place of strength and able to respond to changing conditions through competition and creativity. More than being able to make a livelihood, rural Americans surely deserve to be able to share in and enjoy the country's recent prosperity.

A revitalized rural America is of great importance to society as a whole. Rural problems do not remain so for long. When rural residents are desperate, or merely seek a better life, they tend to migrate to urban and suburban areas, swelling the populations and the social and infrastructure problems in those communities. The problem for rural areas is exacerbated by this loss of the younger, more innovative people from already-declining rural communities, which further accelerates the decline in infrastructure and the abandonment of productive agricultural areas. This process of movement to cities often begins with the exit of youth seeking jobs in the city. Today, this trend may begin with mothers who, of necessity, must take jobs in the nearby rural service centers or cities and place their infants and children in day care close to their workplaces. Such patterns result in the rural community becoming a bedroom community, further increasing the isolation for those who work locally. Bussing children to regional schools speeds up this exodus (Photos 1.7 and 1.8). Closure of small rural schools and associ-

Photo 1.7. Children in rural areas are often bussed long distances to school. This can reduce linkages with the home towns during formative school years.

Photo 1.8. Isolation of farms and farm families is a reality that must be carefully managed if both farm and family are to flourish in the twenty-first century.

ated consolidation of high schools provide examples of the role that institutions play in determining the future rural landscape. There are many such institutions, but it is likely that the changing face of schools is far more critical than one might expect in assessing community viability and sustainability.

The Role of Rural Institutions

Efforts to address problems such as those outlined above have often been economic rural development approaches, combining the efforts of outside experts with federal or other funding sources. Efforts to stem rural depopulation and the loss of family farms through economic incentives are not new, and the task is constantly evolving with new and more complex ramifications. For example, today the farmer and farming communities must face ever-expanding demands from people who want "natural" or organic foods, humanely treated animals in environmentally clean fields and pastures, and easy access to lands and waters for recreation. U.S. citizens increasingly demand detailed food labeling, ecolabeling and certification of products and processes, and green-space conservation, which challenges the very underpinnings of commonly perceived individual property rights in rural areas. Who should work to provide appropriate rural development in these changing times? Who has provided development assistance in the past, and how was it provided?

Rural communities are made up of individuals, families, and businesses, in a specific environmental context. The context of a small rural town in Kansas may be rolling landscapes covered with crops of grain much of the year, with few streams or ponds, and the nearest town many miles away. People and land do not exist separately. They are connected in many ways through the institutions that form the framework of government, economics, education, and spiritual and social life. There are many institutional structures that affect rural communities. Some are obvious, such as the church, state and federal government programs, schools (locally and regionally in community colleges and land grant universities and through cooperative extension service programs), soil conservation districts, banks, the Grange, the Farm Bureau and farmer cooperatives, agricultural service and supply companies, service clubs, and the like. Some are perhaps less obvious, such as the Boy and Girl Scout movements, 4-H clubs, garden clubs, masonry clubs, local newspapers, and others. Many of these communities of people through common interests have contributed significantly to local education and leadership development. Each of these institutional structures has also played an important role locally and nationally at various times in the development of rural America.

As transportation and communication systems and the national economy have changed over the last few decades, so has life in rural communities. When high school became compulsory, children not only attended school for more years but also became less available for family farm or rural business labor. As schools were amalgamated into large, often impersonal regional schools on campuses some distance from homes of rural students, the disconnect of children from home grew even more, and the local (small and rural) community became increasingly less attractive to its youth. As health care providers similarly have changed, rural families must now travel long distances for care from professionals they do not personally know and who probably do not well understand rural communities or rural health issues.

Inexpensive and seasonally available labor has always been important in agricultural communities. Higher rural birthrates have long provided ample labor on the farm, with any "surplus" children heading for the city. As compulsory schooling became the norm in rural areas, and where farm families could not produce enough children for farm labor, the urban poor or orphaned were sometimes sent (via churches and other institutions) to fill the labor gap. Migrant labor has also been a regular feature of rural communities nationwide, particularly in the Southwest.

The role of the church in rural community development remains a strong influence in many parts of the country, such as the Midwest and the South. In other regions, such as New England, it is typically a more minor player as a community force or focus of activities except in limited areas. The Grange, a movement established during the nineteenth century to share knowledge about modern methods of farm husbandry, plays a minimal role in rural communities today. Similarly, community centers, an integral part of early rural settlements (typically one of the uses of the elementary school), may no longer exist in rural settlements. It is difficult to have a community without a community center, or even a school gymnasium for meetings (Photos 1.9 and 1.10).

Another change of critical significance to rural communities has been the rise of interstate banking. Local banks, which could provide a quick loan to a businessperson needing to purchase inventory or equipment or a house mortgage to a farmer needing to construct a barn or

Photo 1.9. Despite national coverage of "Town Hall" meetings during political campaigns, the cost of maintaining historic meetinghouses in rural America is often beyond local means. There is indeed a scarcity of good community meeting places equipped for modern times.

Photo 1.10. High schools like this one have been closed in many rural regions and the children bussed to larger regional high school campuses for "economies of scale."

housing for a field hand, have almost disappeared. In only a decade we seem to have lost the local bank trust officer who knew you personally when you went for a loan. As recently as a decade ago even a new person in town, with sponsorship from a more long-standing resident, could get a loan to start a business or build a first house. The banking laws enacted in rural states by the elected representatives have often reflected urban perspectives of banking industry lobbyists. The new banking laws have been helpful to those seeking resources from out-of-state banks for large commercial loans but have been hard on those who live in rural areas. The result is that low-income housing is often harder to find in rural areas. Loss of locally owned banks has also meant a loss of community leadership and commitment to the local economy. In New England, it has become common over the last two decades to burn down a barn as the most effective way to "renovate" an old barn by replacing it with a new one. Another mechanism has been to sell the old barn to wealthy landowners in another, often urban, region. Some even hire people to take a barn down plank by plank to rebuild on "hobby farms" in the East. And the dairy farmer in New Hampshire or Vermont can build a new barn with the resulting urban income. But the result of such practices has been a tragic loss of rural heritage.

Those who now immigrate into rural areas are a new type of resident, with more disposable income. These people may, however, play an increasingly important role as those who can afford to renovate abandoned agricultural feed supply stores and barns or to take the economic risk of opening upscale restaurants in rural town centers (Photos 1.11 and 1.12).

Rural lives and livelihoods are tied to global economies and trading partners. Observant citizens working in rural areas have, one hopes, considered the implications of current economic trends in Europe, such as changing market demands and the introduction of the new Euro currency. The latter was a historic step in which eleven countries moved to a single trading currency on January 1, 1999, with complete elimination of all national currencies to occur within a few years. The introduction of the Euro could have far-reaching impacts on marketing strategies in the United States and Canada. Given that global marketing techniques are critical for sustainable rural development, rural citizens must learn how to maximize benefits from this new monetary trading unit.

Other institutions that have had a remarkable impact on rural life

Photo 1.11. Stores like this that sell primarily agricultural supplies cannot survive when nearby farms close. Loss of rural infrastructure can be a threshold beyond which farms go rapidly out of production.

Photo 1.12. This "upscale" restaurant is a renovated feed store. Renovation of buildings, especially in downtowns, has been found to be a critical positive factor in many rural regions.

and land use in rural America include land grant universities, agricultural experiment stations, and university cooperative extension services. Their imprint and legacies, however, have been both positive and negative. Although these institutions have changed in the last two decades, an appreciation of how they were established and their overall goals is necessary to understand rural America today.

The Morrill Act of 1862 endowed agricultural and mechanical colleges in each state. These "land grant" institutions promoted agricultural experimentation and a range of technological and engineering training used in building the infrastructure: roads, bridges, buildings, and the like. One of the next significant steps was the Hatch Act of 1887, which created the agricultural experiment stations where research on pests, new varieties of plants, and a whole host of significant agricultural innovations were ultimately developed. The efficient use of natural resources to produce food and fiber needs for a fast-growing rural society, most of whom could not go on to a college or university after high school, was one of the factors that subsequently led to the Smith-Lever Act of 1914. This legislation provided for the cooperative federal-state-county agricultural extension service to provide instruction and practical demonstration for rural residents through the county extension agent system. Extension agents, working out of state colleges, were assigned to every important agricultural county in the nation to teach farm families new farming methods, new ways to combat plant pests and animal diseases, and how to use hybrid species and to provide nutritional information and home economics as a means to "improve country life." They were also assigned the task of tackling special problems arising from national emergencies such as droughts, floods, and related problems. In effect, they helped farmers with everything from loans, to debt adjustment, farm credit, rural rehabilitation and relief, and prevention of soil erosion (USDA 1937).

But higher standards of living in rural areas, primarily a result of federal farm loan banks that provided ready cash for agricultural equipment to implement these modernizations, along with a boost from wartime production and prices, came at a considerable cost to the environment. Decades of pushing the ecological carrying capacity in rural areas using chemicals, energy, and plow methods over vast areas, combined with overcapitalization, indebtedness, international and national market vicissitudes, and periodic droughts and the Dust Bowl, have left their imprint on the rural heartland and to a lesser extent on other areas of rural America.

As the extension outreach work moved from a crisis-oriented mode of operation to an increasingly teaching-oriented mode, it began to use an "expert model" approach to rural development. People outside the community were widely perceived as having the answers to rural problems. Although this may have been the case in the early years of the extension service, now, without the necessary community empowerment, there is no mechanism to "institutionalize" the necessary changes by permanent community members. A model is needed that can be adapted by local residents to meet present needs and to meet changing global and local conditions.

The goals of the land grant institutions and cooperating agencies described here helped rural America to produce more food and fiber and improved the lives of many. However, conservation and environmental concerns have become a serious point of tension in day-to-day activities of many land grant institutions and in related cooperative extension programs. And there is still an unhealthy tension between agricultural and environmental professionals. This tension, as David Helvarg (1994) clearly articulates, must be effectively and rapidly addressed if sustainable rural development is to take place. Helvarg's analysis (based on interviews) shows a collection of unlikely bedfellows, such as the NRA (National Rifle Association), the Farm Bureau, the Heritage Foundation, major timber and mining corporations, resource and trade associations, and even the Moonies (followers of a radical religious sect). In Western mining regions, for example, the DeBeers diamond cartel of South Africa reaps huge profits from its royalty-free gold-mining operations (under the 1872 Mining Law) on the Humboldt National Forest in Nevada, with significant consequent environmental impacts. Sustainable rural development *must* work in a cultural climate where property rights and "takings" are ongoing issues.

Universities and agricultural colleges, as institutions with vested interests in rural communities, must operate in this often-hostile environment, treading a fine line between meeting the demands of both liberal and conservative interests in the context of a global economy. This comes at a time when institutions of higher education are being forced to curtail their rural outreach programs because of drastic cutbacks in federal and state funds, despite the large population of (previously urban) people who now live in rural areas. These "recent arrivals" want clean rural land, air, wildlife, plants, and water, and they seek both working landscapes and wilderness, depending on the region of the nation into which they immigrate. But the institutions that once provided outreach and service in rural areas are faced with budget cuts or are forced to meet quite different institutional demands. These institutions are often working with out-of-date information, concepts, and attitudes, with parochial perspectives—which is like trying to travel across the United States using a map printed before the Interstate highway system was built. One of the results is the continuing perceived dichotomy between environment and economy, a recurring tension in rural towns nationwide. Unfortunately, traditional agencies often blame the landscape when their maps prove inaccurate.

There is an added and very serious problem particularly common among the leadership of institutions and universities: the public relations "face" these institutions present to the outside world. Their reports and speeches produced for public consumption frequently smooth over institutional errors and shortcomings, reflecting their inability to openly admit what is not working, has not worked, and indeed may be making the problem worse. Such leaders cannot then make decisions, because they cannot accept and work from reality. Thus, while the rhetoric sounds right, the reality within the institution is confusion and frustration. (For those who work in a university, for example, it is often a challenge to get a clear organizational diagram of the institution or a chart of the decision-making structure used to make major decisions and set spending priorities.) The faculty and staff of the institution typically report the truth, but the leaders cannot accept it. It is as though they refuse to understand that we often learn from things that go wrong and mistakes that are made. By avoiding the truth these institutions do themselves and the communities they serve great harm.

Conservation *with* Rural Development

Regardless of political persuasion, urban or rural location, or the apparent destruction of the environment in many regions of the country, the concepts of conservation and preservation are strong threads in the American psyche. Although conservation implies multiple uses of available resources, preservation—very much an American concept—proposes limited, if any, use of the resource under consideration. Movements to conserve farmland, family farms, and soils and to preserve wilderness or final remnants of forests or grasslands are common elements in the ecological and cultural histories of the United States. (Good discussions of these topics can be found in Benjamin Kline's *First*

Along the River [1997] and in Richard Knight and Sarah Bates' *A New Century for Natural Resources Management* [1995].) The tensions associated with such conservation or preservation goals continue to be at the root of many of the conflicts that leaders in sustainable rural development must deal with. Although federal and state laws and regulations can both help and hinder the citizen leader, the confrontations are frequently still fought at a local level and with an increasingly vocal "minority" representation.

The European approach to conservation has generally included a strong component of "countryside management," which works, by and large, through complicated economic incentives and redistribution of tax monies to specifically delineated regions. It has successfully permitted economic growth in some areas, preserved human-made rural landscapes in others, and ensured an overall increase in rural standards of living. Some of these concepts are covered in Hugh Clout's *Regional Development in Western Europe* (1975, 1981) and in Mark Blacksell and Andrew Gilg's *The Countryside: Planning and Change* (1981). The "countryside preservation and management" approach has appeal in the United States, especially in regions that have been settled the longest. The use of regional approaches to rural and development issues is a strong principle in the European model and appears to be a trend that will continue to strengthen. If properly done, such a decentralized, regional approach to rural development in America could be used to strengthen individual rural communities as well as the networks and infrastructure that hold them together. This combination of countryside and regional approaches offers a more sustainable approach to development.

Although conservation and preservation have been taking place in the United States for many decades, the perspectives and mechanisms used have changed to meet the changing demands of the people. More changes are needed based on new ecological and economic knowledge, and adaptable strategies must be developed by local leaders.

The nation's attitude toward its natural resource base and the environment is changing, and the availability and use of rural areas by those who live there are often balanced against the desires of those who would like to hike, ski, hunt, fish, or just preserve some areas as wilderness. Tensions between the traditional agricultural and extractive industries and the "newcomer's perspective" on the natural resource base can be found in every corner of the nation.

In the West, where most of the land is publicly owned, tensions over grazing, mining, and forestry rights are not likely to be resolved overnight. Two examples are enlightening. The first concerns the issue of reintroducing the wolf in the West. The wolf is an endangered species, protected by law. But increasing its numbers to stabilize its population brings the animal back into conflict (both economic and value-based) with cattle and sheep ranchers, many of whom graze their animals on public (federal) lands where re-introductions are planned. The second example concerns the desire of environmental groups to save remnant old-growth forests in the Northwest. Forestry communities see an immediate economic loss and total decline of their way of life in their small towns unless they can go on cutting timber as before. The rationale that they can go out of business now (leaving the remnant forest) or go out of business in a few years (when they have cut it all down) cannot be expected to satisfy those whose jobs and way of life may be lost forever.

The apparent dichotomy between what are loosely grouped as "environmental rights" and those of "economic goods" continues to have a serious effect on rural lives in many areas of the nation. Until these competing sides are approached as linked issues and both sides more clearly understand the implications and work toward common ground, this "environment-versus-economy" debate will continue to be destructive to both rural lives and the environment. A useful reference on the economic impact of environmental destruction can be found in Thomas M. Power's book entitled *Lost Landscapes and Failed Economies* (1996).

In a broad sense, rural conservation should integrate natural resource conservation with farmland retention, historic preservation, and scenic protection within the rubric of a sustainable regional context. To be successful in the long term, such activities must involve the local citizenry. Although initial involvement might focus around some of the environmental issues, such as whether a rural community will be the repository for a hazardous waste dump, the longer-term view (beyond the "crisis planning" stage) must involve a conservation strategy. Effective, locally developed strategies will likely include development of leadership seminars and courses designed to address specific conservation topics (such as sustainable forestry); development of institutional structures, such as conservation commissions, that will support conservation concepts into the future; and involvement and training of all of the rural community, including its youth. The mandate for us to conserve and preserve the environment is clearly part of the modern American's experience. The term "stewardship" is used because it is an institutionalized concept in American society. In our academic and religious education we are frequently directed to be good stewards of the land. The commonly accepted meaning associated with the concept of stewardship is that as stewards of the land we take care of all natural resources for future generations. However, "sustainability" and "stewardship" do not necessarily go hand in hand, and a brief digression must be made into the etymology of the word "steward." The Cartesian view of nature as "resources for human consumption" places humans "in control of" nature rather than as "part of" nature. Some go further and see nature and natural resources as "capital" for economic manipulation. These (more limited) perspectives assume that technological control is not only possible but also desirable.

The word "steward" is derived from the Anglo-Saxon work *stigweard,* meaning the person who is the major domo, caterer, or in charge of the pigsty. Although one might smile and consider that perhaps the original meaning is not too far off, there really is a lot more to our natural physical and biological environments than merely meat production and keeping the sty clean. The goal must be to ensure that even when the term "stewardship" is used, for want of a better word, we should always recall that we are not separate from these natural resources but are part of the whole ecosystem.

Property rights are strongly protected under the U.S. Constitution. Private property rights are thus very powerful. Conversely, it is also implicit that private property rights must yield to the public good. These legal constructs produce a tension that is a common feature in battles over rural land use today. The conflicts can, for example, often only be fully resolved in a sustainable manner through "taking" part of the bundle of rights via purchase of development rights. The following roadside sign on private land in Vermont sums up one person's frustration with the diverse perceptions of land use in rural areas: "If your land is posted, stay the hell off mine." Posting private property (by erecting signs on the land) prohibits the public from entering for hunting, fishing, snowmobiling, or hiking. These posted lands are increasing as more and more urban people move into rural areas in search of solitude.

One effective mechanism that might move antagonists is to approach the issue from a community perspective (see Power's *Lost Landscapes and Failed Economies* [1996]). In such an instance, new perspectives and linkages are deliberately sought so that diverse interests in the same natural resources could be refocused on looking for the positive attributes needed in the community to make the whole system work more effectively and accommodate a wider diversity of people. Approaches to rural development in the United States have often been fragmented and single-issue-oriented rather than integrated and system-based. Typically, programs have been created by autonomous public and private organizations, such as those dealing with water, housing, wastewater, health and nutrition, farming, and forestry. As described earlier, such programs have often been delivered to a community by outside experts and funded by federal dollars. Many of these programs have outlived their initial mission or failed to adapt to the complex modern rural environment. Rural development has also failed in many instances because the local rural residents were not involved in determining the needs of the community or the mechanisms needed to address those needs. This book does not attempt to analyze data on past rural development programs but to suggest that present rural challenges need to be tackled using methods different from those used in the past. Differences in private property ownership, including ownership of development rights, coupled with a different approach to taxation and economic incentives to industry permit only broad comparisons with Europe. Nonetheless, given world economic trends, the complex mechanisms used to maintain rural landscapes in Europe are worth consideration.

The enormous complexity of rural issues and distinctive variations in history and geography, intertwined with urban issues and society's changing values and attitudes, means that there is no simple recipe for rural prosperity. One size will not fit all, and even a cohesive group of programs might not begin to meet local needs. It is not a question of having inadequate data; as a nation we seem to flourish on data and the collection of data, deriving solutions for problems through data analysis. The data used, whether national, regional or local, may be accurate, but what is typically missing is the integration of the research with proposed actions, including actions proposed by the community itself.

Integrating Research with Community Action

Each region faces its own problems, challenges, and opportunities. Development efforts, especially those funded by national and local governments, have been taking place in most rural regions for decades. They have helped reduce the impacts of crises, especially natural disasters such as floods and crop loss, and have fostered economic investment in new rural infrastructure through loans. The scope of these efforts has, however, been drastically reduced over the last decade through withdrawal or reduction of funds and personnel available. Local efforts, sometimes with financial assistance from businesses or philanthropic foundations, have been able to fill some of the gaps in some regions, but it has been difficult to determine from past efforts what worked, what did not, and why, so that new efforts can build on lessons learned. Despite the considerable literature on rural development in the United States, research and practice remain largely separated. Traditional research methods use a "scatter-gun" dissemination strategy, where papers and conferences are aimed primarily at an academic community and the population under study is excluded from the dissemination. This traditional approach does not often result in comprehensive, lasting community development. The community development process of research and linkage with the rural community needs to be redesigned to promote change within the community and to affect the broader political processes.

The community must be engaged in the development of the vision, research, and interpretations and in designing solutions. The community too must assess progress and make changes. This has to be an ongoing process with continuous adjustments in vision, problem identification, priority setting, solutions, and assessment. Systems thinking about community cannot take place without this degree of involvement, and community empowerment does not work with the "expert-driven" model for development. In redesigning development efforts, a broad range of tactics is essential.

Promoting Integrative Thinking

Rural development plans, programs, and projects have tended to be developed by people outside the affected rural community and are intended to address one issue at a time. They are not comprehensive, or integrated in design or delivery; they are routinely developed in theory only, or have been used at an earlier time, in a different location. Ideas do have transferability, but they must be carefully adapted to local contexts and approached in a systematic manner, integrated with many other aspects of life in the rural community. Integrated thinking should create linkages between ecology and agriculture, for example, or build partnerships between economic development and environmental conservation. The planner, urban or rural, may, through educational training, approach this "sprawl/growth" mechanistically, providing citizens with tools such as zoning ordinances, impact fees, and transferable development rights to solve the local "problem." Contextual issues are frequently ignored as being less expedient, too politically complex, and too comprehensive to be addressed easily. Decisions over the rural/urban ecotone zone could benefit from a more ecological perspective, in which sustainability is viewed in broader geographical, ecological, and historical perspectives, to provide a sense of the carrying capacity of the local area.

Changing False Perceptions of Rural Areas

There remains a persistent, unrealistic, and often romantic view of the bucolic rural economy, society, and its people. This does a serious disservice to the rural resident who may be running a large dairy or crop farm faced with vagaries in climate and economy, both local and global. The reality is that there are many kinds of people living in rural communities, and the trick is to get them all involved and to use their collective and individual expertise. The stereotype of the farmer who is self-sufficient, healthy, and wise must be tested locally to better understand the real daily lives of farm families.

Making Data Accessible

Similarly, there is a common misconception that if only rural communities had more data, they could solve their problems. In fact, there are actually enormous amounts of data, but they are overwhelming and often inaccessible to most local rural communities. The problem is to find data that are up-to-date, of the right level of detail, and accessible when needed. Too often data are generalized to fit a regional or national census design inappropriate for a community context. It's been suggested that these "facts" are just "bits of information out of context"—answers to the wrong questions. This situation is often exacerbated by the fact that local communities do not always know how best to use the available accurate data. Some data may be too technical, such as geographic information system (GIS) data, which is only as accurate as the ground measurements taken in the first place. Data are important in rural development at certain critical times of development, although often not at the first brainstorming session of a town redevelopment effort. And the data must be accessible to all. They may be needed at the evening meeting in the old school hall at a community meeting, long after agency office hours, so that resources such as Internet access of data in usable form that can be downloaded are important.

Utilizing Local People and Building a Positive Rural-Urban Connection

"Local" people living in rural communities today may come from diverse backgrounds and may have only recently taken up residence, joining "old-timers" and long-time residents. All of these people are "local" and are "stakeholders" in decision making. The goal must be to build collaborative partnerships among and between locals and with neighboring communities. Rural development has too often been designed by policy makers and planners as though there were a rural vacuum, disconnected from urban influence. The opposite is the case today. Local decisions must be made in a global context. The old adage "think globally, act locally" is not as simplistic as some might think, and understanding linkages is key.

Recognizing Women and Senior Citizens as Leaders and Change Agents

Rural development often employs outside expertise but does not adequately use some of the most important local resources: women and senior citizens. Placing more women and senior citizens in leadership roles can be the key to creating successful programs.

Women have played key roles, frequently pivotal to the successful outcomes and sustainability of rural projects. David O'Brien and his colleagues, in an article entitled "The Social Networks of Leaders in More or Less Viable Rural Communities" (1991), working in Missouri, found that the role of women was the critical determinant of viable rural communities. I have found that appropriate leadership development that can draw more women into leadership positions is thus a centrally important factor for sustainable rural community development.

Empowering Youth

There is not much for young people to do in rural areas, from the perspectives of the youngsters themselves, and the sorts of things that draw richer urbanites to rural areas are either things that local children see all the time (open landscapes, "wilderness," and nice farmsteads or small towns and villages) or activities such as skiing that are too expensive for them. Rural youth are not being drawn into farming or into other rural businesses. If they are not college-bound they will receive little environmental education, but if they are college-bound they will probably receive *no* agricultural education. There is thus a great need for leadership development that is aimed specifically at rural youth.

Encouraging Celebration in Local Communities

The role of celebration is very important and has, in many respects, been lost as we become more work oriented and spend more time watching television, videos, and other "modern" forms of entertainment. The home office makes it hard for many to escape e-mail and Internet messages as a primary means of communication (try to re-create in your mind what a typical weekday was like in 1800 or 1900 or even 1970 compared with today). Now, several members of the extended family of today travel to nearby towns to work, and the family's real leisure time is reduced. All of these are realities that must be taken into consideration in rural development efforts. An annual gathering, with dinner and a reception, that brings together farm families, youth groups, business people, local leaders, environmental groups, and many others who might not work together but who could "show and tell" what they had done for their communities recently, can be a significant event where networking and learning take place.

Using Local Newspapers

Dissemination of information, stories of rural development activities, and the roles of individual people take place somewhat informally at celebrations, but news must also be actively provided to the most preferred form of media in the local rural community. It was interesting to find that the local newspaper is the most useful source of information for the majority of rural residents in Vermont. Television and local radio appear to play only minor roles. The local newspaper is also effective in encouraging rural development through feature articles and editorials and plays a leadership role of considerable importance in the agricultural counties with the best coverage.

Protecting the Environment and the Natural Resource Base

Rural development has regularly ignored or avoided considering the ecosystem context within which it occurs. It is as though the perceived false dichotomy between the environment and economic development has become too deeply embedded in the minds of Americans for the interconnections to be seen. This is especially serious in the poor relationship that exists between those who work in agriculture and forestry industries and those who work in environmental arenas. This dichotomy must be addressed if there is to be sustainable rural development.

Key Principles of Sustainable Rural Development

> Like rurality, sustainability is filled with implication and nuance. With its roots fixed in ecological science, sustainability suggests renewability . . . and system integrity . . . within a larger complex of environmental connection, resilience, adaptability, versatility, perpetuation into a fundamentally unknown and uncertain future, and inter-generational equity and justice. (Lapping 1997, 29)

Closely linked with the American preferred vision of the pleasant pastoral life of rural inhabitants is the "presumption of rural sustainability." How can modern rural development accomplish such a complex task? It is my experience that sustainable rural development is best addressed by the community itself. Local residents are charged with the task of doing all they can for the future landscapes and the future children.

As discussed earlier, rural development in the United States and in developing nations has been seen as an expert-based model in which the expert from outside provides advice and guidance, delivers a program, and leads a specific activity of short-term duration. Outside resources, both financial and human, are the norms in this model. In addition, this model assumes the traditional notion that addressing *the* problem or issue in the rural community is best handled by the expert. This focus may permit early measurable outcomes, but the isolation of one issue from the complexity of rural problems will only guarantee that the proposed solutions will not be sustainable. Such single-issue, patchwork approaches mean that the fabric of the rural community is unevenly repaired, "and no one puts a piece of unshrunk cloth on an old garment, for the patch tears away from the garment, and a worse tear is made" (Matt. 9:16).

By contrast, rural development that is holistic in approach, comprehensive, and seeks to be sustainable is far more complex. It is systems based and does not rely heavily on outside expertise. When the community is understood as a living system—social, economic, environmental, political, and cultural, and includes people as part of a whole complex picture—then a far richer fabric begins to appear. It will then be the local people themselves who select the appropriate threads to reweave the local rural fabric. Community members, empowered, will seek expertise from a diversity of perspectives and disciplines to help the process, both from within and from outside the community. Local decisions will shape public policy and government action. Democracy will be strengthened at its roots.

In this systems approach to community-based rural development, linkages between communities in a region will be strengthened, and linkages will be built and fostered between rural and urban regions for mutual benefit. Outcomes of such efforts will be less easy to measure, the process "messier" than in traditional rural development activities, and mistakes will be made. Nevertheless, the long-term effects will be more sustainable and more likely to be beneficial, not only to the rural community but also to society as a whole.

This holistic, integrated approach means that there will be many more factors to consider in the rural development process than with the traditional model. Throughout this book there are numerous lists of working criteria, lessons learned, and outcomes measured. Appendixes present various templates for rural leadership development courses, forest stewardship programs, and other transferable models. In this comprehensive approach to rural development, it is easy to get overwhelmed by all the parts and all the interconnections. Such an approach may appear to the skeptic to be scattershot, lacking specific objectives and spreading resources too broadly. My experience has been that complexity need not overwhelm the process. As with the study of ecological systems, a coherent approach is possible without losing track of all the parts, or their validity and meaning.

Certain key principles for attaining sustainable rural community development can be drawn from the range of lessons learned, including mistakes made by those who have been and are now involved in the processes of rural development. These principles can be used to provide the frame of reference necessary to handle large amounts of data. This is a vision of complexity.

Change Is Inevitable

Rural regions do not exist in a state of homeostasis. Both natural and human landscapes change constantly over time albeit at different speeds and in different directions depending on the combined factors that influence the speed and type of change. Rural, urban, and the fringe between them are all changing. How society manages those changes will determine the long-term sustainability of communities, both human and ecological.

Key Principles of Sustainable Rural Community Development

Empower Community Members. It is of paramount importance to engage and empower the community so that development is, in reality, community-based and community-driven, and a more diverse group of citizens become the leaders.

Strengthen Democracy. The democratic system of government must be strengthened through the development of this new leadership and by encouraging their participation in community governance and the crafting of public policy.

Encourage Women to Be Key Leaders. Women are an essential ingredient in bringing community values and complex participatory skills to the processes necessary to make sustainable rural development work in practice.

Involve Children and Adolescents. Engagement of youth in the community development process is critical to future sustainability, as well as to broaden and strengthen the democratic process.

Encourage Systems Thinking. Rural communities are living systems functioning as integrated parts of larger systems, both cultural and ecological. Therefore, rural development must be holistic in approach, actively using systems thinking and seeking leverage points (a key factor or issue critical to a specific situation or community that can be used to build interest).

Encourage Innovation. Innovation must be fostered at many levels, both within the local community and outside, including those institutions that frame our societal structure; this will require changes in the present concepts of formal institution-based education.

Foster Rural and Urban Linkages. Given that rural and urban communities are not separate but are intricately interwoven social entities, these linkages must be built, strengthened, and fostered in a manner that is mutually beneficial and sustainable.

These key principles provide a guiding framework throughout the book and can be used by community leaders as they begin to reassess development needs. Connected to these principles are a number of related concepts that will be identified and clarified through specific examples. However, there is no simple cookie cutter that can be used, and what worked the first time a community tried to do something may not work a second time or in another community. Rural areas are changing and diverse.

Although changes in rural America are not new by any means, the scale and type of change deserve a closer look. Devastating crop and property losses from "natural" disasters, coupled with global competition, have contributed to agricultural instability, linked with economic and ecological instability. Use of natural resources is a major issue in rural regions. The real connections and impacts of these phenomena on rural life are not well understood. We know that the number of agricultural jobs has declined and that there is instability in many rural communities, with lower property values and smaller tax bases. We also know that most new jobs in rural areas are, increasingly, service-sector related and often do not provide important employment benefits, such as health and dental insurance. However, the problems that an outside person might perceive in a rural community might not be the same as the needs identified by the local population, and there is rarely a simple (and certainly never a single) solution to the issues identified in a given community or region.

Effective planning and development in small rural towns and rural landscapes as varied as those of Iowa, New Mexico, Georgia, Vermont, and Idaho require a delicate balance between conservation of valuable resources, both ecological and economic, and encouragement of sufficient change and economic development to improve the living standards of rural Americans. However, sustainable rural development—even if we really knew what it meant—is not likely to be determined by planners and politicians in the national or state capitals. The perspectives of the diverse citizens living in rural communities, who are at once dedicated to their environment and who wish their children and grandchildren to remain there and enjoy prosperity, are essential to sustainable rural management.

Sustainable rural development is thus defined as a collaborative process that strives to reconcile the promotion of economic opportunities and livable communities with the conservation of ecological integrity and biodiversity, a process of change in which exploitation of resources, natural and human, direction of investments, orientation of technological development, and institutional trends are made consistent with future as well as present needs. Sustainable rural development is not a fixed state of harmony.

Rural communities must thus be seen and understood as complex systems with their own histories and geographies. Successful long-term strategies for change in the face of globalization of many major issues of concern, from toxic air pollution, to climate change, to market economics, will require that local leaders craft the mechanisms to adapt to these phenomena and to reweave the fabric of their metaphorically threadbare communities. Although there will be discussion of national trends and reference to written materials, much of this book will deal with the role that individuals, working together, can play in determining the future trends in their rural communities. The goal for those involved in sustainable rural community development will be "to help people help themselves."

Chapter Two

The Need for a Systems Approach:
Integrating the Elements
of Rural Development

Communities, like Nature, are multidisciplinary, interconnected, and interdependent living systems.

Two approaches to problem solving in America have traditionally been employed: the disciplinary approach and the systems approach. Both have merit, and knowing when to use one or the other is important. The disciplinary tradition employs the scientific method to solve specific research problems. Items to be studied are isolated by categories and disciplines for which there are distinct names, such as economics or chemistry, with subdisciplines within each discipline. The disciplinary approach permits a perceived problem or issue to be isolated and then analyzed in depth. The downside of this approach is that the context within which the problem exists, such as present land use or political control, may be changing quite quickly. Such contextual change will affect the problem under analysis. Still, by isolating the problem in order to determine a solution, the research is clearly focused and provides probabilities or measurable outcomes, or similar data results.

The systems approach, in contrast, has its roots in ecology and is more concerned with the interrelationships among the issues and the disciplines than with answering an isolated question. Systems are seen as living. Thus a systems approach is more dynamic, is able to respond to feedback, and is better able to respond to change.

The Disciplinary Perspective and Its Limitations

> We require a new paradigm for community development and for university outreach, research, and teaching. Solutions must include a radical change in education curricula to include community-based study and interdisciplinary analytical skills in elementary, high school, and post-high–school education.

The challenges facing rural America reflect historical biases in our education and thinking. Rural, community-based development demands a comprehensive and integrative approach, and yet research funds, funds for economic development, and private investments have more typically focused on single issues with measurable outcomes. A comprehensive approach, where as many aspects as possible of the rural context are considered together, is complex. It is especially difficult to identify and measure outcomes. Indeed the whole range of what might be described as "lessons learned" may be far more extensive and comprehensive than "measurable outcomes" alone and demand additionally a multi-disciplinary interpretation. Furthermore, experts in one arena of knowledge may have little understanding of the concepts, information, and data available from even closely related fields and indeed may feel in competition or conflict with other approaches. These considerations hinder the necessary efforts at a truly integrated approach to rural development, an approach that must, of necessity, change and adapt in response to continually changing social, economic, and environmental contexts.

Certainly the "land grant" university approach to rural development, as suggested in the first chapter, has tended to reinforce many often-conflicting approaches to rural development. Unfortunately, limited approaches such as these are doomed to produce situations, businesses, and environments that are almost certainly not sustainable. All aspects of nature are connected, and rural communities, the lives and landscapes of rural people, are integral parts of the whole. Why not approach rural development with a more holistic perspective? Even better, why not approach it with systems thinking—call it rural community development, but in addition, acknowledge that sustainable communities need a sustainable environment?

Over the last few years universities have been proposing innovative ways to encourage interdisciplinary research, collaborative, community-based outreach and engagement, and interdisciplinary teaching that will change our way of thinking as an educated society. At the moment this is mostly just talk because it is difficult to break down the multitude of departments, disciplines, and subdisciplines into which academic knowledge has been fragmented over the last 200 years. The reality is that most of the older universities in the nation began in the late eighteenth or early nineteenth century with two departments (e.g., natural science/philosophy and classics). Such a university today probably has over eighty departments ranging from English to history, from computer science and political science to plant and soil science and microbiology. These disciplines, each with their own concepts, theories, philosophies, and jargon, are then grouped into departments and colleges under the watchful eye of administrative deans. Liberal arts professors rarely consider that their university professorship job description involves any kind of community outreach or service, and they rarely mix with their land grant colleagues. Indeed a negative, competitive atmosphere pervades many of the Halls of Academe, and few university leaders seem willing to do more than tinker with the arcane structure of the university, let alone consider the revolutionary change that is probably needed. Even in high schools there are clear lines between disciplines taught and the career tracks set out for students to follow. This becomes especially problematic for the rural child who is tracked into a set of courses that poorly prepare him or her for rural agriculture or rural business in the twenty-first century, when a more holistic, global perspective would likely permit greater adaptability to the challenges ahead.

The resultant fragmented approach to education with emphasis on narrowly defined "scientific" approaches, and skepticism about intuitive approaches, means that although we do have excellent research in highly focused arenas, we often fail to understand the context of the research. We have, in effect, fragments of information out of context. This is not to discredit the need for focused research and focused grant programs to address specific rural needs, but rather to recognize the often-missing contextual dimensions and necessary linkages among such efforts. In our collective societal belief in the power of science, we seem to have forgotten that science does not prove anything; it disproves. We need also to recall that it is often the "confounding variables," the contextual information, that can lead to a more complete research answer or permit the postulation of a better research question. Such research data and information can then help inform rural development, especially when the research questions are at least partially identified by community members who then assist in the analysis, interpretation, and implementation of potential solutions.

Rural community challenges reflect the need for comprehensive, integrated rural development that takes into account the environmental, economic, and social contexts of the given community or region. One cannot describe a rural community without acknowledging the interconnections among the environment, the economy, and the social, historical, and cultural contexts. No part of the community exists alone; changes in one aspect affect the entire system. We need to use data and information from many diverse disciplines, including our various cultural histories, to more fully address the present challenges in rural regions and to consider more carefully the needs of future generations.

In the first chapter, I alluded to problems in rural America arising from the past and present roles of institutions in rural areas and to the fact that rural America does not exist in the same type of physical and cultural isolation from urban America as in decades past. Other tensions must also be addressed in effective rural development. One of the most serious tensions is that between the environment and the economy, a false dichotomy largely fueled by ignorance and fear and one that ignores the ecosystems in which we live. I contend that economic development and environmental preservation and conservation (two quite different things) are not only compatible but also must be addressed together. Somehow, arising from our more recent settlement history and the myth of American abundance, there is still a great reluctance in American society to accept the need for changing attitudes toward the environment and for a changed structure in our education system. The present status of education reflects an inability to understand the whole system, an inability to ask the right questions, a parochial, isolated culture, too much discipline and not enough interdiscipline, too few risk takers, few good leaders, too many experts, and not enough integrating pragmatists. In many ways, we have not been provided with honest, accurate, and up-to-date "maps" in our education or in the information sources upon which we depend. Our entrepreneurial skills seem stifled. Also missing in our education today is development of problem-solving skills, critical thinking skills, and effective collaborative skills for the good of the community.

Just as important is the need to reassess and probably drastically change the size and structure of high schools. When several thousand children under the age of eighteen are held together for much of the year in large campuses some distance from their home community, how can we effectively teach community-based thinking? The intent of every citizen should be to see the context of community life, to understand its integrated wholeness, and to recognize the interdisciplinary nature of nature.

EPIC—A Rural Development Model and Catalyst for Change

> The EPIC model is comprehensive, integrative, community-based rural development linking together many projects and guided by a vision of general goals.

Environmental Programs/Partnerships in Communities (EPIC) is premised on the belief that rural communities are whole systems with environmental, social, and economic components. The EPIC model was not created to identify and directly tackle specific problems but rather to emphasize the long-term functioning of the entire community system. For example, the goal may not specifically be "to save family farms" but rather to work with community members, such as farm families, to identify a range of perspectives about the agricultural ecosystem, which include the farmstead, and then identify a more effective way to care for the land and water that will also support the farm family. The EPIC model does not seek specific measurable outcomes but instead looks for a broader range of lessons learned. Thus we would not count the number of farms saved from going out of business, but we would assess the increased diversity of social and economic activities taking place, the changes in values, the levels of innovation, the diversity of new leadership in the community, and so forth.

Even more critical is for EPIC staff to be "invisible" in the community. Typically, outside "experts" come to the rural town, identify a "problem" or deliver a "program" on a minimal budget, and then leave town to write the follow-up report or journal article. In contrast, the EPIC model specifies that a staff person from the outside must ensure that the ideas and concepts being encouraged are really those of the local community.

The EPIC approach also encourages the use of experience and intuition as well as analysis and science. Every problem or challenge has a context. Natural systems are inherently complex and inextricably interwoven within the cultural context. Indeed, rural and urban landscapes are not merely backdrops for our lives; we are part of those landscapes. Cultures are intricately woven together with the physical and biological landscapes where they have evolved, and one cannot resolve a problem in isolation from the context within which it developed. In recognition of this, EPIC involves community citizens, community development practitioners, and academics from diverse disciplines as sources of essential references to guide a more strategic approach to rural development.

People outside the community may conclude that the community needs more data, or a "needs assessment." But the reality may be that too much data exist for the local populace to handle effectively and that in fact what are needed are very basic skills, like how to run a meeting. In addition, of great significance to the young and old is the longing for encouragement and celebration of one's ideas.

Thus the EPIC approach is always to work with the local people, to help *them* to identify their community's needs (as opposed to its problems). EPIC provides resources where possible and "gives away" ideas to allow the community to conduct its own work, finding new partners with new perspectives within its own towns. Then EPIC staff quietly step back. Success is measured by the fact that people had only a vague recollection of EPIC and its staff. "Who was that masked woman?" they might ask, soon believing that they had done it their way and with little, if any, external help.

The vision and goals are at first those of the EPIC director and the team of leaders, each working on a separate but linked aspect of the whole. But as the rural community development effort begins to evolve, the vision and goals are regularly reassessed and modified by the community groups and individuals with whom the EPIC staff interact. Learning is seen as a two-way process; the EPIC model does not have an institutional structure or a specific agenda for each community.

Perhaps a bit of the history of EPIC will provide insight into its institutional framework and demonstrate as a case study many of the perhaps conflicting perspectives raised earlier. The idea of EPIC was based initially on my life experiences living, working, and raising a family in rural regions as far-flung as Northumberland on the Scottish border, East Africa, New Zealand, and Wisconsin and Vermont in the United States. Each rural community within the dominant culture of the society had its unique sets of mores and attitudes toward the land and the people making up the community, always with a unique local history.

The acceptable roles for an active woman scientist with innovative ideas, raising a family with her husband while running a small farm, were clear in each of these diverse communities, and yet not immutable. New ideas could be introduced, and women seemed to be able to move new ideas into the community with less negative response than some males might engender. Volunteer work on local boards (from being the "mother as leader" in children's groups, to schools, planning commissions, zoning boards, and conservation groups) followed over the years by participation on state, national, and international boards as a professional have all affected my perspective on rural community-based development and strategic leadership.

In 1989, after some years as a professor at the University of Vermont, a land grant state university, I gathered together a group of other "maverick" professors, including extension faculty and interdisciplinary scholars from across the campus, as well as community members, to form what we later called the "EPIC Core Team." Out of these early brainstorming activities came a grant proposal that was generously funded by the W.K. Kellogg Foundation from 1992 to 1999.

EPIC was ideally located in the Environmental Program, a university-wide program that reported directly to the President via the Provost. From 1992 to 1997, the EPIC team consisted of invited faculty from the Business School, College of Arts and Sciences, College of Agriculture and Life Sciences, School of Natural Resources, and Cooperative Extension. Its members also included varying numbers of graduate and undergraduate students who worked with us as key leaders in the community-based initiatives. It should be noted that some university administrators do not support the idea of senior faculty helping communities. Although the trend now in universities is toward more community engagement, it is still hard for many administrators to accept and reward this as appropriate university conduct.

The off-campus members included an ever-changing mix of people from various nonprofit organizations. We shared ideas and knowledge across a diversity of disciplines and life experiences, treating each other as equals. We met regularly over the years, and our morning meetings, normally ending with a long lunch, were a bit of a puzzle to the rest of the university, given that we seemed to laugh a lot and enjoy our collaborative efforts. We actually looked forward to our meetings.

We developed an overall vision of EPIC, with general goals for each of the component parts but also with considerable flexibility to handle the unforeseen and the ambiguous. Over time, as we tried to address all aspects of rural life, we identified elements that defined the EPIC approach; these are presented later in the chapter. These elements were not necessarily universal in the minds of all who joined the team over the years. Faculty and off-campus core players each led a project of their own, but with critical (albeit challenging) links to each other. EPIC provided seed money for these leaders in their research and outreach efforts while still aspiring to maintain a working environment that could foster collaboration and shared learning. As director of EPIC, I was known to describe myself as a circus leader who let all the disciplinary beasts out of their cages. I had to direct them, yet not constrain their innovative ideas and enthusiastic approaches. Not all of the original members stayed. Those few who preferred not to be team players (for example, those who wanted to take their perceived "share" of the money and go off on their own or those who would not share lessons learned and mistakes made) were encouraged to leave the project. This is an important aspect of managing a highly diverse group and trying to build a team. Some players were encouraged through individual meetings with the Director to modify their styles of operating so that they could better collaborate and address more completely the desires of community members rather than inject their own expert perceptions of community needs. This worked well with almost all of the original core team members. The leaders met individually with the Director in order to share focused details of the various aspects of the whole project. The role of the Director is thus critical to the EPIC model and must focus on community needs, not on personal professional needs. Thus the whole project was able to move forward.

We were encouraged by the foundation that was providing funding to establish both an on-campus executive advisory group and an off-campus advisory group. The executive advisory group proved to be helpful in the first years as a means to share general ideas, but because of both lack of support from the university administration (which kept changing) and university politics, the group was disbanded after two years. In contrast, the off-campus—external—advisors proved very useful throughout the project. However, rather than set up yet more meetings for the Director and the people working in the field, external advisors were used by core team leaders as resources—individuals to whom we could turn with specific questions and, often, as people to be asked to help in the various communities.

We also built evaluation, assessment, and feedback into the entire EPIC endeavor and modified our efforts over the years as the component parts evolved and community needs changed. However, the evaluation was not aimed at determining measurable outcomes in the traditional sense of the word, but rather used to identify lessons learned and to enable us to meet the needs of the various community endeavors in which we were engaged. But more on evaluation in Chapter Three.

The organizational structure and operation of a rural development project is thus not simple if it is going to be effective. The structure must be dynamic. To be community based means to think in a different paradigm, with the university office not seen as the center and professors and staff not seen as the only experts. The experts can be found at many levels, but to be effective over the long term the experts and expertise must reside in the local community, which in turn must be the center of all development activities.

Not surprisingly, this apparently amorphous rural development project did not sit entirely comfortably with some. For those who could not envision the system as a whole, we developed a model to help better explain it. This model initially placed EPIC at the center (Figure 2.1), but this centric perspective, while perhaps appropriate to explain what EPIC intended to do in the first year, seemed almost arrogant if we really believed that the community must be at the center. We realized that the model had to be reversed to be effective in the long term. Drawing the model was always a challenge, but Figures 2.2, 2.3, and 2.4 show the evolution of our thinking. Such models may oversimplify the actual multidimensional nature of reality, but the EPIC model is rather complex and is not necessarily easy to understand through words alone. It is hoped that the graphic format will clarify the model approach.

Most radical of all was our vision for the ideas and the generous resources placed under our control. EPIC was funded primarily through a university, which used foundation funds to provide resources, personnel, information, and leadership, yet our actual goal was to "give away" these resources. Rather than form a permanent Center at the university or in state government, EPIC worked from a "virtual" center. Thus, one of the measures of its success is that EPIC is not a permanent, self-perpetuating, institutional structure, but rather that it nurtured dozens, if not hundreds, of diverse community efforts that have themselves resulted in new structures, organizations, and activities at local levels and that these new ventures have continued and have become sustainable. The work continues in a low-key way, within new networks established and new organizations founded. Some of these new organizations, ad hoc groups, approaches to agriculture, Environ-

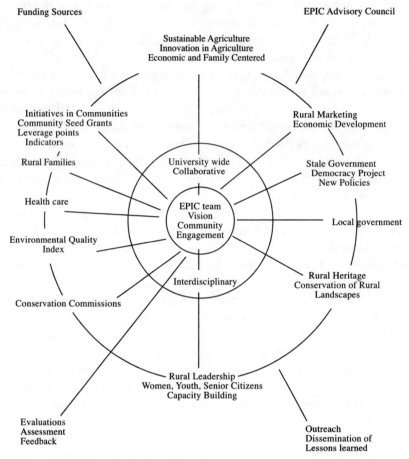

Funding Sources

EPIC Advisory Council

Sustainable Agriculture
Innovation in Agriculture
Economic and Family Centered

Initiatives in Communities
Community Seed Grants
Leverage points
Indicators

Rural Families

Health care

Environmental Quality
Index

Conservation Commissions

Rural Marketing
Economic Development

University wide
Collaborative

EPIC team
Vision
Community
Engagement

Interdisciplinary

Stale Government
Democracy Project
New Policies

Local government

Rural Heritage
Conservation of Rural
Landscapes

Rural Leadership
Women, Youth, Senior Citizens
Capacity Building

Evaluations
Assessment
Feedback

Outreach
Dissemination of
Lessons learned

Figure 2.1. The rejected model.

mental Indicator Reports (discussed later), and the like, are acknowledged by many to have "spun off" from EPIC. Others do not know that EPIC ever worked with their organizations, which have taken on a new lives, often with new leaders, and the role of EPIC is already obscured by history. Others have deliberately taken ownership or claimed credit for projects, ideas, or results, and we must accept that too.

All this is critical to understanding the role of the EPIC model as a catalyst in a series of actions and reactions carried out by individuals and communities in rural areas, as well as by the university faculty and staff, who also function as a community. Success in transferring the model to a new region of the country and adapting it to local conditions

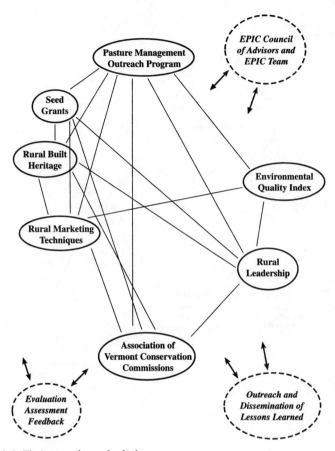

Figure 2.2. Trying to show the linkages.

may depend on the lessons that we learned in Vermont and New England.

The integration of research and outreach, which is essential for effective modern strategic rural development and planning, means that EPIC draws heavily on local citizens, local community development practitioners, and academics from diverse disciplines as reference sources to guide this interdisciplinary approach. The EPIC model means that one actively seeks to find leverage points and to provide levers. The ideas and the detail of the work had to be adaptable and flexible over the months and years as the work continued to grow, change, and flourish, often heading in directions that we could never have envisaged at the outset. Serendipity was often important. Those

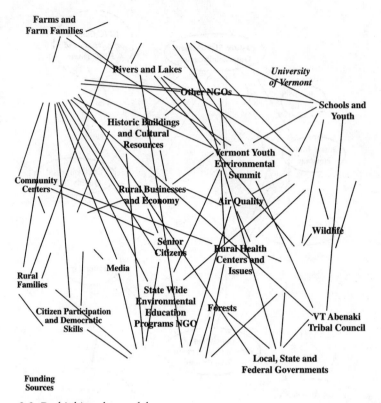

Figure 2.3. Rethinking the model.

involved can become energized by the successes but must also learn from the mistakes. It is of considerable importance to note that many private and government sources will not fund programs with changing goals, flexibility, and a commitment to people at the community level.

Innovation continues to play a key role in sustainable rural community development. Implicit in the concepts of a self-directed community is the theory that grassroots efforts are the best way to influence the community over the long term. No one person or local organization acting alone can deal effectively with the complexities of rural problems. Cooperation and collaboration are crucial to improving community life. It is also important to recognize that the EPIC project as such was funded for only four years, and that after that time, funding continued in only a limited way. This is too little time to be certain of long-term results. Rural, community-based development is an evolving process, one of the hallmarks of sustainability.

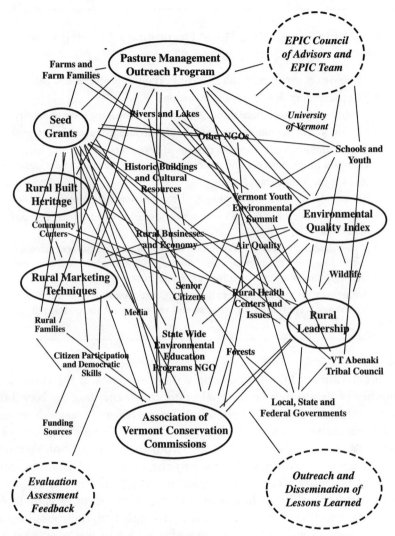

Figure 2.4. The EPIC rural development model.

The EPIC Rural Community Development Model

Certain key elements of sustainable rural community development have evolved during our work with communities. These can be used, along with the list of key principles outlined in Chapter One, by community leaders as a sort of checklist for preparing funding proposals or evaluating community efforts.

Elements in the EPIC Rural Community Development Model

- Participatory processes result in identification of problems and issues.
- The community develops a shared vision.
- Priority setting takes place through a process of engaging the community.
- Women in the community are mobilized, encouraged, and empowered.
- The community encourages its citizens in systems thinking, with special attention to the linkages and connections among the component parts.
- Innovation is encouraged.
- The community directs goal setting, plans of action, and implementation.
- The knowledge base of the community is strengthened as one component of capacity building.
- A continuous process of assessment and evaluation of progress toward goals to improve the program (and not to prove something) occurs from the beginning and must involve the community.
- Adjustment of the goals, priority setting, and assessment about reaching the goals is an ongoing process and must involve the community.

In determining how best to apply these elements in the rural communities of Vermont, with the goal of not only benefiting the New England rural region but also of providing lessons learned and guiding principles for others across the country, several program areas were identified. A diverse group of people from the University of Vermont, the University of Vermont Extension, the business community, nonprofit organizations, community groups, and agriculture met and identified critical rural issues in our region, innovative ideas already under way that could have major impacts if strengthened, and possible key team players willing to facilitate this effort. Out of this meeting came ideas for rural leadership programs: seed grants for communities, programs for youth in community and conservation, innovation in agriculture (especially intensive pasture management), new ideas for rural marketing, rural heritage, and new mechanisms for information dissemination and sharing.

The key to the success of the EPIC model and its potential for increasing sustainability has always been the energy and involvement of well over a thousand people in one state alone, who, over a period of several years, developed a vision and worked hard to help make the world a better place for their children and grandchildren. Most of these people have carried on with the work that they began in partnership with EPIC several years ago.

There are many possible outcomes to rural development work, and the lessons learned and mistakes made are not always noted in reports that merely describe "outcomes." In an effort to ensure that lessons learned as part of the EPIC experience could subsequently be shared with others, mechanisms for assessing progress, measuring success, and assessing failures were put in place at the outset of EPIC that are used even today. These include assessments at a personal level with EPIC volunteers, at the family and community level, and at the local and regional levels. Even influences at national and international levels can be seen.

It is not easy to use this holistic, comprehensive approach to rural development. The whole still has to be divided into bite-sized pieces, but the necessary integration of ideas and linkages that one desires cannot be forced onto a community. It has to happen with a mix of careful strategic forethought by the Director and team leaders (including local citizens), with the hope that serendipity will play a role, because the full extent of the local complexities may not be revealed for several years into the process. Rural development is a dynamic system, a process in time, and not something with a beginning and end.

A Strategic Ecosystem Approach

The EPIC approach is thus one that seeks to integrate community development with research and teaching by considering communities as whole systems. The approach is somewhat similar in philosophy to "action research," in which all members of the involved community take part in the process, from asking the first question, to setting the goals, to measuring the results, to changing the path of research and its associated activities, to interpreting the outcomes. This involves a process of education, self-education, enlightenment, and adaptability.

An example taken from the intensive pasture management component in Chapter Six demonstrates this approach. Intensive pasture management includes basic research on pasture species, cow behavior, animal feed intake, economic data analysis, environmental impact, conservation mechanisms, and self-education of farmers and university faculty and staff. Ultimately it resulted in farmer-led information-exchange walks on active farms and to farmer-run organizations that replaced the need for university involvement. Other impacts that were far broader than the initial research affected family life in positive ways not thought of at the outset. The new agricultural methods changed the farm workday, which in turn changed family life and provided more time for community interaction.

Women played a key role in making this innovation in agriculture successful, both initially and later, by developing organizations that supported its sustainability. For example, in trying to build new partnerships, meetings were held at which farmers, university faculty and staff, extension faculty and staff, leaders of nonprofit conservation organizations, and others shared ideas and brainstormed about new, more innovative ways to make money on the farm while still conserving the landscape and its rural heritage. The women representatives of these groups more easily crossed the boundaries between disciplines, were somewhat less worried about making mistakes, and were more willing to try new ideas. It was also found that women farm technicians were more likely than men to establish a close rapport with farmers (often men), could more easily share their advice and ideas, and had a greater likelihood that their ideas would be successfully used by farmers, perhaps because women seem less threatening to a male farmer. Whatever the reason, when a new nonprofit organization was proposed by the farmers, they asked for a woman leader and voted many women onto the board.

The innovations made on the farms working with new ways to graze cows resulted in economic improvements, but probably more importantly, they brought about social change, reducing farm-family isolation and freeing up time for farmers to get involved with the broader rural community or township. We EPIC staff came to believe that such integration is key to successful community development because it involves a commitment to problem solving *with* people instead of *for* people. Research thus becomes an integral aspect of a holistic, integrated strategic process of community development built on systems thinking, flowing from and to the action. Problem solving becomes a joint effort based on an informed negotiation among people at all levels.

This is a strategic, ecosystem approach. It is not linear in approach and does not favor addressing single items of concern to a community in isolation from the whole. It demands that the connections between the component parts of the whole system be identified and that major and minor impacts be assessed and addressed where possible. The analogy in an organization is the difference between long-term planning and strategic planning. The strategic ecosystem approach demands that we see the whole and recognize that any action will affect all parts of the whole in some way. It may also permit the rural development "players" to help local residents more clearly identify the key factor that may be the leverage point in their community or that may be the catalyst for moving change in the right direction. This approach requires that the rural resident/developer see the landscape as natural systems, from bedrock geology to watersheds populated by complex ecosystems, that have been modified by human use over time. Human landscapes continue to evolve from the underlying natural landscapes, and the two cannot be separated, especially in decision making. This view will permit a more comprehensive approach to sustainable rural community development. A strategic ecosystem approach is, however, messy because so many variables are handled simultaneously and measuring the synergistic results is problematic at best.

Some aspects of this approach, although not specifically identified as such, can be seen in various forms in Western Europe beginning before World War II and increasing in effectiveness during the 1960s and 1970s. European scholars such as Halford Mackinder in his article "The Human Habitat" (1931), Alexander Von Humboldt in his book *Kosmos* (1845), Alan Ogilvie in his article "The Relations of Geology and Geography" (1938), Paul Vidal de la Blache in his articles on the principles of human geography (1896, 1925), David Linton in his inaugural lecture entitled "Discovery Education and Research" (1946), Jean Gottman in his article on methods analysis in human geography (1947), Georges Chabot in his article on French conceptions of human geography (1950), Harald Uhlig's article on research in northern England (1956), G. Wibberly in his article "Some Aspects of Problem Rural Areas in Britain" (1954), and John House in his book of geographical essays about northern England (1966) provide examples of a more comprehensive ecosystem perspective on rural life and landscapes. Similar perspectives have been provided by American scholars in books and articles such as George Perkins Marsh's *Man and Nature* (1846), Carl Ortwin Sauer's "Man and Life" (1967), David Lowenthal's analysis of Marsh (1958), C. Glacken's *Traces on the Rhodian Shore* (1967), Rachel Carson's *Silent Spring* (1962), Aldo Leopold's *A Sand County Almanac* (1947), and Richard Hartshorne's *Perspectives on the Nature of Geography* (1962). A common thread in the writings of the foregoing scholars is integration, whether in systems thinking or in regional analysis, whether pure science or applied research.

The concepts of integrating research with action, if not explicit, were certainly implicit in the premises underlying the establishment of the Cooperative Extension Service in the United States and the British Town and Country Planning efforts in Britain during the past five decades. A somewhat analogous approach was articulated in the recent *The Keystone National Policy Dialogue on Ecosystem Management* (Keystone Center 1996).

The synergy between research and community action (engagement) is essential for modern strategic rural planning and development. Research is both a tool and a way of answering questions. In community development it is also a way of demonstrating the positive outcomes of the processes through which the community goes to achieve new goals. Such work also serves to link similar initiatives across the country.

Outside "experts" and researchers do have a role to play in sustainable rural community development. They can be involved in problem identification, vision development, assessment, and so forth, with the proviso that the community leaders set the rules of engagement. This allows the university and cooperative extension service programs to provide assistance to rural communities only where it is asked for.

Systems Thinking: Looking for the Leverage Point

Small, well-focused actions can sometimes produce significant, enduring improvements if they take place in the right location and at the right time. And if there is a perceived local need, a project begun for other reasons might gradually come to be seen as a rural development project. For example, in the rural community of East Fairfield, Vermont, people came together around the issue of how to best use an old building in the center of the town. Local values proved to be more complex than economic interest alone. On the one hand, some wished to renovate the building to house a new business; on the other, a group of mothers did not want a business placed in what had once been a public school. Although the community needed economic development, it eventually decided that its greater long-term need was for a community gathering place and space for local services—a place where children and seniors could stay more connected to their community. The result was a community center that subsequently became a major catalyst for local change in many other aspects.

In another example, a group of university students, working with community-based input from state experts, produced an index of environmental quality for the state of Vermont. The indicators were qualitative and descriptive in nature and clearly expressed concerns about the lack of environmental information easily obtainable by the public and a lack of information and data on the true quality of the rural environment. This quickly stimulated state government to reassess the state environment, publish its own annual environmental report, and begin to better assess the environment.

System thinkers refer to the principle illustrated in these examples as "leverage." A biological metaphor of this principle is a species whose growth depends on a combination of factors or limiting conditions. If one critical factor is in short supply, the species growth is stopped, even though all other necessary factors may be present in abundance. Identifying and supplying more or less of this critical factor, or changing or removing the limited conditions, allows the species to utilize the other factors and grow.

Rural development in diverse forms has been taking place for several decades. It has helped small rural communities in numerous—especially short-term—ways. In many of these cases, however, outside third parties have superimposed "master plans" on small communities or simply delivered limited services that ignored the uniqueness of a town or denied a small town's capacity to work independently. Too often, answers provided were to questions that no one in the community was asking or were answers to the wrong questions. Today is a time of tremendous change, a time when the old approaches used to address rural problems are of limited effectiveness, especially in the long term.

The EPIC model encourages and supports those who show interest in making a positive difference in their community. It also supports the efforts of individuals and groups to join with others from diverse backgrounds and, where appropriate, encourages them to work with others in nearby communities to foster the growth of a network of active volunteers over a larger region, thereby creating new linkages.

If a project is to change the system through people, the leverage point can best be identified by the people in the community, based on personal interests, shared values, and common ground and not by an outside assessment of needs. This citizen-driven approach is more likely to succeed in the long run because it strengthens the abilities of the citizens in the community rather than deepening their dependence on outside experts and outside funding, both of which are of limited duration and often come with strings attached.

Because the leverage points and the limiting factors that inspire change are different for each community, EPIC projects undertaken in each community will vary enormously. The EPIC approach looks for ways to revitalize connections within and between communities and to revitalize their connections with the greater environment in the complete sense of the word—physical, biological, and cultural.

The ambitious, comprehensive scope of EPIC is the result of an appreciation for the interrelationships of the environmental, economic, historic, and social processes that make up rural communities. The focus of each individual project or component within the whole model is, however, limited. The EPIC approach tries to provide a situation in which each project, or part of a project, could affect the larger system and where the larger system would, in turn, affect each project. It also permits participants to identify situations where a proposed activity might not work or where it might even exacerbate existing problems. Providing opportunities for citizens to see and understand the larger system and to observe its interconnections gives both balance and inspiration to their efforts as a community (Photo 2.1). Such work is simultaneously humbling and inspir-

Photo 2.1. Here children at a high school youth environmental summit learn about the interconnections in nature.

ing for those who serve as resource people, facilitators, and citizen leaders.

Innovation

Innovation plays a key role in rural development. Not only does it ensure that new ideas are drawn from the local population, but the very process of encouraging innovation is, in itself, a stimulus to other individuals and to the community as a whole. One of the key elements in the EPIC model is to encourage innovative thinking and action by community members in all aspects of rural development work.

In the EPIC model, innovation is encouraged through verbal expression and by providing seed grant money for innovative projects. In the leadership workshops, for instance, workshop facilitators (who may be both internal and external to the community) verbally encourage workshop participants (who are from the local community) to come up with more "creative" and "new" ways to be persuasive when role-playing situations of possible conflict in the community and for devising scenarios for long-term success. Likewise, awarding seed grant monies to leadership workshop graduates allows them to try out innovative ideas in their communities. Seed grant projects that EPIC has funded in Vermont include connecting all the town leaders with a free local e-mail system and converting an abandoned storefront to a cafe to serve as a community meeting place. Other seed grant projects are described in Chapter Five. As a part of the EPIC application process for small seed grants (which are typically less than $2,000), applicants are encouraged to be innovative, to build new partnerships, and to do something that is not just "more of the same." EPIC staff take risks by awarding these funds to individuals and ad hoc groups and expecting them to be used on new and unproven ideas. But, in doing so, we show our trust in these people at a deeply human level, encouraging them to take risks.

What makes an idea innovative will be different for each group in each community, and, perhaps, in each state. What seems innovative in Vermont may not seem so in California (Photo 2.2). In the agricultural component of the application of the EPIC model in Vermont, New York, Quebec, and elsewhere in the northeast innovative ideas about intensive pasture management and other new farming techniques proved to be of critical importance (intensive pasture management and related topics are discussed in Chapter Six). In brief, intensive pasture management involves working with farmers to encourage them to use

Photo 2.2. Innovation will mean something different in each community. Here, a group of Mennonites gather to learn more about holistic resource management and intensive pasture management.

grass as a primary feed source, allowing their cows to graze each day instead of feeding them under conditions of confinement. This change takes place in the face of many traditional comments that it has been "tried before and failed, so why try again?" But, while not preferred by all farmers, it works well for many and has increased profit margins, prevented small farms from going out of business, improved farm family life, and sparked more farmers to become active leaders in their rural communities. This support of innovation is done in several ways, some quite substantive in the funding basis, for example, by providing skilled technicians capable of learning alongside the farmers, on the farm, and by answering the questions that they asked us, rather than providing set answers based on past ideas or on thoroughly researched concepts. For a number of years we were also able to support innovative farmers by simple steps like spreading the word that we would supply relief milkers at no cost to farmers, so that busy farmers could get together for a meeting or come to the university to take part in a celebration and share their ideas with a broader spectrum of rural residents. This human element is as critical to long-term positive benefits to society as the necessary scientific measurable outcomes. The innovative farmer is still a risk taker, but more people appear to be sharing that risk.

Innovation usually occurs as a problem or a need is recognized—either as a social problem rises to the top of an agenda or as an individual perceives a future problem and begins to seek solutions (Rogers 1983). The EPIC model itself is innovative, and it acts as a catalyst to encourage community members to make substantive, locally based changes on their own.

This is not to suggest that all reinvigorating ideas will necessarily be "innovative." They may be old traditions, rediscovered and modified for modern times, using modern technical information and meeting modern needs—such as building a community center. Certainly an innovative idea must be compatible with local mores. One cannot be too innovation-oriented but rather must be client-oriented. EPIC staff and team leaders strive to provide an environment in which innovation can flourish, while being mindful that innovations perceived by individuals as having more advantages, compatibility, and less complexity will be adopted more rapidly. One example of how old traditions can be revived involves the Abenaki, a tribe in northern Vermont. Through the support of an EPIC seed grant, Abenaki leaders held a Heritage Festival, the first ever for this tribal group. After the festival, one of the leaders commented, "EPIC leaders thought we had a good idea, and they gave us the encouragement to try it out." The EPIC approach is based on the premise that with community members themselves initiating innovative action, a planted seed would more likely grow into a successful community improvement. In fact, after two or three years of initial funding through small seed grants, the festival became self-supporting, and the idea was adopted by other tribal groups in the Northeast.

Figure 2.5 reflects a generally accepted profile of innovation, in which the small number of initial "innovators" (1–3 percent of the community group, for example) increases as "early adaptors" begin to modify the original innovation to better fit their local situation. By the time 13 to 14 percent of the relevant community population are using the idea, the early adaptors are joined by an ever-increasing number until the "early majority" (30–40 percent, for example) are using the idea. Thus the recent innovation becomes an institutionalized, commonly accepted idea. I say "recent" because, as can be seen in the discussion of pasture management in Chapter Six, it can easily take twenty years for the early adaptors to catch on to the idea and adapt it appro-

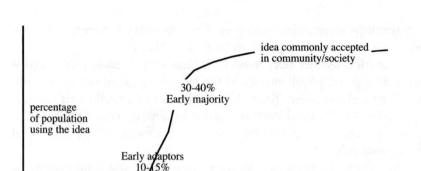

Figure 2.5. Generalized profile of innovation acceptance over time.

priately. Similarly, two decades of persistence was necessary for local conservation commissions to become generally accepted, as will be discussed in Chapter Four.

Principles for Self-Directed Community Development

In addition to integrating research and outreach (or "community engagement" in recent jargon) and using an interdisciplinary lens to focus on leverage points and inspiring innovation, EPIC concentrates on the people. For, in the long run, it is the community that must be able to direct its own development and success. The following aspects of self-directed community development are essential to rural community development efforts such as EPIC.

Locate the People with Vision at the Grassroots Level

Stohr (1987) shows that, frequently, people in rural areas become accustomed to living in crisis systems in an atmosphere of increasing apathy and passivity. As a result, local adaptation and innovation mechanisms in these areas become increasingly eroded and suppressed, leading not only to severe economic repercussions, but also to social and environmental problems. (As an aside, this is not only a concern in rural communities, but also can be found in many institutions and communities, such as universities.)

To address such situations, EPIC seeks out those in communities with leadership qualities and helps them develop the skills and confidence necessary to guide their communities forward. The theory behind this approach is that people, helping themselves, are the best way to influence the system over the long term, and that as William Lassey points out in his book *Planning in Rural Environments* (1977), citizen awareness and support are the basis of successful planning efforts. EPIC begins this process of identifying potential leaders by holding a series of leadership workshops in a community that bring together a local people to brainstorm about possible local and regional leadership. Often, potential leaders are not even aware that they are seen by others as leaders. The workshop participants, usually local town officers, extension agents, business people, youth leaders, and so forth, must be representative of the regional (county level) population and include the "disenfranchised" as well as the established, more women than men, senior citizens, and youth. Representation at the regional level is important because it helps to link otherwise-isolated small rural communities. Those identified during the workshop as possible leaders are then officially nominated, making them eligible to attend an intensive leadership development course. It was found that often the very act of being nominated stimulated many to become strong leaders.

Challenges to rural development often revolve around the relationship between "top-down" and "bottom-up" processes. Top-down "New Deal"–style mechanisms must give way to bottom-up entrepreneurial mechanisms that satisfy grassroots needs through information and innovation. Although the initiative to make this change must come from rural local inhabitants, leadership, financial support, and decentralized government at a state level are also key to its success.

Both the United States Department of Agriculture and the state cooperative extension service system emphasize the fact that long-term success will occur only when local "grassroots" people are key players. Their policies have proved effective in some respects but have also caused the USDA Cooperative State Research, Education, and Extension Service to become less community-focused, responding poorly, for example, to the environmental impacts of agriculture.

The cooperative extension system is an intriguing and frustrating institution with respect to its work at the community level. Its early efforts to empower local grassroots movements were less effective in the 1960s and 1970s because agriculture was no longer the dominant community force. The more integrative approach used by grassroots groups was abandoned for a top-down programmatic approach, an "expert-driven" model in which rural services came to mean delivery of packaged programs. But agriculture as "industry" is not the same as agriculture as part of the whole integration of rural life with land and water resources. More recently, the rise of agribusiness has made the extension's role even more confusing for both rural families and the extension agents who serve them.

Cooperative extension, while much reduced in terms of federal funding, is still a significant player in grassroots work; however, the rules for many extension agents have changed radically from the original concept of the extension service described in Chapter One. Now, many extension personnel are required to publish peer-reviewed articles, and some must raise a percentage of their annual salary by writing grants; such institutional demands by universities that administer extension services are hardly conducive to effective grassroots work.

States vary greatly in their operational structures, their effectiveness, and the efforts of their extension agents and educators to assist local communities. The task for effective rural development is to draw out the citizen leader, encouraging his or her innovative idea and vision. This citizen leader will in turn, be able to draw out the collective vision of the community as a whole.

Build Community Empowerment, Including Skills and Confidence, for Social Improvement

Research in citizenship training has shown that while having the skills to engage in public life is important, it is even more important to have the confidence to use them. Citizens are more likely to participate in improving their communities if there is an opportunity to make a real difference and a way to participate that is comfortable to them.

This idea of community empowerment is central to the EPIC model, which describes it as social action that encourages those who might feel they have little control over their lives to participate in the community decision-making process in order to gain more control over resources and improve their quality of lives (Wallerstein 1993). Such empowerment, to be effective, must rely on genuine local preferences (Galston and Baehler 1995).

In many rural communities, there are large numbers of people who do not feel comfortable serving in an official capacity and, in fact, will rarely voice their opinion in a public setting. Some find public roles too controversial or believe that they do not know enough to serve on a planning board or conservation commission. Others prefer to avoid the conflict political tensions inherent in debates concerning limited resources.

The leadership component of EPIC is probably the most direct route to helping citizens gain skills and confidence. Some of those enrolled in EPIC's leadership workshops may already be involved in their communities in some capacity, although many may not be members of municipal boards or other established organizations and, initially, might not have consider themselves leaders. Ideally, the leadership workshops and seminars should focus on personal empowerment, helping participants to see themselves as more effective "change agents" in facing new challenges and providing each with a toolbox of abilities from which they can draw for most situations they encounter.

The intensive pasture management project discussed earlier and the rural marketing approach also aim to strengthen citizen confidence in themselves, each other, and the market and to de-emphasize the idea that citizens need regular, "expert" guidance.

Encourage Cooperation and Collaboration

We live in a society that admires individual performance and achievement. There are few rewards and little recognition for effective community work requiring cooperation, collaboration, and freely given time, energy, and thought. But no one person acting alone can deal effectively with the complexities of rural problems and challenges. Important parts of any rural development initiative are the promotion of local cooperation and willingness to share information and to identify common objectives and values. Such collaboration must be initiated by leadership and requires joint ownership of decisions and a collective responsibility for future action (Murray and Dunn 1996).

As EPIC progressed through the first few months of 1992, it became clear that the "P" in EPIC stood for more than "Programs"; it also represented "Partnerships." The emphasis was on a two-way exchange of ideas, not on one-way programs delivered by "experts." Thus, university personnel learned a great deal as they shared knowledge and exchanged ideas with community members, and the synergy was beneficial to the entire rural community and even the university.

Stimulate Capacity Building and Long-Term Self-Sufficiency

Successful rural development must consider the future when working with communities and must build efforts based on a clear understanding of the past history of the area ("The past is always prologue"). Rural communities must be able to manage their own affairs once the outside force has gone. When long-term change is the goal, it is more important to influence the functioning of the entire system than it is to provide a thing or service that may be needed in the immediate present. The whole system thus can be changed in the long run by the people who live there.

Effective change is probably created when the community finds the leverage point for themselves and they gather and direct resources to achieve their goals. This "reweaving" process of revitalization is ongoing. The goal of EPIC is to leave the citizen leaders, farmers, business people, students, and organizations with a greater capacity and inspiration to do the reweaving themselves.

Capacity building, an essential component of rural development, is basically the ability of local people to solve their own problems. It means that community leaders must demonstrate strategic thinking and offer a planned program for community involvement in which strategies are devised in response to opportunities or decisions (as opposed to the often-favored "long-range" planning, which sets goals and benchmarks in advance). Strategic planning is thoughtful of the future and concerned about the wider quality-of-life issues. Strategic leadership assumes that communities can respond to the situations around them and understand the nature of change (Richardson 1997).

Initial accomplishments with capacity-building processes may be modest, but over time they can translate into even greater successes. Changes in people mean that the change process can continue into the future.

Short-term successes tend to increase peoples' awareness and make citizens more likely to initiate another project, which in turn improves the efficiency of future projects and strengthens the capacity of more citizens to create change. Long-range self-sufficiency helps the community sustain themselves through indigenous activities or through relationships with other communities (Galston and Baehler 1995) and also becomes a self-reinforcing process. It is strengthened when community efforts are measured as they progress and are publicly recognized in newspapers, through interviews, by visitors from other towns and states, and by holding regional celebrations.

In Fairfield, Vermont, the town was able to build capacity through a group of related projects that were able to meet the new and changed needs of the community. The initial goal for the Fairfield Community

Center was simply to save a building in the town center and use it for a meeting place. Then another subset of local people suggested the need for an after-school program; another suggested senior programs. Others were empowered and energized by their friends' ideas, and gradually the accumulating synergy led to a health clinic, leadership workshops, summer programs for children, and so forth. This capacity building affected leadership by empowering a wider range of participants, both women and men. This in turn increased the sense of self-sufficiency of this rather isolated rural agricultural community, decreasing its dependency on the larger town some distance away. From such capacity building new leaders emerge, and a new sense of a revitalized community can be seen. Neighboring communities learn from this and seek to copy the process and join a network.

The self-directed nature of sustainable rural development discussed above appears to make it easier for innovative ideas not only to flow into a community, but also to increase the likelihood that the innovations will be tested for local efficacy and adaptability. The capacity-building approach is also more likely to permit a systems approach where key factors can be more easily identified.

Chapter Three

How Are We Doing?
The Need for Ongoing Assessment

Asking the Right Questions—Over and Over Again

Although there are many books on rural development, it is usually difficult if not impossible to determine how their conclusions were reached. How and when was the work evaluated? What was the scope and extent of assessment? Over what period of time? What lessons have been learned and how were they learned? By whom? How often are the development mechanisms used? Who were the players? What evaluation formats have been developed and how have they been used to report back to funding organizations, whether public, private, or corporate? Can evaluation and ongoing assessment of projects be used to increase the effectiveness and long-term success of a rural development project? Have we asked the right questions in the first place? Are we asking the right questions now? Has the work been synergistic? If so, what have been the spin-offs?

Although I have drawn on my personal and professional experiences in writing this chapter, I have also drawn on the results of the ongoing assessment of each linked component part and the entire EPIC system approach as applied over the last eight years. These assessments, using both qualitative and quantitative evaluation instruments such as those found in Appendix B, provided measurable results, many of which are described in Chapters Four through Eight.

We also wanted to know if we could understand and capture the synergy that might possibly be taking place at the linkage points of different activities in the rural environment. For example, if stimulus for new, innovative ideas for farming became more common in a region, were the social and economic spin-offs that occurred—although not specifically part of the written goals of the separate-but-linked rural development components—nonetheless an added benefit? If so, was the entire system activated in ways that resulted, for example, in a more integrated farming system in the community? Did farmers become more active in other aspects of the rural community as a result of improved farming techniques being used on the farm? We found that, yes, farmers and their families, as a result of applying new agricultural techniques and reassessing their life values, increasingly participate in community activities, build and take an active part in new farmer-run organizations, and even feel happier. This is discussed more fully in Chapter Six.

In pulling together the findings of our rural development work, we have also used publications and reports written by others involved in EPIC over the years. Some of the EPIC evaluation tools (in generic formats) and other assessment tools can be found in Appendix B (B1, B2, B3, and B4). They are presented so that others involved in rural development can copy and modify them for use in their own communities. The bibliography also contains many references relevant to evaluation, and special note should be made of the work of Patton (1990, 1997), Bliss and Martin (1989), Graham and Jones (1992), and Kellogg (1998).

This chapter is placed near the beginning of the book because, although I do report some of our research findings for the period 1992–1999 in later chapters, its purpose is to discuss evaluation and assessment as an integral, ongoing aspect of rural development activities, not as a separate activity taking place after the project is over. It is also hoped that by discussing the scope and significance of evaluation here, the data, information, and analysis presented in later chapters will prove more useful to others involved in rural development.

Evaluation in General

Most rural development projects are short in duration, usually about three years. They are typically evaluated at the end of the project in a retrospective report (frequently narrative in nature), which is submitted to the provider of the funds. These documents, usually written by project staff, tend to be colored by bias and by the desire for funders to feel their money was well spent. However, even if reports to the sponsoring government agencies and private foundations are reasonably accurate, they are often just stored on agency shelves for record-keeping purposes and not used to enhance the longer-term success of rural development efforts. When this happens, there is no way to share what was learned on a project with other funding agencies, citizens, or leaders of other projects. Often, results are hampered by a lack of scientific credibility so that scientific journals are reluctant to print them, with the result that an even broader audience misses out on learning what worked for a project and what didn't.

Evaluation is not easy to do, however, and it is technically challenging. This is especially the case when dealing with the many human dimensions in the montage of rural development. It also means that funding used for evaluation might be perceived as having been diverted from the main task at hand—a diversion of resources rather than an essential cost of good management.

There is much in evaluation and assessment that produces tension, and that tension must be carefully managed. Thus, it is necessary to articulate the goals for evaluation so that all players understand them. The use of the term "assessment" rather than "evaluation" often helps to reduce some of the tension for the players involved.

The intent of evaluation/assessment should be severalfold:

1. To strengthen projects and permit learning to take place, making changes where needed as the project evolves.
2. To encourage multiple approaches to the problems at hand: to be both multidisciplinary and interdisciplinary.
3. To be grounded in the local community, creating a participatory process, allowing for flexibility, especially when dealing with complex, comprehensive efforts aimed at systematic community change.
4. To build capacity in the community.

The Scientific and Other Methods in Evaluation

Our education has tended to lead us to a reductionist, or simplified, view of the world. There are strengths in scientific perspectives, but sometimes they discourage contextual thinking. Because ongoing assessment/evaluation is an essential element of sustainable rural development, it is necessary to compare the scientific method with other research methods, understand the differences, and acknowledge the need for a more than one approach to rural development research and project work.

As a whole, science and the scientific method are held in high repute in Western society. Our basic education is built on scientific principles. The scientific approach is used by almost all of us in our day-to-day work, whether we identify it as such or not. We begin with a perceived problem and move from there toward a resolution. We begin with a guess as to why we have the problem and seek to address it in a systematic fashion. Good science is based on an "educated guess," a hypothesis based on an understanding of the scholarly literature. An experiment to test the hypothesis is designed with controls and measurements that will produce quantitative results capable of being precisely replicated by other scientists. Scientific measurement permits the demonstration of a causal relationship. For example, it allows us to test the hypothesis that air pollution damages vegetation, including crop plants, and in doing so introduces toxins into our food chain.

Natural science research based on a hypothesis works relatively well in situations where only a single component is being measured. For example, dioxins, potentially unhealthy toxic chemicals produced by the incineration of plastics, reach cows' milk when the animals eat air-polluted crops. The scientist wants to know where the dioxins originate. This can be done by tracking dioxin emissions from known sources to the site of deposition in a distant geographical location and then modeling the results on a computer using a highly selective number of variables. Measurements of dioxin in plants at ground level can validate the model. This is complex research, but even so it only attempts to measure a very limited number of variables. In rural development, however, the number of possible "variables" is much larger. For a given community, all the ecological, economic, and sociocultural components that might affect the desired outcome must be considered. This task is far more complex than the pure or applied research in traditional science. Human values are not easily measured. Furthermore, the scientist is not typically involved the next step, which is to put in place the policies necessary to prevent further pollutant output. And the policy maker responsible for such decisions might not be a scientist. The criteria that each profession uses to measure the success of their work are different.

In science, the researcher is trained to measure only a limited number of variables in order to gain the most clear picture possible of a limited area of study. In the process of designing such research, possible "confounding variables" are identified that might impact the clarity of outcomes of the research. These are contextual complexities in the research environment.

The scientific approach is not perfect. It cannot guarantee that we will find "truth," only probabilities, and it assumes that the right question was asked in the first place. Nonetheless, it is important to understand the scientific method and its limitations in rural development work. We need scientific research from a variety of disciplines, each providing data that may be useful in rural development work. Equally essential is the need for a variety of evaluation techniques not only to interpret data and information, but also to permit regular adjustment of actions to meet the overall goals of sustainable rural development. The EPIC model approach, for example, included pure and applied research within the intensive pasture management demonstration project, and this was shared with farmers and policy makers as it evolved. Some of this work can be found in Sarah Flack's research on white clover and light (1995), in Bill Murphy and others' research on Kentucky bluegrass-white clover (1997), and in Michele Witten's research on farmer participation in federal cost-sharing programs (1996). Critical findings in the field research led to refinements in the actual ecological advice given to farmers. Thus, the intensive pasture system evolved in a practical manner, adapting to the local agricultural ecosystem. It was also found, from ongoing discussions and from periodic social-sciences evaluations of farmers and their families, that the integrated farming systems approaches had social and economic impacts.

Typically, scientific research begins with field or laboratory work conducted in order to answer a predetermined hypothesis. The results of the research are published and undergo the rigor of peer review. The application of these results may take many years. By contrast, working with farmers as research partners in the learning and assessment process blurs the lines between research and evaluation. A clear set of scientifically determined findings may not easily flow from this type of field work, but the positive impacts on the farming community and agriculture are seen more quickly and some of the more serious pitfalls of scientific research may be avoided.

The natural science research model by itself, filled as it is with "variables" for us to "measure," is ill-equipped to help us understand comprehensive community initiatives that are collaborative in design and management. Such initiatives can be an action or series of actions taken by a community. Rural development, which must reconcile data from numerous disciplines with the human values that communities live by, is far more complex than can be measured using only the scientific approach.

In rural development, much energy is expended in ensuring a synergy that generates the energy and interest of the community and that, in turn, may ensure its sustainability. Synergy, the concept that the total can be more than the sum of its parts, is extremely difficult to measure, whether from a natural science approach or from a social science approach. Conventional methods of evaluation have not adequately addressed issues of process, implementation, and improvement, nor have they captured the complex and often messy ways in which these initiatives affect change (Connell et al. 1995, Schorr and Kubisch 1995, Kellogg 1998).

> In community initiatives the need to "prove" something is far less important than the need to "improve" something.

This does not mean that we should avoid evaluation but rather that we should adopt several approaches, be open to intuitive understanding, and try to clearly handle the biases of our own values and politics in the evaluation process. Based both on the EPIC model approach (1992–1998) and on the W.K. Kellogg Foundation's work (1998), the following are some recommendations for approaches to assessment and evaluation in rural development projects.

Learn and Use Several Different Approaches to Evaluation

Interpretivism/constructivism has its roots in anthropological traditions that rely on accounts, rich in description, of close, ongoing relationships among individuals. Such holistic accounts are often lost in evaluator-determined categories of data collection, which do not take into account contextual factors. The interpretivism/constructivism approach focuses on implementation and process, allows us to understand the context and the complexities of programs, and helps improve project management and delivery.

Open-ended interviews were used extensively in EPIC evaluations (samples of the interview guides used can be found in Appendix B). These interviews were used in all components of the EPIC model to strengthen, modify, change, and better integrate the activities in which we were involved. For example, we funded a school-to-work project that our ongoing assessment showed did not work well, and thus we did not continue funding this endeavor. We had also set aside funds to pay for data and data analysis requested by communities. But interviews revealed that the rural communities in which we worked did not in fact need more data. The data may still be needed at a later stage, but what these communities really wanted at that point was community development and small seed grants (these are discussed in detail in Chapters Four and Five). This may partially be accounted for by the fact that we sought out those communities that were the most isolated, the least developed, and the least desirous of rural economic development.

Social science surveys permit both quantitative and qualitative data to be collected in a relatively simple, standardized fashion. In EPIC, because our aim is to be as inclusive as possible, surveys must not rely on complex quantitative statistics but rather aim to be community-friendly and educational. This does not necessarily produce clear, publishable data, but it does help build community. The process is sometimes more important than the data produced. Several sample survey forms are included in Appendix B. Interviewing is another data-gathering technique used. Often conducted informally or in focus groups, interviews also aim to build community in addition to collecting data. Simple surveys and interviews are critical in permitting us to learn more quickly from our mistakes and to use those lessons to improve our work. Surveys and interviews are used in each component of the EPIC model on a regular basis, because they permit adaptation of ongoing work. For example, they can reveal when changes are needed in the agricultural advice being given or on the substance and mechanisms used in leadership development programs.

Economic analysis can be of considerable help to a community that wants to develop mechanisms for encouraging economic development appropriate to its region and to garner support from those who feel more quantitative data are needed in decision making. In EPIC, economic analyses were performed in conjunction with the pasture techniques used by farmers. Farm data were collected and provided in formats useful both to farmers and to resource and agricultural economists. For some towns, standard marketing analyses were also used (see Ron Savitt and Pauline Sullivan's *Developing Marketing Plans for Redeveloping Small Rural Communities* [1995] and Pauline Sullivan and Ron Savitt's *Store Patronage and Lifestyle Factors: Implications for Rural Grocery Retailers* [1997]). Economic analyses were especially useful for towns that had completed leadership development and needs assessments for their community and region.

Feminist methods in assessment and evaluation efforts will ensure that women, girls, youth, and minorities will be included. The feminist approach is "contextual, inclusive, experiential, involved, socially relevant, multi-methodological, complete but not necessarily replicable, open to environment and inclusive of emotions and events as experiences" (Neilson 1990, 6; Reinharz 1983).

Feminists methods are a dominant component and became a key principle of the EPIC rural development model initiative. Feminist methods, whether used by men or women, have contributed considerably to the success of many EPIC components as well as to the evolution of the project and its absorption by communities. The application of feminist methods and approaches is clearly going to affect the long-term sustainability of rural communities.

It is significant to note that the individuals (women and men) not comfortable with feminist methods removed themselves from the EPIC core team early on in the project. This resulted in a team predominantly made up of women, but it worked to the benefit of all, because women were found to be more effective listeners and better at sharing and learning in the rural communities. The men who did take part in EPIC, especially in the early years, were open to diverse perspectives, were comfortable with ambiguity and complexity, and thus were able to play significant and sustaining roles.

My observations over the last thirty years of similar interactions in rural communities in East Africa, New Zealand, the Lake Baikal basin region of Siberia, and Western Samoa have shown that the role of women (and of men who use feminist methods in their roles as leaders) in the core teams involved in rural development is critical to achieving community stability and sustainable development. The significant role that women play and of feminist approaches in general is inherent throughout the discussion of the pasture management outreach program in Chapter Six and in the case studies of seed grants and related activities discussed in Chapter Eight.

Theory-based evaluation is based on the premise that combining outcome data with an understanding of the process that led to the outcomes teaches us a great deal about a program's impact and its most influential factors (Schorr and Kubisch 1995). The process includes the development of a program logic model or a picture (such as those presented in Chapter Two). These models can be used by team leaders and citizens to guide the project and to explain it to agencies, policy makers, and other collaborating organizations and partners. Such models can provide information about how to implement similar initiatives and how to identify linkage points between integrated parts of the whole system. They can also be used to identify core elements, possible pitfalls, and lessons learned along the way. They also allow newcomers to the project to see more clearly where they might best fit.

Because it is important to involve both men and women in sustainable rural development, the use of theory-based evaluation, which provides a basis of communication between men and women, is recommended. It can also help to increase the total number of project participants.

Question the Questions

All players in a rural development initiative must be encouraged to ask questions and to question each others' roles and approaches. What is working? How are we measuring it? What (or who) are the blocks to progress? This is a tricky task. Many of us have been trained in specific disciplines. Since rural development is intrinsically multi- and inter-disciplinary, we must be comfortable challenging and being challenged by our peers, our colleagues, and by the citizenry we serve. Adaptable team players who are tolerant and supportive of ongoing project assessment are essential to successful rural community development.

As discussed earlier, this has meant that the EPIC team of university, state agency, nonprofit organizations, citizens, and students must participate in this process of questioning and discussion on a regular basis. Some were and are better at it than others. It is interesting and perhaps significant that women tended to be more willing than men to participate. Those men who actively participated for several years appeared to think and work within broad contexts and enjoyed working with many different evaluation and research tools. Some experts, trained and comfortable in distinct, narrow disciplines, may not be comfortable working on teams that include experts from other fields, nonexperts, and people with little formal education. The opposite also holds true: the local citizen who has worked in the rural community since leaving high school or eighth grade may feel intimidated by those with university degrees. Other participants may have personal or professional agendas that make it difficult for them to work collaboratively with others toward community-based goals. Still others find it difficult to listen actively or to cope when their ideas are challenged. Defensive responses to questions will hamper sustainable rural community development.

> Adaptable team players, able to work with a diversity of perspectives and tolerant and supportive of regular and ongoing assessment, are absolutely critical for successful rural community development.

Take Actions to Change the Initiative as It Unfolds

There are no perfect answers to the questions posed by those working in rural communities, and, indeed, there may be several answers to a question. As described above, many of the evaluation and assessment tools used by EPIC over the years led to changes in the approach and the mechanisms used to help maintain the community in a healthy, sustainable state. Identify mistakes and learn from them. (A note of caution: Organizations that fund these projects are often less flexible than the communities with which they are working, but it is still important that they remain an active part of the team.)

Be Open in Communication and Maintain a Clear History

Our assessment work has shown that successful projects take place in an atmosphere of openness and collaboration. This does not just happen—it must be a conscious effort. Meetings should be as convenient to participants as possible: hold them at a variety of times—during normal working hours as well as evenings—and serve refreshments. Newsletters, meeting minutes, and other informal mechanisms for communication are also vital to success. The goal must be true communication and not just to provide information on a need-to-know basis. In addition, all decision making must take place in meetings that are open to all and be clearly documented in ongoing records that are easily accessible by the public. This is particularly important for long-term projects in which participants, both community volunteers and outside experts, tend to come and go, taking their accumulated knowledge with them when they leave. Project information needs to be systematically recorded and preserved.

The form of open communication found in project history records will differ markedly by culture and geographic region. Some cultures and socioeconomic groups prefer the written word. Others rely on stories passed orally from generation to generation. For instance, the First Nations of the Canadian North, the Eskimo and Indian tribes of Alaska, and the indigenous peoples and other cultural groups in the

United States have long traditions of oral history. For rural development projects in these areas, oral modes of communication, such as television (both cable and local) still work best. Newspapers and other methods of written communication are not as effective. Methods of oral communication are further discussed in Chapter Seven

We have also learned that, under the EPIC model, the number and type of participants will (and should) change over the years, so that only a few retain a full sense of a project's history, and not everyone will understand its holistic nature. Indeed, some who joined EPIC after the first year or so were quite clear that they were primarily interested in the money we provided. Our tasks then were to redirect their energy to benefit the "wholeness of the system" and show them how their specific expertise could contribute to the overall long-term success of the project.

> There is no "best" approach to evaluating a rural development project. The project manager, while encouraging team players to conduct research in traditional ways, must keep in mind that her or his primary goal is not to *prove* something but to act as a catalyst for community revitalization. The leader must be able to work with those who are willing, available, and adaptable players and to be transparent in all actions. Suggestions for conducting evaluations of rural development projects can be found in Appendix B.

Evaluating the Context—Especially the Natural Environment

When a rural development initiative, or project, is evaluated, there is usually a desire to measure outcomes or at least to produce measurable data. But if it is to be replicated by others, there must also be some means of assessing, or evaluating, the context—the environment within which the development takes place. Knowing the context makes it easier to transfer ideas and the lessons learned to others and for communities in other regions to adapt them for their own purposes. This relationship between a community and its physical and biological environment must be a two-way exchange for long-term sustainable development to occur.

Context evaluation, which usually takes place in the early phases of a rural development project, assesses all aspects of a community that might affect the project. These include the ecological (natural) environment, the cultural environment (including historical settlement patterns), economic trends, and sociopolitical trends. Unfortunately, rural development often begins only in response to a serious problem faced by a community. The result is that all too often the rural development expert called in to solve it addresses only the economic implications of a crisis to the detriment of the other "environments" also affected (ecological, cultural, and sociopolitical). All too often, when the economic argument takes precedence over all else, the natural environment is ignored. And to ignore nature is to take its benefits for granted.

> To assume that we can ignore nature in this way is to place a rural community in serious peril and to guarantee that there will be no sustainable development there.

My experience worldwide is that the natural environment, the stresses upon it, and its potential carrying capacity tend to be ignored, or at best given only token acknowledgment. Good rural development must consider the basic ecological concept of carrying capacity—how much an area is ecologically capable of supporting—even before assessing the socioeconomic needs of communities. A complete community needs assessment tends to focus on socioeconomic factors and may or may not be what the region wants or needs. A good example is that of a case study community assessment of the town of Superior, Nebraska, found in Luther and Wall (1989), which does not include any assessment of the natural resource base and the carrying capacity of the natural environment. This case study will be further explored in Chapter Eight.

The long-term implications for human health in rural communities are also often ignored when it comes to determining where to locate waste depositories for hazardous materials, strip mines, or military operation and training sites or how to evaluate groundwater contamination, air pollutant impacts on animal feeds, and other related by-products of our modern world. Such oversight probably reflects continued tensions over environmental protection versus economic growth—tensions that must be overcome if sustainable development is to succeed. It may also reflect the fact that most people are truly overwhelmed by the enormous set of interconnected facets that must be considered as a part of a comprehensive rural development effort. Those involved in rural development would do well to learn from recent work in ecological management. See, for example, *The Keystone National Policy Dialogue on Ecosystem Management* (1996).

There are many methods for evaluating the natural environment of a community. In the EPIC model, we developed a simple system of identifying rural "environmental indicators." These included (essentially) qualitative assessments of water quantity and quality, air quality, agriculture, forestry, energy, wetland protection, and rural heritage.

> Environmental indicators (discussed more fully in Chapter Seven) are an effective mechanism that communities can use to stimulate state and local policy. They can also be used to highlight community volunteer activities and to involve children and schools in local projects.

In many cases carrying out only an informal assessment of population size, structure, and trends; socioeconomic trends (from census data); general land-use trends; and the names of local leaders and organizations may provide an adequate foundation for a rural development project. We Americans like to gather statistics, but for many rural communities, more numbers and data might not be of use. We found that at the grassroots level there was a far greater need for basic assistance, such being taught how to run meetings, how to apply for funding, or how to set up not-for-profit organizations.

Evaluating Outcomes, Lessons Learned, and Sustainability

There is an important, albeit subtle, difference between "outcomes" and "lessons learned." An outcome is typically a measurable effect or result of some activity. "Lessons learned" is a more far-reaching concept that seeks to capture the subtleties of process, values, and other essentially immeasurable effects. Identifying lessons learned relies on a careful analysis using a more creative, intuitive perspective. It is necessary to understand both outcomes and lessons learned to move toward sustainable development, because both process and cultural values are vital ingredients for a healthy community and society, and they play a critical role in determining long-term success.

In rural development work outcomes can be observed at many levels: the program level, family level, community level, and regional and state levels. Outcomes for specific economic sectors can also be determined. Some outcomes will have been determined before the project begins, but most will (and should) evolve as the project progresses. Both outcomes and lessons learned must be specifically sought out if a rural development project is to be successful in the long term.

> If the rural development project is set up primarily with "measurable outcomes," then the rural development project will likely be doomed to failure.

Of paramount importance is to determine before a project begins whom it is intended to serve. If the project is indeed intended to serve the rural community (by which I mean both the natural environment and the people who live there), then the project must be capable of constantly evolving, as a result of input from the local community, as it progresses. This approach, applied in a creative manner, will provide an environment in which the unexpected can take place. The result will be that new ideas, or modified old ones, will evolve to suit the local circumstances, permitting greater likelihood of sustainability in that region. The goal that could be measured in such work might be that the idea no longer "belongs" to the EPIC staff, or to any other group of "outsiders," but has become absorbed into the fabric of that specific rural location. Indeed the original idea behind the project may have been so transformed that it is barely recognizable.

EPIC measures its success by the fact that most of those people benefiting from the work have no idea who or what EPIC is or what it did. Because of this, we have had to use myriad ways to collect data and to assess the outcomes and determine the levels of sustainability. Later chapters describe some of the successes and failures of our work and try to suggest why certain projects succeeded or failed. Some of the most meaningful outcomes and lessons learned, especially those that relate to the human condition, are very difficult to measure, and yet they may be the most significant aspect of the rural development work.

One final note on assessment. The EPIC model includes core team leaders, each of whom is responsible for one aspect of the project undertaken. Each is expected to conduct periodic internal evaluations of his or her team's work (by using surveys and interviews, for example). The EPIC director continually assesses all parts of the project and periodically asks for short narrative reports from the team leaders. Team leaders discuss their work with everyone involved in the project at the regular meetings (held every five to six weeks). Ideally, these are stimulating, enjoyable meetings held over a long lunch. Virtually all core team leaders and technical staff and community leaders attend, although the ratios of players change over time as people move on to work independently in communities. Every team leader is encouraged to listen and interact with the entire group and to modify his or her work based on input from all.

Many in this collaborative process will be unfamiliar with work conducted by others. I offer an anecdotal example: One core leader, whose expertise was in historic preservation, listened to a farmer talk about his family's rural heritage and how he adapted his early-nineteenth-century barns to modern farming. Following the farmer's description of changes in barn use, the academic expert expressed amazement at himself for "not really realizing that barns had cows in them!" He was able to laugh at his simplistic view of the barn as a wooden structure with certain architectural characteristics and design features. He was able to change his view of historic preservation to include a viable farming community.

Working with a diverse group of people demands that meetings are run efficiently and clearly by sensitive leaders. People must want to come. Expectations and outcomes from the meetings must be very clear. Meetings must start and end on time. Provisions may need to be made to ensure that there is funding to pay for someone to have a babysitter at home, an extra assistant in his or her store or business, or a relief milker to milk cows so that busy community members can not only attend but also take part in the meeting without worrying about what is going on at home or in the barn. In geographically isolated communities, telephone conference calls could be substituted, and other creative ways to meet can be thoughtfully developed.

The EPIC model also includes an external evaluation. In Vermont, this role was filled by a person who conducted regular ongoing assessment of all aspects of EPIC throughout its five active years, interviewing people in rural communities, attending meetings, and providing feedback to the director and team leaders. She was hired as an independent consultant, selected in part because she lived in a rural community and had many years of experience in several fields. Her findings were important and strengthened our methods of action. This person was selected specifically because she perceived issues differently from the director and staff. She was initially very interested in measuring outcomes and in finding economic measurements of success but was quickly astounded by the lessons learned. It was hoped that this "external evaluator" would enable us to gain different understandings and insights into our work. Although we did gain some insights from the external evaluation, it proved more useful in giving us the confidence to build on our strengths and verified our instincts about the aspects that weren't going so well. The external evaluator was well respected in the region and was of critical importance in providing unbiased feedback.

The primary funder of a project can be a helpful partner in evaluation. For example, one of EPIC's funders is the W.K. Kellogg Foundation, which has funded projects similar to EPIC's all over the world.

EPIC has been able to benefit from many of the lessons learned by the Foundation staff and their other grantees on its other projects. One example that was helpful in the early stages of developing the EPIC model was a project in Georgia that utilized seed grants. Others included the economic development work of the Heartland Center in Nebraska, work in the Dakotas on leadership, and work with integrated farming systems in Michigan and Ohio (several of these projects are listed at the end of Appendix C). In developing the EPIC model, I learned what I could from these and other projects. The EPIC model became more comprehensive and kept evolving as the assessments and evaluation continued to bring new ideas and information to us in our core leaders meetings. Regular discussions with the program officer at the W.K. Kellogg Foundation proved invaluable.

If rural America is to have viable and sustainable communities, we need to know what has been tried elsewhere, what has worked, what has not, and why. We need to be able and willing to share the lessons we have learned from the rural development projects in which we are involved, and we need to be adaptable. No one person leading a project in a rural community can know all the right questions to ask or have all the answers, especially at first. Outside and local experts as well as community volunteers must all be involved in the project and its assessment. An adaptive approach, which can meet both the community's needs and the needs of the changing economy and environment, locally and externally, requires ongoing assessment and evaluation of effort, using a wide diversity of mechanisms, and a wide diversity of participants. The resulting data, information, stories, and concepts developed from such diverse approaches will not provide the perfect scientific answer with guaranteed results. But these data will require the rural citizen and the expert to thoughtfully consider the findings of others as they determine which ideas adapt to their local community to forge a stronger community for future generations.

Chapter Four

Lessons Learned about Leadership

If I were pressed to select only one from a list of the ten most important components needed for sustainable rural community development, it would have to be leadership training. A few hours a week, spread over about two months, in the company of other local citizens in a nonconfrontational setting, can lead to individual and community empowerment, often with unexpected spin-offs.

> The most significant results from the leadership course are the multiple connections that were made during the program. The awareness of the multiplicity [of perspectives] in managing the forest also became evident. . . . The need for areas of large acreage to be managed in a coherent manner and the fact that there is more to managing the forest than just marking timber became evident through the leadership course. . . . This was critical new knowledge of broader ecosystem understanding.
>
> —James Roberts, community participant in a forestry leadership program in New England

Most of us work and play in a relatively isolated manner, with family, friends, and work colleagues. These are "safe" settings. We come together in larger groups at family functions, funerals, sports events, school gatherings, and so forth. When we meet as a local community, it can be stressful. There may be an issue in land-use planning, zoning, or citing of a landfill or jail, any one of which can cause conflict. Leadership training can provide new opportunities for community collaboration with synergistic results.

Strategic rural leadership is collaborative. It involves a diversity of people, opinions, and perspectives and is grounded in an understanding of the physical and cultural environments of the local communities. Such leadership can understand, at least to some extent, both the component parts and the whole system of the rural community in its context, local and global. It demands a look back at historical patterns of behavior and a clear look forward to a preferred vision of the future, grounded in knowledge of the present. Such leadership is not simple, and it is hard to find. Strategic leaders must be dedicated. These individuals may be local citizens, agency representatives, academics, or business people, but all must be committed to a community-based and community-driven approach to rural development. The strategic leader knows and understands a diversity of styles of leadership and management and knows which to use in a given situation. Because a new, more strategic leadership is urgently needed, those people who are presently involved in rural development must work to encourage local citizens to learn more about leadership and to prepare themselves to play leadership roles in the future. In this chapter, I will take a broad look at leadership and then present and assess a sampling of leadership development mechanisms, workshops, written materials, and training programs that appear to work well.

Perspectives on Leadership

There are many books on leadership, some of which are listed in the bibliography. Given that there is no one style of leadership that will meet the needs of every community, or every challenging situation, some knowledge of the many approaches to leadership is essential. Those working in rural development need to be conversant with a range of approaches to leadership, able to use several styles, and able to share this knowledge with collaborating citizens. When I take part in leadership development seminars, I bring a couple of canvas bags filled with books and articles about leadership, which the participants may borrow during the course. These are books that they may not find at the local bookstore or lending library (assuming there is one locally).

Some leaders provide the classic, military style of the top-down approach, such as Perry Smith's book *Taking Charge* (1988) presents. The title clearly reflects the message. This approach is still common in many arenas but has limited application in most rural-community situations. It is, however, vitally important to understand the clear structure provided by this traditional model because for some activities it may provide the most useful structure—for example, when setting up a nonprofit board in which roles must be clearly established at the outset. The "in-charge" leader might have the necessary vision and might be the one to set up the board, but, as the organization takes on a life of its own, a new type of leader will be needed and the old leader will have to step aside.

Others, such as Warren Bennis in *On Becoming a Leader* (1989) and John Gardner in *Leadership Papers* (1987), provide foundation leadership concepts that are comprehensive and, while traditional in some approaches, still offer a wide array of choices based on carefully reasoned rationale. Similarly, Burt Nannus, in his book *Visionary Leadership* (1992), provides some useful albeit traditional perspectives on corporate leadership. However, given that in many rural regions the citizens are traditional in outlook and conservative in perspective, knowing these types of approaches is helpful, especially for the outside person trying to effect change in a local community.

Robert Greenleaf's book *Servant Leadership* (1977) provides a new perspective. According to Greenleaf, the true leader may not be in the number one, out-front, position of chair of the board or of senator, but through more subtle and facilitative mechanisms (often as the "number two" person) can quietly move an organization or idea forward. This can be a very effective mechanism in a rural community, especially where there may be religious communities directly or indirectly active in community development.

Women scholars have developed other views of leadership. Ann Morrison in *The New Leaders* (1993) assesses leadership issues in the corporate world and the particular problems for women wishing to move into leadership positions. She also addresses some of the very difficult issues of diversity in the workplace, expressing concern over the backlash likely from the cultural correctness forced upon institutions. Her observations are well worth attention. Dean and Mary Tjosvold, in their book *The Emerging Leader* (1993), look at corporations and describe mechanisms that can and should be used to build teams and foster collaboration in an atmosphere that has traditionally used, and worked in favor of, individual competitiveness as a sign of success. These books seek to clarify the problems in corporate leadership. Harnessing the corporate skills of retired IBM engineer and computer expert Brad Murray, with his newly learned local leadership skills, proved beneficial for several towns in rural northern Vermont; he was able to foster greater collaboration between town leaders in a whole region through use of computer technology (Photo 4.1).

By contrast, Larraine Matusak (1997), in her recent book *Finding Your Voice,* based on her decades of leadership experience (including

Photo 4.1. Following the local, multicommunity EPIC rural leadership workshops, Brad Murray, a retired IBM engineer, applied for a major national competitive grant to link people and organizations in his rural community by developing a community-based e-mail and Internet system that improved communications between conflicting groups.

being a Mother Superior, a college president, and director of a foundation-based national leadership program) emphasizes "transformational" leadership. Such leadership cuts across all sectors of the community and deeply influences many aspects of an organization or system. John Adams, in *Transforming Leadership* (1986), also emphasizes the need for a clear vision and a transforming style of leadership. Such leaders have as their underlying goal the desire to empower others, a trait absolutely critical for leaders in sustainable rural development.

There are many models available for facilitators of leadership development activities that are especially useful in community empowerment efforts. Those presented in this book appear to provide readily transferable templates suitable for adaption in diverse communities across the country. Several of these programs were developed as part of the EPIC model approach to basic leadership development. Fran Moses of Georgia, Vermont, for example, said, "I had never thought of myself as a leader until I was nominated to take the EPIC leadership workshops. And now I am not scared to speak up at Town Meeting or anywhere. I even got the town fathers to agree to set up a conservation commission, although I let someone else actually run it" (Photo 4.2).

Other leadership training might be only tangentially related to rural development activities such as seed grants and agricultural innovation (Photo 4.3). Focused leadership development built around forestry and conservation is commonly used in the East, Midwest, and West.

Youth leadership, a "key principle" intrinsic to EPIC, is also an

Photo 4.2. Fran Moses of Georgia, Vermont, is interviewed by the author at an annual gathering of EPIC. She said, "I had never thought of myself as a leader until I was nominated to take the EPIC leadership workshops. And now I am not scared to speak up at Town Meeting or anywhere."

Photo 4.3. Sally Forgues, right foreground, is a farmer, grandmother, and pediatric nurse. She and her husband have turned their farm over to their son, who, with his wife and baby, works in a family partnership on a diversifying dairy farm near the Canadian border. Sally's leadership and support in the family, the pasture farmers' network, and farmer group meetings continue to be essential in bringing needed changes to their rural community. Sally also links the farm to the urban medical center where she works part time. There she can find outlets for organic chickens, which they now produce as well as organic milk.

Photo 4.4. Youth leadership, planting trees with a group of volunteers as part of a Youth Environmental Summit (YES). Such hands-on efforts help to connect the children with their local communities and build a network of similar-minded teenagers from other schools.

important component in rural development. Convincing youth to accept leadership roles is not easy. One method might be youth summits that include hands-on activities such as planting trees (Photo 4.4).

Strategic Rural Leadership: Making Sense of the Complexity

Given the complexities and problems in rural America and the many leadership styles that have been identified, are there explanations of why so many rural problems remain unresolved? Many contend that it is because there is plenty of chaos but not enough clear leadership.

When asked, many rural residents say they are troubled by the apparently limited understanding of rural America by our national leaders, who spend so much of their time "inside the Beltway" that they have lost connection with the day-to-day realities of America. There is angry confusion both within Congress and toward Congress. The evening news is filled with numbing accounts of murder, bombings, war, and international summit meetings. How can anyone lead effectively in the face of such chaos?

Images of rural America often imply the idea that everyone will get together to rebuild a burned barn or bring in the hay. Although that certainly does happen in some locations, rural society, as discussed earlier, is far more complex than these simplified images convey, and many of the traditional institutions no longer operate or operate with less vigor. Similarly, there are more complex and changing leadership roles in rural regions than in decades past, and yet, despite the sophistication of American society, those filling these new roles often have more basic needs than one might assume. There might be a greater need for a short workshop on fundraising than for a complex computer software package. The important challenge for rural leadership is to help residents, old and new, understand the new local and global environments in which they must operate and to recognize potential opportunities, choosing and acting upon only the most sustainable. These opportunities may have some traditional components, but radical changes are needed to ensure long-term improvements. We need to not merely tolerate maverick suggestions but to carefully implement them for long enough (maybe for years) to truly test their validity. The present fear of failure among leaders, and their lack of understanding of the historical, geographical, and ecological contexts of rural communities, stifle innovation and hamper progress.

Those of us living and working in rural communities who are concerned about agriculture, environmental protection, natural resource conservation, economic development, and other factors that influence sustainable development are troubled. We perceive a limited understanding of the true nature of rural life by leaders who spend so much of their time in the "ivory tower" of universities or in the halls of the nation's government buildings. Their comments and actions seem to have little connection with the day-to-day realities of rural America. By and large, rural communities seem forgotten or misunderstood by most Americans, and yet there are many leadership needs in rural communities similar to those in urban and suburban communities. In rural work, only the scale is different: daily challenges for leaders seem more local and more humanly sized.

Imagine, for example, that you, the reader, are at your town or regional meeting to determine what to do with solid waste in the community. You have heard that incineration, no matter how technically efficient, will put into the air a range of toxics such as mercury and dioxins from burning plastics, all of which come back to us through the food chain as serious health problems. Thus, safe local or regional disposal of trash is vitally important. You come to the meeting having appropriately identified all the "stakeholders," from engineers, to politicians, incinerator operators, environmentalists, and health care professionals. The town has completed an informal needs assessment. The town leaders have reviewed the capital assets of the town, buildings, road maintenance equipment, and the like; they have looked at total town population, socioeconomic data, and the natural resource base; they have probably taken a survey of all the town families regarding their vision for the future of the town.

There at the meeting, perhaps in the elementary school gym, are all the players: the NIMBYs (not in my back yard); the engineers who have all the technical answers and who really believe that a landfill can be safe; and the self-righteous, elite environmentalists (sometimes called "green sneakers" and "tree huggers") who appear biased and simplistic (to the engineers with whom they are probably squabbling). These environmental idealists often want us to reduce waste, change our values, and take care of the indigenous peoples, the rainforest, and the poorer members of society who live in the section of town sited for the regional landfill. They demand that we all pay attention to Environmental Justice.

At the same landfill meeting there are farmers and loggers who quickly set up in opposition to the environmentalists, whom they perceive as "enemies," while appearing to ignore the implication of the possible pollution of their fields, grazing animals, and forests. There, too, are the "logical" scientists, university professors, and economists "assessing risk" and giving "probabilities." They can point out the clear economic benefits that accrue from "tipping fees" from the several states who will send their trash to your town landfill. Also present are the "greedy" lawyers, demanding "due process" and civil rights for the poor and the Native peoples. The environmental lawyers want legal enforcement of policies and regulations that are based not only on limited understanding of science and economics, but also are based on compromises reached with corporate businesspersons and with national and regional politicians. In attendance, too, are the frustrated town officers: leaders desperate to help their town function better, seeking safe, sustainable economic growth and yet tired and frustrated to the point of anger and fearful of what will happen to business locally if the income from the landfill does not come to town.

The conflicting values of society, together with the lack of interdisciplinary analytical training, seem to encourage a destructive form of competition within our own habitats. This leads to the so-called "tragedy of the commons," a term first used by Garrett Hardin in an article by that name published in *Science* in 1968. This term refers to the degradation of common-property resources. It takes place when each user reasons, "If I do not use this resource, someone else will, and the little bit that I pollute will not make much difference." When there are only a very few users of a resource (such as a large pond) this logic may be correct. However, over time, if no one is actively trying to conserve the natural resource for future generations, the cumulative impact of many people trying to use the common resource will result in either the resource being used up or being contaminated. No one intended that the pond be destroyed, but it happened nonetheless. Once destroyed, no one can use (and benefit from) it, and therein lies the tragedy.

This rather crude depiction of a typical local meeting is presented to demonstrate the impact of stereotypes and the very real fears and conflicts that must be addressed if a sustainable future environment is to be attained. By labeling all the players and all the stakeholders at the meeting, everyone is put into a "box." They are given all the values that we assume they bring to such a meeting, even though we know that we are all far more complex than that. But the labels are there, and they make leadership difficult—especially for the local community citizen—and make negotiating almost impossible.

Yet scenes like this have been going on for a long time. Environmentalists have fought with the corporations, businesses, and governments from local to global. There have been wins and losses on all sides. Farmers have often been caught in the middle, unwilling to be treated like business and regulated, but unwilling to be labeled "environmentalists." The typical local citizen remains silent, often lacking confidence in his or her more practical perspective on what they might see as pretty obvious. The backlash against the conservation and environmental communities should not be taken lightly, however. As the journalist David Helvarg points out in his book *The War Against the Greens* (1992), there are many whose extreme views hold serious implications for those whose perspectives are more in balance with nature. Fear tactics can thus reduce the numbers who will have the confidence to stand up at meetings, or write to the papers, or serve as town leaders. With so many remaining silent, the local communities that do try mediation, negotiation, or holding "town meetings" of various sorts have seen limited results. Sometimes mediation has worked, but all too often the battles have been fought in the courts, where it has been the experts on the witness stand who have determined the outcomes. The perception is often that these experts have been manipulated by lawyers, many of whom have little understanding of science or of local communities and no understanding of daily life on a dairy farm, or of cotton and soybean production in the South, or of picking apples in Washington State. The gaps in understanding seem to have increased phenomenally, and the political backlash is complicated by angry confusion. We need new understanding of the changing paradigms. We need to ask some questions about how and why we have come to this serious decline into instability in our rural communities, with only limited leadership at all levels of government. We also need to recognize the rapidly changing global context within which we must function.

To understand why the old paradigms no longer work, we must recognize that our education has failed to prepare us for a world of increasing unpredictability and complexity. For the most part, we have been trained to see complexity as a set of singular problems to be resolved by specific predictable technological solutions. If the air is polluted, you write a clean air act requiring scrubbers. Lawyers, scientists, and economists (the "experts") argue over costs and benefits, risks and responsibility, endlessly tinkering with the regulations necessary to resolve "the problem." But somehow, the goal of clean air is never attained. We never reach homeostasis. And, today, after decades of regulation, a third of all Americans still live in areas, which include many rural areas, where the air is unsafe to breathe and the water unsafe to drink. And, although we now talk a lot about "ecosystem management," "sustainable agriculture," and "sustainable development," we still see the young families and teenagers moving to urban areas. In many rural towns and villages, mothers with young children must work outside the home, just as in urban areas, leaving the infants and children in daycare facilities in the city. Rural villages have, in essence, become suburban in function. Rural isolation increases; farmers are especially isolated from the day-to-day activities of their families and their local community as well from urban America. Stable, sustainable rural communities are a rare phenomenon. Indeed, I am not sure that I would know one if I went there.

Somehow we seem to have forgotten what we all know intuitively: that every so-called problem has a context; everything is interconnected. Wildlife, rare plants, forests, industry, rivers, and people coexist in a region. They function together, for better for worse, for richer for poorer, in sickness and in health. But, unlike the marriage contract that those simplistic phrases suggest, there is no divorce from the environment. You have to work it out. This requires the recognition in our daily lives, in our science, and in the way we seek and order knowledge that nature is interdisciplinary.

Challenges of Rural Leadership during Chaos

The trend in education over the last 100 years has been to increasingly fragment the "body of knowledge" into many disciplines. Teachers and administrators themselves educated in such a structure have carried it into high schools and elementary schools. The result is an educational system that does not easily permit an understanding of the real nature of the world around us.

Margaret Wheatley, in *Leadership and the New Science* (1992), reminds us that we live and work in organizations designed from seventeenth-century images of the universe, seventeenth-century (Newtonian) physics. Our fragmented education has resulted in confusion of the mind, which interferes with perception and leads to conflict, as David Bohm suggests in *Wholeness and the Implicate Order* (1980). But if we are to help rural communities to help themselves, then we need to at least ground our work in the science of our times rather than working with our fragmented perceptions of reality and fragmented approaches to research and to rural development. Certainly there are some who are trying to change to the way we approach science. For example, many uneasy collaborators are struggling with concepts of ecosystem management, trying to make sense of the whole but still deriving their data from fragmented sciences.

It is easy, however, to find examples of the results of fragmented thinking and out-of-date science in the maze of state and federal agencies that directly affect rural regions. The scope of laws and regulations are beyond the understanding of any one person, and the resulting jurisdictional patterns are daunting for the best political geographers. We may be the only major nation on the planet without a minister of the environment in the cabinet, and the management of forests, agriculture, parks, energy, water, wildlife, and minerals is scattered among several federal departments and hundreds of agencies.

This fragmented approach to natural resources management has serious implications. For example, a number of rural residents in the large lake basin of Lake Champlain (which is shared among parts of Canada, New York, and Vermont) wanted to develop a plan for the basin, a natural ecological unit. The U.S. Congress agreed, and the Lake

Champlain Management Conference was established. But in the end, the fragmented governing units could not reach any kind of agreement. This example makes clear that the number of government stakeholders eligible for a seat at the table is too great. There are myriad national, regional, state, county, and town governments with direct jurisdiction on Lake Champlain. Some agencies, such as the Environmental Protection Agency (EPA), have been divided into two subagencies because of regional boundaries that bisect the lake. Not a single agency unit boundary reflects the lake's watershed boundaries and rural townships. Almost every state and local town boundary is an artifact of seventeenth-century exploration and wars, rigidly enforced by constitutional prohibition against interstate treaties. The fragmentation that Wheatley discusses clearly makes it difficult to plan strategically to address rural problems in a manner based on ecosystems as dynamic whole systems.

Of course, there is not just one context within which our facts must be understood and within which our leadership must operate. There are many integrated and overlapping contexts that must be considered. For example, America is the geographical and political context within which our strategic environmental decisions must be made about pressing problems both locally and nationally. The United States is itself a land of contradictions. It is easy to point to our profligate use of natural resources, yet the United States has some of the strongest and most consistently enforced environmental laws in the world. For example, over 100 years ago, the United States established the first national park and has gone on to effectively protect a higher percentage of land area in public parks, forests, refuges, and reservations in North America than any other country in the world has. And leaders worldwide look to the United States as a model of democracy and a model of environmental protection within a thriving market economy.

Our American cultural contexts are complex both in geography and in history. Deciding what to do in regard to rural community revitalization and its linked environmental protection and economic development will take some visionary thinking, visionary leadership, and revolutionary, deliberate, changes in our cultural values and attitudes, all based on a good understanding of our cultural history and geography. This process must begin in schools as we reassess and change formal and informal education to meet the needs of a sustainable world, community by community.

The approaches to sustainable rural community development thus need to be adaptive, making the best use of available science and data and drawing to the table the right mix of stakeholders who are prepared to build trust and act in a truly collaborative fashion. The necessary collaborative process must promote leadership, and the leadership must itself be diverse and adaptable, recognizing the limits of the skills and available time of team participants.

Successful leaders can be found, however, exhibiting many styles of leadership. The kinds of leadership roles a community or organization needs will also change over time as the organization and community change. Certainly community ownership of the rural development project is enhanced where there is clear leadership by local citizens.

Attributes of the New Rural Leader

> The tone of a meeting, with diverse stakeholders deliberating over a difficult environmental issue, the tone of an organization, the tone of a town planning commission, a university, a state, or a nation is set by its leaders.

The Leader Sets the Tone, the Atmosphere

Tasks can be delegated, but the vision of the leader cannot. The vision, once it is clearly articulated by the leader, must, with the leader's guidance, be developed by the group. Often, it is in the process of developing the community's vision that a leader emerges or a new leader steps up to replace the original. Leaders must display trust and confidence in the participants, ensuring that the work is meaningful and that all are free to express their ideas. For example, there was a nurse who recognized that her rural area was poorly served by health care and that existing services were fragmented. With a vision and a collaborative style of leadership, she was able to establish a regionwide network of collaborating health-care practitioners, despite the adversarial politics and competitive economics. Once the organization was firmly established, she quietly stepped aside and let the next leader take over.

As we consider rural leadership, we need to recall how many hats we wear or have worn. Think through all the leadership positions that you have held, from Girl Scout leader to director of a board. It is this training over the years in diverse settings that will influence how we establish discourse in professional arenas, determine how well we adapt ourselves to complex situations, and color the approach we take to

Photo 4.5. Rural isolation is a reality for many, and most rural people do not find it easy to share some of the innovative things that they are doing on their farms. This rather shy farmer is speaking in public for the first time, with considerable encouragement from his daughter.

leadership education. Volunteer activities undertaken from childhood to old age are fine leadership training grounds.

The strategic rural leader may have a charismatic quality, yet not necessarily be a traditional "out front" type of leader. Such a leader may be a quiet leader (Photo 4.5). Strategic leaders are rare. When such a person happens to come from the local community, long-term sustainability is more assured than if he or she is from a government agency or university outside the community. However (and most importantly), the outside person can and should function as a catalyst to trigger and stimulate local action and leadership. This planner, university faculty or staff person, funding agency personnel, capital extension agent, government official, or regional businessperson must understand and use strategic thinking to be a good catalyst for community change.

The most successful leader will set a tone that promotes professional development and skill building in all of the collaborators. This tone inspires people to take risks, to collaborate more, to share ideas. What tone does a leader set? Would you follow this leader? Do you see her or him as a role model for others? These questions are the first and most important to ask about a leader.

Builds Trust

This is not a simple activity, and it does not occur only once, after which you can forget about it. Trust building is an ongoing process and requires constant attention. The mix of stakeholders that the leader draws to the table must also be prepared to build trust and to act in a truly collaborative fashion.

In the Commission for Environmental Cooperation (CEC), a NAFTA (North American Free Trade Agreement) commission, people gathered around the table from three very different countries. When the CEC first set to work in 1994, much effort went into building trust, establishing a "transparent" process, and working toward consensus; people tried to be sensitive to cultural nuances. Everything got off to a pretty good start, but, after a year or so, people fell back into their traditional cultural- and gender-biased roles as the political machinations of such a highly political body began to take its toll. Interestingly, the most effective chair of the Joint Public Advisory Committee, the public component of the Commission, was a First Nation woman. She had honed her skills for years in working with diverse Native American groups and the dominant Canadian nation. Her quiet, yet firm leadership demonstrated a strategic style. She combined verbal leadership with nonverbal and, through clearly written statements, captured the needs of each party for the maximum benefit of the whole.

Trust building is an active, not a passive, process. Leaders must regularly ask themselves how they are working at building trust among those who look to them for leadership.

Knows When to Lead and When to Manage

Leadership requires a risk taker with vision, clear values, the ability to communicate, and adaptability. A manager should probably not be a risk taker, but should carefully care for (manage) the resources under his or her jurisdiction and must be prepared to take orders from a leader. A leader needs to be both a good leader and a good manager, knowing when to lead and when to manage in the many diverse settings that present themselves. A good homemaker can thus be as good a manager as the CEO of a corporation. The context is different, but both home and corporation must be well managed.

In another example, a local group of leaders planned the construction of a new community center in town that would offer all sorts of programs for the young and old, sick and downtrodden. This group forged ahead with their ideas, taking risks as leaders must. But they needed funds and a range of resources to make their vision work. They not only had to figure out how to get these resources, but also they had to carefully save and stretch their funds to last as long as possible. From a management perspective, this meant not taking many risks; it meant managing the resources carefully. There had to be a balance between leadership and management.

Remembers We Are All Human

Although there are many situations of conflict that must be overcome in rural development work, there are also plenty of opportunities for negotiation. Negotiation requires that we enlarge the "pie" in order to broaden the discourse and, eventually, to broaden the size of each participant's "slice" of the outcome. Negotiation also requires that we recognize the fact that we are all human. This is more than just being sensitive to others and their needs; it should include positive activities that build a feeling of "belonging." For example, serve food at the meetings you call. Do not ask others to bring their own food, or they will also bring their own agendas. The brown bag lunches so common in the United States need to be replaced by shared pizza and milk, or by whatever the locally preferred food is. In addition, before and after the meeting, talk about your children, the dog, and families, rather than limiting conversation to sports stories or business talk.

The former topics about commonplace human activities will be more likely to promote a collaborative attitude around the table; the group may be able to better integrate new ideas, avoid single-issue approaches to the problem, and listen and communicate in a more open manner. If one of the goals of the rural development effort is to create partnerships, then these actions and attitudes will be more likely to lead to a sustainable outcome.

Understands Herself or Himself, and Others

None of us can understand complex problems let alone know how to best resolve them until we understand ourselves—all our strengths and weaknesses—well. There is a tool used in leadership workshops called the Myers Briggs Indicators (see, for example, Otto Kroeger and Jane Thueson's book *Type Talk* [1988]). I have used the Myers Briggs preference assessment for about fifteen years, and I find it a helpful guide. It identifies sixteen personality traits and asks you to identify your preferred style of functioning in order to determine, or indicate, your personality type. No style is right or wrong: it's just your preferred style of operating, the place from which you draw your strength. We use this tool early in the EPIC leadership model (discussed in detail later in this chapter).

The person in a leadership position needs to really understand self and then hire people whose personalities complement each other, building a group that not only wants to work together but also has the combination of characteristics that will be more likely to work synergistically. Use of such tools as the Myers Briggs Indicators of personal preference can help us to understand the others in our community group of volunteers as well as in the professional workplace.

If leaders use something like Myers Briggs to understand themselves, then they will be better able to appreciate the others in the group as human beings before labeling them by profession, expertise, or weaknesses. So aspiring leaders should try to consider the preferred styles of operating that others in the group might have and how they might approach problems. Some people quickly make decisions with few facts; others prefer all the facts before reaching a decision. Some find it almost impossible to see the whole context; others never can see the need for details.

By clearly understanding the people who see you as a leader in the rural project, you will be better able to recognize and address limitations on participant time and resources. Volunteer burnout is common and can be avoided by being sensitive to the operating styles and needs of individuals.

Builds a Diverse Collaborative Group and Shares Knowledge

When a leader understands herself, she will feel secure enough to share ideas and leadership concepts, to mentor others, to hire those whose personalities complement hers, and to build a group that can work together. We cannot succeed by working alone, and the old, top-down leadership paradigm is not only passé, but also it does not work well in most circumstances. So, there is a need to build teams and groups that want to work together. To be successful, groups must draw on many strengths, and so such groups must be as balanced as possible in personality types and in gender makeup. This does not mean looking for "one of everything," but rather staying aware of the group's makeup and seeking balance when possible. Several authors, such as Dean and Mary Tjosvold in The Emerging Leader: Ways to a Stronger Team (1993), describe a range of techniques for team building, recognizing that different work environments will provide different challenges for leadership and management.

The results sought must include addressing any cultural or power imbalances in the group, such as imbalances brought about by generations of stereotyped gender roles, cultural and ethnic differences, and also those imbalances resulting from differences in education or socioeconomic status.

Seeks Consensus, When and Where Appropriate

A word of caution about consensus: Consensus is much talked about today as the most desired form of decision making. It sounds inclusive. It is certainly a mechanism that can and should be used to build a collaborative approach to problem solving and to build a group that feels inclusive to the participants. However, there are often occasions when consensus is not the most effective mechanism and indeed can actually destroy the harmony sought.

Although consensus can be used effectively to build a collaborative group, it can also be used to force out the minority opinion and to push a group agreement to the lowest common denominator. There will be many times when formal rules of parliamentary procedure for conducting meetings (presented in *Robert's Rules of Order* [Robert 1990]) must be used so that minority opinions can be clearly preserved for the record. Many important Supreme Court decisions have come in a later generation of interpretations built on the minority opinion. *Robert's Rules* also helps the Chair impose a structure on the meeting, so that results can be clearly recorded.

In other situations, such as when the organization spends all its time trying to build consensus, no decisions get made. Such a situation is disastrous both for the leader and for the organization. A leader must be willing and able to make critical decisions. For many aspects of rural development there is no time to wait for complete consensus. The solution arrived at might not always the perfect solution, but the leader needs to know when it is best to be firm and make the decision alone or, alternatively, through a subset of executive team members.

Recognizes the Limits of Volunteers and Defines Participant Roles

Much of the work in communities is undertaken by volunteers. These people are women and men whose children and homes are major priorities. Volunteers can and do burn out, often after about six months of hard work on a task. It is important to recognize the limits of volunteers' skills and time and to be thoughtful about lightening their load where possible or, as seen in Chapter Five, to provide honoraria when appropriate. Volunteers need to know in clear terms (preferably written) what they are expected to do, how they are expected to it, and for how long. The ground rules need to be set out as clearly as possible, recognizing and articulating the need for flexibility. Further, if consensus can be used in decision making, to a large extent many of the tensions in collaborative efforts may be avoided.

Promotes Leadership by Others

Everyone is replaceable. It is of paramount importance that the leader promote leadership in other people. This can be done indirectly by assigning more tasks, praising work, electing likely leaders to office, and so forth. And it can also be done by funding development workshops and by sending individuals and groups from the community to leadership seminars fundraising seminars or to other activities important to the community.

In a similar vein, it is important for the leader of the group or activity to be able to permit members of the group to leave and go on to other tasks and to bring new participants into the activity. Often a committee will set up in a town but there will be no turnover. The result is that no new people feel empowered, and if it continues indefinitely, not only are no new ideas incorporated, but also the project itself will fail to keep pace with community change. Thus, there must be a consistent effort to encourage the periodic replacement of participants, including leader.

Knows When to Move On

As alluded to in the item above, a good leader knows when to step aside and let someone else lead. Indeed, the person who begins an organization or community effort might be a great visionary but may not be the right leader once the organization is established or when undergoing its next major transition. In training and in mentoring a number of potential replacements, the strategic leader will have laid the appropriate groundwork and not left the organization high and dry.

Remembers the Children

In building a local, community-based team, one should not neglect the significant role that children and youth can and should play as part of the team effort. Indeed, one cannot expect a young adult, a newly voting citizen, to be able to effectively play his or her part in the political debate over the landfill or whatever unless he or she has some previous experience. The fresh, open perspectives of a fifth-grade class of children can often inspire the battle-weary groups in conflict over an issue whose resolution is clear to a child's intuitive sense. Similarly, the use of college students working with schools and communities to bridge the range of perspectives can allow all parties to "win" in the planning process.

Knows the Local Culture and Its Carrying Capacity

All too often we fail to really understand the history and culture of town, region, or environment. Successful strategic leadership requires a thoughtful, often detailed understanding of past events, characters, religion, politics, ethnic heritage, and families that influence the issue under consideration. This is not easy in an era of political correctness, but no less important. The local leader must help residents think about the nature and realistic capacity of their community. He or she can inspire a shared vision, challenge traditional notions, and enable others to act, but only with sensitivity to those who have gone before. Such leadership may enhance the possibilities for the community to be innovative and flexible in its actions, managing available human and financial resources for maximum effectiveness.

Uses All Available Scientific, Technological, and Other Data

Although the project priorities may not include a needs assessment, it is still important to consider all available data. The context of the issue at hand requires an analysis of present knowledge on the subject, which means that the leader should work with the collaborating group to clarify where each participant will go for his or her data and information. State agencies, universities, web pages, or the local town municipal offices? Although the scope and depth of such a wide range of data can be overwhelming, some of it may be critical to the groups' success. Of greater importance than just listing data and data sources is determining how accessible these data are at the community level. Knowing when to call in experts and when to send them away is important, too. The community project will work best if the data are locally accessible and locally handled.

Is Transparent, Open, and Accessible in All Actions, Running an Efficient and Effective Process

Successful rural town leaders, such as Michele Bessett, a businesswoman leader, have described the factors most critical to the successful establishment of a village community center: She reported that "transparency of actions was vitally important." Leaders such as Bessett make an effort to always have open, well-advertised meetings in public places and to distribute meeting minutes. Even more importantly, they are sure to mention upcoming meetings to those persons—whether mail carrier, town clerk, or storekeeper—in the rural town who most likely to pass on the useful "gossip." The openness of such communication increases the likelihood of truthful exchanges. Trust building is a function of leadership everywhere. And trust is built on transparency of action.

Transparency, an atmosphere that is open and accessible to all, will be enhanced if there is an ongoing evaluation process and will ensure that accountability and a commitment to attaining project goals are built into the process.

Seeks Early Results

It is easier said than done to produce early tangible results from a rural development project. The most important results may not be measurable for several years. However, it is advantageous to construct the project so that some measurable "outcome" can be reported early on and will help to link additional decision making to actual on-the-ground implementation. Both participants and outside observers will be better able to identify the actions with good outcomes.

Tries to Avoid Labeling People

The description of the landfill meeting at the beginning of this chapter highlighted the fact that judgmental labels do not encourage productive discourse. How often do I flinch to hear "You Environmentalists!" Everyone wants to be an environmental person and a leader of one sort or another. Be gentle, try to see the human being, the whole person, and avoid assuming that one knows everything about the person at the confrontational meeting. Individuals are always quite complex and often wear many hats.

Understands the Interconnections in Nature

An intentionally multidisciplinary and interdisciplinary approach must be adopted and continuously monitored in all efforts if sustainable rural development is to be the result of good leadership. This is much more difficult than one might possibly assume.

Asks the Right Questions

Old attitudes and old leadership styles won't work any more. To make a difference locally or globally we must change the way we handle facts, in teaching, in thinking, in lifestyles, and in values and attitudes toward each other and toward the environment. We must be more humble and less arrogant, more willing to listen and to understand the contexts of our work. In all rural development work there needs to be a regular assessment regarding whether the community has asked the right question and identified the most key problem. In doing so, there is a greater likelihood that the money and human resources applied to the problem are focused in the right place.

Understands the Basics of the Legal and Governmental Structure and Operation and Public Policy Formulation

When a local planning commission, water board, or zoning board is faced with a request or complaint, the volunteer or appointed members often find themselves in a situation in which legal advice is needed. In many instances, the local board feels threatened or actually is threatened with a lawsuit by the attorneys attending for the complainant party. The lawyer is only doing his or her job, but the volunteer board is often intimidated. Citizens who have taught themselves the basics of the relevant law and the appeal structure and perhaps have even studied case examples are going to feel better able to stand up to the aggressive attorney threatening to sue and less like retreating in fear and ignorance. Ignorance of the law and of the legal and political processes surrounding it may open up the town, for example, to the very large development that the town planning commission is trying to conserve.

Of paramount importance to the rural community leader in these legalistic times is to understand the dynamic nature of the United States legal system, founded as it is on English Common Law and strengthened by the Constitution. This is the finest legal system in the world, highly adaptable, built on a long history of case law and precedent, and, based on new ideas, new data, and modern interpretations, capable of overturning old decisions. Having a good understanding of the balance of power between the three branches of government (at both theoretical and the practical levels) will strengthen the abilities of the local leader and reduce fear and confusion. Each rural community member has far more power than they typically use. And remember, judges are human too.

Closely linked with overcoming legal barriers is the need to understand where policy comes from and the precise mechanisms for effecting changes in public policy. These should be included in a good leadership development course.

Is Adaptable

There is no one "cookie cutter" profile for the "right" kind of leadership. A complex issue may require that a leader use several leadership and management techniques, depending on the precise context and sequence of events. Greek mythology tells of the goddess Athene, a mentor-leader, who was peace loving yet strong, capable of going to war or running a home; she could take on the form of man or woman depending on the circumstances. Like Athene, the strategic leader selects the appropriate style of leadership for the circumstances.

Tries to Be a Strategic Leader

Strategic leadership integrates all facets of the problem at hand. It is multidimensional and holistic and makes every effort to avoid a fragmented approach to issues. Indeed, deliberate fragmentation of the issue is often a typical tactic used by those who seek a less sustainable rural environment. We can find many examples of projects that failed because of a unidimensional approach; the old leadership styles will rarely work any more. Or, as Southern senators have been heard to say, "That dog won't hunt any more."

To make a difference locally or globally we will have to change the way in which we handle facts, in teaching, in thinking, in lifestyles, and in values and attitudes toward each other and toward the environment in which we live. We will have to be more humble and less arrogant and more willing to listen and understand the contexts of our work. In the end, it may turn out that the most effective strategic leaders, those most likely to make a long-term difference, are those who give away power,

---

The Strategic Rural Leader Will

- Have a collaborative style and bring that attitude to the table
- Clearly address cultural differences and power imbalances
- Run efficient meetings
- Trust the others in the group or around the table
- Be open and accessible
- Show that she or he is not afraid to make mistakes
- Share his or her vision with others, developing and strengthening it with participant input
- Know when to step aside and let someone else lead and how to do so gracefully

dispersing it among those concerned with the complex problem under consideration and willing to risk themselves for others.

The EPIC Model Rural Community Leadership Program

Given that leadership development is needed in rural communities, we need to look at programs and approaches that can most easily be shared with other regions and communities. The leadership programs discussed in this chapter were developed in response to the needs articulated by rural citizens around the country. These initiatives include not only EPIC programs, but leadership models from a diversity of perspectives and locations. They contain elements of the EPIC model of rural development and are reflected in the key principles described in Chapter One.

The leadership model used in EPIC derives in part from my experience as a W.K. Kellogg Leadership Fellow and Advisor over the last decade or so, working with a diverse cross section of citizen leaders from across the nation. Leadership workshops have also drawn on the work of USDA Cooperative State Research, Education, and Extension Service professionals such as extension professor Lois Frey in the northeastern United States, whose leadership work evolved in the field during the 1980s. Lois became the key person leading the EPIC community leadership workshops as they evolved. This was modified by Lois Frey and the author to meet the comprehensive goals of EPIC.

Objectives and Program Structure

The objectives of the EPIC Rural Leadership Program are for participants to

- increase their understanding of the public policy process
- increase their ability, individually and as members of groups, to participate in the resolution of public policy issues
- understand the various methods of decision making and how to implement them
- enhance communications, group processes, and their own leadership skills
- understand how governments function and how to affect the process

This leadership development model has a community focus. Its goals include the requirement that participants address an issue of concern in the community and identify possible policy solutions. These goals should be clearly articulated in writing at the outset of the course. Although individual mechanisms and tools used to teach might vary among groups, the goals should remain central. In EPIC's case, it provides EPIC facilitators and resource people the ongoing opportunity to promote the democratic form of government.

Prior to offering leadership workshops in New England during the 1990s, and before determining the actual structure of the program to be offered, we analyzed other leadership programs offered in the region. We found that short seminars were periodically offered by organizations such as the cooperative extension system. These seminars and workshops were typically of short duration, usually a day or less. They were often directed toward town officers or others already in leadership positions and were not necessarily called "leadership" training, although in essence their goals were the same.

In determining the best niche for EPIC-style leadership, we also looked at community development projects undertaken in the past and in particular examined how their leadership likely operated (although they might not have used the term "leadership"). Some communities took part in the program "Take Charge," which was, essentially, a community-initiated and community-run needs assessment activity facilitated by an outside coordinator. The program was developed by the North Central Regional Center for Rural Development and was actively taught in many regions of the United States. It is more fully described in the report "Take Charge: Economic Development in Small Communities" (Ayres et al. 1990).

The Take Charge program is aimed at communities wanting to develop strategies for change. In the program, leaders in a town are brought together to analyze its problems. The program is usually run by an outside facilitator, but its goals are, through brainstorming, nominal group processes, and data collection, to determine the basic needs of the town in order to be better prepared to meet future challenges.

Of particular use in building consensus about the concerns common to most people in the gathering is the Nominal Group Process. Here the group is broken into smaller discussion groups, all of whom are given identical sets of questions such as "What are the most serious problems in town?" and "What are the greatest things about this town?" A representative from each subgroup reports back to the whole group, and the ideas are recorded by topic on a flip chart. The entire group then votes on the items of greatest significance by tagging them with colored labels, and out of this a plan of action is developed. The underlying hope is that the exercise will encourage community leaders to reassess their approach and will develop a plan of action for the community as a whole.

The EPIC model of leadership is very basic, and we found as the years went the communities that had taken part in Take Charge programs were better able to handle change in the community and that individuals in those towns were able to more quickly access newly available EPIC seed grants.

There is a follow-up program called "Re-Charge" for communities four or five years later. The Re-Charge program is similar in design to the Take Charge program; both programs have proved very effective at the community level.

However, we found that in rural Vermont there were essentially no programs or courses available to the typical rural community volunteer, none that prepared individuals to run for local offices, and none designed to attract new leaders, young or old. Consequently, the EPIC leadership model was able to fill an important niche in rural communities.

The importance of networking must also be pointed out. After the first or second series of EPIC leadership workshops, another leadership program was started in the region. Its director met with EPIC staff to discuss additional niches needing to be filled. As a result, this program was designed for community leaders wishing to learn more about government and preparing to run for office. This government leadership program complemented well the more basic EPIC leadership program, which was designed for a more specific grassroots community-based audience.

The EPIC leadership program is a ten-week (45-hour) program with eight 3-hour evening meetings and two retreats each lasting from 5 p.m. Friday to 3 p.m. Saturday. Participants are selected based on a number of criteria about the region they come from; preference is given to regions with high levels of agricultural activity, economic stress, unemployment, underemployment, and poverty. Participants are selected through a nomination process whereby local leaders are asked to form a short-term steering committee and nominate up-and-coming leaders who would likely enjoy and benefit from a leadership course. These individuals are invited in groups of two or three from all towns in the region so that the twenty-four participants will be clustered by township and region. A effort is made ensure that plenty of women and seniors are included. During the course of the program, participants role play, practice coping with tensions over local issues (such as the citing of a landfill), learn how to access resources, learn how to give a television interview, write a press release, and persuade a reporter to write about their work. Throughout this process they are encouraged to learn more about themselves. The lessons are basic, but we found that they were very much needed and that they had a profound effect on participants and their communities.

Community Access to Resources

Rural development projects often begin with a needs assessment—frequently with strong economic underpinnings—using a cluster of communities to ascertain a baseline of needs and problems. While needs assessments can be useful, they can also be expensive and time consuming. Economic data are certainly available, but such a needs assessment may not be what a community wants. In conversations across the nation, the new burgeoning leaders are not looking for data, but for information (data in context). Community leaders soon find that there are many sources from which communities and involved citizens can obtain data.

Data are primary tools for the outside experts that tell communities what is wrong and how to fix it. In the expert-driven model of rural development, data are critical. The test for a sustainable rural development model is that the data become more readily accessible to a wider range of community leaders who, in effect, take ownership, using the data themselves to guide their steps.

The United States is a nation of laws and data. Most public datasets are readily available, and when the response from a state or federal agency is "no," the Freedom of Information Act (FOIA) permits access to almost all data you are likely to need. Although it takes longer to request data through FOIA (usually by writing a letter), it is usually worth the extra time if the data are important to the project. The EPIC leadership development program includes a section on how to access data of various types.

Data need to be accessible and in formats that are useful. Many federal and state agencies house data and provide funding for rural improvement projects, but, with materials scattered in many locations, they can be quite difficult to track down. However, if data sources are recorded into a single community-based resource booklet, then all parties can benefit: Agencies get contacted appropriately, and landowners have all the sources at their fingertips. In EPIC, this meant finding a graduate student to collect all the data on resources, both technical and financial, for land conservation—and especially for stream erosion control (agricultural runoff is the primary source of water pollution in the state). The end result was *The Green Guide: Conservation Funding Opportunities for Vermont Landowners* (EPIC 1996), which was delivered to all state legislators, as well as to farm groups and town offices.

Another guide that we published provided a list of all the organizations in the state involved in conservation work, listing all known environmental, land-use planning, and natural resources groups and agencies both locally and at the state level. Appendix C provides information at a national level, but includes as many local and regional sources as possible. It is not meant to be comprehensive, but it forms a foundation for community research and networking.

EPIC published a quarterly newsletter, *The EPIC Journal,* for several years. A useful tool, it helped to keep EPIC participants and their friends informed about the organization as it continued to develop. In some communities, the use of e-mail and bulletin boards has proved important. In one town, a retired IBM engineer (Photo 4.1) and EPIC leadership program graduate secured a federal grant to fund the development of a system in his rural town so that between meetings school board members, planning commission members, and other municipal leaders could exchange ideas and information via e-mail and public bulletin boards with the hope that conflict might be reduced and quicker results be achieved. A philanthropic organization, the Together Foundation, provided e-mail services free of charge for this endeavor, which has subsequently spread to other towns.

Publications, e-mail, and the Internet were not the primary focus of EPIC, and their applications in rural development are limited, but the right combination of useful data in one place can provide community leaders (often attending meetings after regular work hours) with sources of information and data at their fingertips. It is data in context, accessed at the right time, from which they can better assess their own needs.

From Confrontation to Discussion

The so-called "research discussion" used in the EPIC leadership model tries to move the participants beyond the traditional debate format in which opponents argue to "win." Instead, each participant is given the opportunity to present a five-minute talk using researched information, the goal being to encourage a more civil discussion. Knowing how to take part in a discussion without becoming confrontational is an art that must be learned and practiced. EPIC developed the following guidelines for successful research discussions:

- Each topic is divided into two components: pro and con.
- Each topic is addressed by a team of two, four, six, or eight people. Half the members discuss the pro side of the topic and half discuss the con side of the topic.
- Each member has five minutes to present information on his or her topic. It is helpful if each side coordinates its presentations. For instance, material covered by a member of the pro team should complement that presented by his or her teammates.
- One member of the pro side and one member of the con side each has an additional five minutes to introduce his or her topic. Likewise, at the end, one member from each side has up to two minutes to present a wrap-up.
- The audience listens for factual information and for its source.
- It is helpful to better focus the presentation by limiting the number of points the speaker makes to two or three.
- Provide overhead projectors, easels, and pads, but other equipment such as slide projectors and VCRs must be signed up for in advance.

The discussion guidelines outlined above describe a process that enables individuals to take the necessary risks to apply abilities and learned skills in the public arena, broaden the base of community volunteers, and expand the community leadership capacity beyond the present "doers."

Although the EPIC leadership model includes lecture presentations to demonstrate a variety of leadership styles, participants are very much encouraged to "learn by doing." The range of participant activities include finding out how to access information, participating in a community simulation called Libertyville, making a video production, using the nominal group process for decision making, and presenting a "Speak-Out" along with an evaluation. Finally, each EPIC leadership program "class" selects a public policy issue that is most important to their town or region. Topics are selected by the participants and are relevant to the local issues; they might include whether to change the annual school schedule, where to locate the landfill, whether to permit an incinerator to come to the area, how to best deliver social care to those in poverty, or how to select the most appropriate rural development for their region.

Throughout the program, participants are provided with as many leadership styles as possible, both by observing each other's styles and by observing outside presenters of both genders and of diverse ethnic origins and ages. Similarly, a wide range of consensus building and negotiating tactics are introduced, including clearer definitions of words such as "coalition" and "network."

Building a Coalition

A coalition (adapted from material in the Family Community Leadership Program, Cooperative Extension Service, New Mexico State University) may be thought of as a temporary group of organizations or individuals working together for a common purpose. Coalitions may be service-oriented, social, religious, educational, issue-related, or governmental (town, county, state) in nature. Some coalitions may be permanent; others are formed to deal with one issue only, and they disband when the issue has been resolved. The single-issue coalition is easier to put together because the organizations only have to agree on one particular issue. A coalition is needed when you recognize that your organization alone does not have the power to win.

When forming a coalition, your organization's self-interests should be analyzed. Before asking other groups to join the coalition, ask yourselves the following: Will some of the groups make our members uncomfortable working with them? Are the demands other groups make to join the coalition acceptable to our members? If a much larger organization than ours joins, will we lose power to make decisions? Only ask an organization to join your coalition if the organization will contribute more than it demands and if that organization will not create problems that will weaken your organization or cause a split on the issue. There is no sure way of preventing problems among organizations in a coalition. Therefore, knowing your organization's self-

---

Organizing a Coalition

- Consider all possible groups that might join your coalition.
- Classify each by type of organization: service, special interest, social, or religious.
- Do some homework on each group. What does this organization do? Has it been involved in community problem-solving situations before? Has it supported issues similar to yours?
- Decide which organizations you think would support your issue.
- Approach these groups.

interests and being familiar with the self-interests of other organizations before forming the coalition can prevent possible major disagreements. Factors critical to the success of a coalition:

Goals. There must be common goals for the coalition and a sense that the coalition can accomplish more by working together than individually.

Outcomes. It is important for members of a coalition to identify the benefits to be achieved by working together. What will be the payoff?

Leadership. The leadership in a coalition must be able to move the group toward its designated goal, and there must be confidence in the leadership by constituent groups.

Commitment. Each person must be committed to working together toward established goals and to support the methods and decisions of the coalition.

Communication. Good communication among groups, along with a clear understanding of each person's role concerning publicity and the dispersal of public information, is critical. A system for information sharing should be developed.

Turf. Clearly defining the responsibilities and roles of each organization helps to eliminate "turf" issues. Any concerns of partners need to be openly discussed and resolved in a timely manner.

Diversity. A coalition should have a diverse gender and racial composition.

Forming a coalition is not difficult. It takes time and a well thought-out and planned strategy. Forming a coalition is not without problems, but the problems will be outweighed by the advantages. Too often organizations exist unto themselves. Not knowing what other groups are doing in your community means not knowing you share the same concerns and share the same visions.

In addition to knowing what a coalition is, the rural leader also needs to understand what a network is. The following is adapted from the Family Community Leadership Program, Cooperative Extension Service, Oregon State University.

Building Networks

A network may be thought of as a collection of acquaintances whom you can count on for help. The four kinds of help you can expect from network contacts are information, services, support, and access.

Of these, information is generally regarded as the most valuable, especially if it is current, "inside" information. Services offered by network contacts generally depend not on what a contact knows but on the skills and resources the contact can offer (e.g., a lawyer contact might help with preparation of bylaws). The third kind of help, support, can take many forms, from simple acts like offering encouragement or publicly recognizing a colleague's accomplishment, to more complex forms like building alliances and coalitions. You can also benefit from networks by gaining access to other networks—a brokering process in which you refer one contact to another. For example, a network contact may know the governor and helps you gain access to him or her.

In networking, cooperation rather than competition is the underlying attitude. Interactions are characteristically based on people-to-people contacts, irrespective of their status, role, or rank. It is a flexible, innovative, low-cost, and efficient way to provide support and often occurs as an incidental event or series of events. The challenge is not simply to develop contacts, but to develop useful contacts and to use them.

Guidelines for developing network skills (Lois Frey, EPIC team leader):

- A network of contacts should be tailored to your own interests, community activities, or career goals. Clarify as best you can what you want to accomplish. Then you can select the people who can help you.
- Don't ignore your existing contacts. Take a look at the informal relationships you have already developed. Analyzing them first is a good strategy.
- If you find that other contacts are needed, look for ways of approaching potential sources. Take the initiative. If you see someone who has a skill that would benefit you or your group, ask for his or her help. The objective is to choose a method that is both appropriate and comfortable for you.
- In forming a network, know what you are able and willing to give in return for the help you expect. Once you begin to practice networking regularly, it will become second nature to you to look for connections yourself and to link with others for possibilities of exchange.

To increase networking skills:

- Attend meetings on topics that address your concern. Let the decision makers know why you are there.

- In addition to listening when you attend meetings, talk to as many people as you can about their ideas and what they can do.
- Carry a notebook for writing down ideas, people's names, and contact information.
- Have cards printed with your name, address, phone number, and possibly an e-mail address. Handing out your card is an invitation to call on you.
- Think of yourself as a resource. Be willing to help others who are looking for information and skills you have or know how to find.
- Study how the organization works. Don't let the special words or names intimidate you. Ask questions. Seek information.
- Form a study group with an eye toward action. If a group already exists, join and participate in it.

Confidence in your ability to make changes in the system comes with practice.

The support of an understanding friend or group is invaluable as you begin. In networking, everyone wins by sharing.

Catching the Attention of the Media

There are several mechanisms for both advertising what you are doing and expanding your activities in a manner that will enhance community development.

THE USE OF VIDEO IN COMMUNITY WORK

We produced a short, twenty-four minute video about EPIC, *The EPIC Project* (EPIC 1993b). The video was all filmed out in the communities, not in a studio, but on farms and in the community centers and other gathering places, demonstrating community-based activities and allowing the actual voices of the citizen leader to be heard. It was professionally (but very economically) produced with the assistance of staff at the university. We found that the video was a very useful form of reporting our activities to funders, enticing other funders to provide grants to communities, and more effectively sharing lessons learned with similar communities across the United States and Canada. The video continues to be loaned out to communities across the country.

USING THE MEDIA

It was found that local newspapers provided better coverage, and had a greater and longer-lasting impact, than did television and radio. So the EPIC model of rural leadership includes the following guidelines for getting media coverage.

For print media:

- Develop regular calendars of newsworthy meetings.
- Develop an "expert" reference list for reporters' future stories.
- Produce short articles on timely issues in press-release format.
- Integrate your news with mainstream news.
- Provide leads to appropriate reporters for possible stories by phone calls or fax.
- Get to know key reporters at the local and regional newspapers who cover your kind of activities.
- When appropriate, follow up an initial press release with a call to your favorite reporter.
- Write carefully drafted and edited letters to the editor.
- Inquire about writing a short opinion piece.
- With their permission, suggest local people as subjects for a possible feature story. An example is a demonstration of sustainable forestry practices.
- Keep a file of ideas, from all kinds of sources, for news stories and radio programs.
- Be aware of trends in news, and key your stories to them.
- Be aware of the political scene, whether local, county or region, state, or national: Who is up for election? What is his or her position on your organization/community activities? Can you capitalize on the political climate and invite one of them to your fund-raiser, to talk about your work in an interview, to be quoted, and so forth?
- Alert reporters to events they may want to cover, and offer to provide follow-up calls or press releases if they can't cover the event.
- Develop a column that is a special series.
- Contribute to regular sections, such as on education or the environment.
- Target press releases to special interest groups and other organizations with newsletters. Is there a state public relations publication that would be interested in a story about your organization's community activities?

For broadcast media:

- Produce a series on a timely topic.
- Produce public service announcements (for example, tips during insect season, unusual happenings with the forest resources, a special event notice).

- If the station produces "live remotes," suggest an appropriate event.
- Offer free give-away items to attract listeners to events.
- Avoid scripted interviews.
- See if your state cooperative extension system or university has a regular television series that features rural activities, and determine if they would like to present a feature about you and your organization's community activities.

Research on the EPIC leadership model indicates that graduates showed improvements in individual effectiveness, increased self-confidence, improved group-process skills, improved ability to participate in group decision making, and a better understanding of leadership styles (see Lois Frey and Christine Negra's "Community Leadership Education in Vermont" [1996]). Leadership training also often resulted in participants requesting seed grant funds to conduct work in their community.

Leadership training can take place in a structured manner, such as in the ten-week EPIC programs, but it also can occur during the project itself. For example, farmers who volunteered their farms to serve as demonstration farms in the EPIC Pasture Management Outreach Program (discussed in detail in Chapter Six) were, while leading pasture walks and in other gatherings, able to gain practice in public speaking and in presenting information about their work as innovative farmers. In several cases, it was the children of these farmers, attending EPIC's annual meeting, who would urge, "Daddy, tell everyone what we have been doing on our farm!"

Dakotas LEADers Program and the Heartland Center, Nebraska

Similar leadership education models can be found in other areas of the nation. For example, in North and South Dakota the LEAD program evolved into the Dakotas LEADers program. This, too, was a project funded in part by the W.K. Kellogg Foundation, an organization that has been involved in leadership efforts for many years. Organizers in the Dakotas wanted to craft a program that took advantage of leadership training offered in urban areas and tailor it to the "stagnating and declining rural communities" of North and South Dakota. Janet Moen and Kim Nesvig write about this in an article entitled "Collaboration and Community: How Small Towns in the Dakotas Organized for

Leadership and Economic Development" (1993). The regional efforts of citizens were collaborative in nature, bringing diverse communities together around common issues. Sponsoring organizations, including the Center for Rural Health, asked each targeted community to nominate a team of six people, representative of the entire community, who would go through a leadership program. The fact that the sponsoring organizations had national connections meant the potential to establish networks that could lead to long-term changes.

In the Dakotas leadership project, the concept of community was deliberatively expansive, combining towns, counties, and Native American reservations. Participants undertook community assessments and selected viable economic development projects for their communities. Seed grants of $7,500 were provided to each community for economic development, with the community itself providing another $7,500. The Dakotas project clearly focused on economic development; leadership and seed grants were closely tied (not loosely linked, as in the EPIC model). The impact on public policy and sustainable environments is not yet known. The EPIC leadership program did not provide seed monies as part of the leadership programs, and it supported a wide range of local rural development needs; in only a few instances did EPIC leadership program graduates focus their work solely on economic development, and only those graduates who were highly motivated and expended the effort to develop a group project and apply for a grant got any seed money. We viewed this as helping to expand the potential number of community participants.

Yet another leadership program emphasizes capacity building as a critical aspect of its strategic leadership approach to community planning: the Heartland Center for Leadership Development, in Nebraska. An example of the work of this Center can be found in Vicki Luther and Milan Wall's monograph entitled *Studying Communities in Transition: A Model for Case Study Research and Analysis, Featuring a Case Study of Superior Nebraska* (1991). A key component of the Heartland Center's work, as well as in the EPIC and Dakota models, was learning to confront and deal with change by forming strategic leadership teams.

Appendix C lists leadership and rural development projects that formed the Rural America Initiative of the W.K. Kellogg Foundation. Kellogg has been the pioneer in sponsoring leadership training efforts nationwide, and it has sustained its interest in this field. Some of these efforts are ongoing, but all of them have some lessons that can be shared with local citizen groups. These lessons cannot all be presented here, but, in brief, each region of the nation will have different issues and cultures that must be accommodated in the leadership programs offered. There are, however, several common elements that constitute general lessons learned.

Lessons Learned about Community Leadership Programs

The phrase "lessons learned" is used here rather than "outcomes" in order to capture some of the more subtle, and less clearly measurable, aspects of the project outcomes. Lessons learned include the actual structure and delivery of the leadership workshops because process was found to be a characteristic important for success:

- Leadership programs that last several weeks and include retreats can have longer-term positive effects on both individuals and groups than do shorter courses.
- Group learning (as opposed to an individual learning on his or her own) leads to clearer understanding of how decisions are made, how policies are made, how to identify and influence key leaders, and how one person can be an agent of change.
- When leadership programs are combined with seed grants, communities benefit considerably. This linkage can be direct, as in the Dakotas LEADers project, or indirect, as in the EPIC model.

Rural communities strongly desire leadership programs for many reasons. The EPIC model leadership course:

Teaches collaboration. Leadership programs permit people from all walks of life to work collaboratively in a neutral, enjoyable setting. This collaboration increases the likelihood of cooperation later. Such programs provide opportunities for people to build confidence and relationships and to try out new methods and leadership skills in an atmosphere that is supportive.

Enhances networking. The program attempts to bring together people from towns and neighboring towns, who otherwise might not have met, with the goal of expanding networks within a region.

Empowers some volunteers more than others. Women and retirees benefit in significantly different ways from men and from volunteers who are employed full time.

Empowers women to accept leadership roles. Women play a critical role in rural leadership, and this role must not be underestimated. Women often assume several leadership roles and even take on other less-clearly defined roles or tasks. They gain leadership skills through courses such as those described here, but also indirectly through the operation of their homes, farms, or other businesses. If there is a single significant lesson to be learned from the rural leadership programs and follow-up interviews, it is that the presence of women in leadership positions is associated with community viability. In this instance, viability does not mean the ability to survive; it means that all activities in the community will be enhanced when women are encouraged to be leaders and that there are many tasks that require consistent leadership, both in the traditional sense and in the newer sense of the definition of leadership described earlier in the chapter. Women leaders were found to be more willing to share leadership positions and to "give away" power rather than hold on to it. They seemed to have a greater sense of community, could collaborate more effectively, and were less likely to let their egos get in the way of the community goal.

Increases self-confidence in citizen leaders. Individuals increase their ability to handle conflict and make decisions and strengthen their self-confidence (Photo 4.2).

Improves information access. Participants learn where and how to access information and how to determine its usefulness.

Teaches negotiation skills. Participants learn how to approach an issue by seeking common ground rather than by using confrontation.

Improves communication. Participants learn how to use new modes of communication (such as e-mail) that can promote collaboration within and between communities (Photo 4.1).

Offers a transferable leadership model. There is a generic leadership program that can probably be used in most rural communities, with minimal modifications to address local culture.

Teaches about interconnections. Some, but not all, will learn to understand the interconnectedness of all factors in a community and linkages between communities and regions.

Community Forestry Leadership and Urban Stewardship

The community is a system, and, in keeping with the elements of the EPIC model and its key principles, forests, as part of the community, must be included in leadership work. The natural resources base and its conservation is an obvious approach. Some volunteer to plant trees or establish community gardens; others might prefer land conservation work; still others are interested in land trusts. Forest cover in the United States, especially in the East, has increased as actively farmed acreage declines and forests reclaim the abandoned land. There is therefore a need for forestry leadership programs, both in rural and in urban areas; some successful models have already been developed.

The diversity of ecosystems that make up the "natural" and human-modified ecosystems of rural America include vast areas of forest and scrub. Much of the forestlands in the West are in federal ownership, while in the South and other regions corporate ownership of large tracts is more typical. Forestry issues in the West and the Northwest are fiercely argued in local communities, and international markets will likely increase tensions about forests and forestry practices over the next decade. In the East, as will be further explored in Chapter Six, forest ownership is highly fragmented into small privately held parcels. As broad categories of rural land use change, and with less land in agricultural production, unmanaged second-growth forests have increased in acreage. Despite the need to address forests and their management at the community level, we found, through EPIC work conducted in New England, that thoughtful engagement of the forestry community—with the exception of isolated individuals—was almost impossible. Its anti-environmental attitude (with or without justification) by and large precluded our efforts to provide seed grants to forestry groups or to draw them into community-based leadership or conservation programs.

However, Lois Frey and others were able to develop a separate leadership program aimed solely at the forestry community. Individual foresters felt more comfortable coming together with people with similar, narrower, interests. These single-issue leadership programs also tended to attract people interested in how best to manage the increasing acreage in private forest land (whether for wood or for other forest products) and interested in developing "natural" forest buffers for wildlife and native plants. Frey's forestry leadership program has been very successful and has used some of the same components as the EPIC leadership programs, but focuses on the hands-on aspects to forestry projects at community level. An outline for a sample forestry leadership program is provided in Appendix A1.

Another variation on these community-based leadership programs can be found in the Stewardship of the Urban Landscape program that incorporated tree planting, tree maintenance, and other related skills (details about this program are found in Appendixes A2 and A3). In the South and other rural regions, such "new" urban forestry projects might sound familiar given the long history of the Shade Tree Association and its equivalent—often women-led—organizations of the nineteenth century.

Based on the utilization of several of these models of rural leadership programs—some focused, some more integrated—and on the continuing assessments and modifications we've made as we gained experience, it is believed that almost any of these forest leadership models are transferable. Each community should, of course, carefully adapt them to fit their local community.

Lessons Learned through Community and Forestry Leadership and Stewardship Programs

Leadership development focused around the topic of forestry may in some ways be easier to organize and run and may show early results for than the broader-based EPIC leadership program. Forestry programs attract a less-diverse range of participants, which permits a community action plan to be put in place more quickly. Such programs may be important for sustainable forestry.

Changed perceptions and approaches of individuals may be less obvious in these leadership groups, but tangible results may be more measurable, making the forestry leadership model more acceptable in more conservative rural environments.

Conservation Commissions and Leadership

Conservation commissions are another community-based and community-driven idea, fitting the EPIC model and its key principles. Such commissions or similar approaches are an old concept: "It would be worth the while if in each town there were a committee appointed to see that the beauty of the town received no detriment"(journal entry of Henry David Thoreau, January 3, 1861). Conservation clubs or commissions are locally based and run, typically at the town or village level. Normally organized and run by local volunteers, they may simply be a town committee or a nonprofit organization. In some states such groups may be able to become established through state statute as a town commission with diverse legal rights. The conservation commission, or whatever name is common in the state or region, can undertake diverse activities. Some towns might choose to be more like the Shade Tree organizations traditional to the South, especially in the nineteenth century, setting up mechanisms to plant and maintain trees to provide shade during the high heat and humidity of the summer. Other towns find the conservation commissions helpful in organizing recycling programs, preparing natural history inventories for planning commissions, or helping to establish town forests or to conserve farmlands. Others are able to use the commission to hold development rights. Thus, for example, when a farmer determines that there is a need to ensure farm or forest preservation, perhaps at the time of retirement or when passing the farm on to the next generation, a mechanism is found to retire some or all of the development rights. Such a commission can purchase or be given the value of the development rights that are removed from the farm as a parcel of property. By holding the development rights in perpetuity, the community takes responsibility for ensuring the sustainability of land to grow food and fiber for future generations.

The first community-based conservation commission in the eastern United States was established in Ipswich, Massachusetts, in 1956 to save a marsh from development—an example of a single issue becoming the impetus for action. Since then, all six New England states as well as New Jersey and New York have established conservation commissions or the equivalent.

One of the main goals of these organizations is to take the town's basic environmental data and weave them into the historical, cultural, and economic life of their town and region. This can be done in a number of ways, from holding conservation fairs, to organizing recycling efforts; planting trees, windbreaks, or community gardens; to building new partnerships with other local organizations such as the historical society, 4-H Clubs, or local schools. At a later stage, the conservation commission may be able to work with the municipal planning and zoning boards or their equivalents to build natural resource data into the plans and into the zoning regulations; as a consequence, the community begins to experiences a new sense of self-worth and identity, seeing itself as a part of an integrated whole, as part of the state and of the region— no longer as just a mere dot on the highway map. In this way, conservation becomes part of the community, which in turn becomes part of the conserved resources for future generations.

Conservation commissions differ in structure and function from state to state. For example, in Massachusetts commissions have regulatory authority—no wetland development can occur without a permit from the local conservation commission. By comparison, Connecticut's commissions only have regulatory authority if they opt to function as a combined conservation-inland wetland commission. In New Hampshire, where 206 out of 234 towns have commissions, and in Vermont, where only 74 out of 246 municipalities have commissions, there are no regulatory powers. In these states, the function of the commission varies from community to community. Some inventory natural resources and provide the information to the local planning commission; others establish themselves as not-for-profit organizations and legally receive, by purchase or gift, conservation easements in trust. The conservation commissions in Vermont can hold easements and fee lands by statute, or in other words hold the development rights as described above. These community-based commissions can be either for-profit or not-for-profit organizations.

Conservation commission work in communities includes habitat restoration, streambank stabilization, tree planting, land conservation, recycling, composting, educational forums, and document preparation. Some town conservation commissions also include conservation strategies for large tracts of land designated as town forests.

In New Hampshire about 25 percent of the commissions receive funds through a use change tax imposed on land that becomes ineligible for current-use assessment. Christine Negra provides further information about conservation commissions in her monograph *Identifying Factors Leading to Effective Conservation Commissions* (1998). She shows that in Vermont, for example, most commissions rely primarily on community fund-raising efforts, with a only a few towns receiving appropriations. In Vermont, one of the useful spin-offs from EPIC has been the formation of the Vermont Association of Conservation Commissions, a statewide not-for-profit organization that publishes a newsletter, *The Seedling*, and the *Vermont Conservation Handbook* (Rasch 1998). Virginia Rasch, a community leader who participated in EPIC leadership workshops and served as an EPIC team leader, spearheaded the conservation initiative and now works with conservation commissions throughout New England.

Conservation and preservation of natural resources, as discussed earlier in the book, are touchy issues in the United States, given the power of private property rights. Each region will need to determine how to best balance conservation of natural resources (to ensure a more sustainable future environment) against the rights of private property owners to use and develop their land. Consequently, the concept of conservation commissions is not easily transferred to other communities without considerable groundwork and adaptation. The community leader may want to consider some of the roadblocks to community stewardship efforts that have been identified (adapted from conversations with Beth Humstone, a planner in Vermont):

- Private property rights pitted against community needs and responsibilities.
- Conservation efforts viewed as opposition to economic development.
- Local need to generate property taxes viewed as conflicting with better community development.
- The emphasis on "local control" and "home rule," which makes it difficult to look at broader regional considerations and puts up barriers to working with others outside the community, who could help.
- Lack of respected leadership with a broad vision for the community.
- Inadequate planning and/or implementation of a shared community vision.
- Inadequate understanding of the terms "rural conservation" and "steward."
- Failure to build coalitions and networks.
- Tendency to overlook social needs of a community when trying to identify and conserve the local "sense of place."
- The perception that there is not enough money or resources to accomplish the long-term goals set by the community.

Communities must be able to understand and articulate the points above to be able to work toward a more sustainable future. Conservation commissions are one of the component parts of the EPIC model of rural development and are considered an important tool for moving rural communities toward sustainable patterns of thinking and action, especially in regard to natural resources. They are not easy to put in place because they must be initiated by local people in the community. In the EPIC development model, efforts were made to inform the participants in the leadership program of some of these roadblocks in the hope that they would be inspired to go home and work to establish conservation commissions in their communities. Seed grants were offered as added "carrots." Some graduates, including graduate Fran Moses (Photo 4.2), did help to establish commissions in their communities, but so far not many have been successful in doing so.

Stewardship, an important concept for community conservation efforts, has several connotations, so a few simple definitions may be useful:

Stewardship: Caring for the ecosystem—land, air, water, plants, animals—in a sustainable manner.

Community Stewardship: Understanding the interconnections in the local ecosystem and caring for all community resources. This includes all the resources listed above, plus the cultural, historical, economic, and human resources that compose our collective inheritance and our legacy for future generations.

Lessons Learned about Conservation Commissions (adapted from Christine Negra's 1998 monograph)

The commission must:

- Be patient and willing to wait—often up to twenty years—for the commission to be accepted locally and regionally.
- Understand the whole—locally and regionally—and to "chip away" at pieces of it.
- Be flexible and open to new ideas.
- Recognize that building trust is a permanent and ongoing activity.
- Be transparent and honest about its activities.
- Reach out to new members on an ongoing basis, including working with children and in schools.
- Identify and be willing to ask for outside help if needed.
- Accept and work with other boards and commissions in towns and regions and with coalitions and networks.
- Use diverse strategies to reach all ages in the community.
- Publicize and "brag" about accomplishments, publishing them in the town annual report or newspaper.

Obstacles commissions often face include lack of confidence, lack of volunteers, frustration with the slow pace of change, frustration with state agencies, local apathy, weak local environmental laws and poor enforcement of them, severe development pressures, and confusion about purpose.

Engaging Youth in Conservation Leadership

One of the key principles of rural development is that of empowering youth. If we are to have sustainable rural communities, then it is imperative that youth are directly involved through schools and through youth organizations like 4-H. Involving youth will not only improve present-day rural communities, but also will benefit (eventually) communities they live in as adults. Encouraging volunteer efforts early and with regularity is also important to the social development of children. At the risk of sounding like an old-fashioned parent, it is vital to instill in a child a strong sense of responsibility for self and for others. Such service to society will teach about civics and leadership and ultimately contribute to a healthy democracy.

How to accomplish such lofty goals is not necessarily easy, but the EPIC model attempts to focus youth leadership through conservation-related activities. This is envisioned as a mechanism for building an environmental ethic, reinforcing the connected nature of nature even though the subjects taught in school are presented in a more fragmented manner. Youth who are actively involved in the community will be building civic responsibility, which will lead to more sustainable communities in the future.

Involving youth in rural development activities is no simple matter. Many stumbling blocks exist, including the difficulty in engaging schools in community projects. Teachers, even when offered seed grants, often felt too overwhelmed with curricula requirements to add anything extra. Some did, however, apply for seed grants to develop wildlife guides to the state with their classes, planting school vegetable gardens, setting up nature trails, and similar projects.

There are several other factors that make it difficult to engage youth. Although our children and grandchildren are very important to us, as pointed out earlier, we do not usually include children and youth directly in decision-making processes, whether for rural or for urban environments. The younger members of society today are isolated from local or regional decision making and policy formulation, typically throughout their school years, from about age five to eighteen. While some schools and—later—colleges and universities might make use of community experience as part of the education process, it is usually minimal.

In rural environments of the not-so-distant past, children were very important to farm life, helping with farm chores and other activities from early childhood. Children were woven into the fabric of rural life much more than in the urban setting. Today, children go to regional high schools some distance from their communities, and the urban influence is strong. These youth often migrate to the city.

The problem of inequity in funding of schools in rural areas is also of considerable concern. Rural children do not always have access to the best-quality education, especially in terms of facilities and equipment. Rural salaries are often also low and may result in a loss of experienced teachers to "better" schools. There is undoubtedly an unequal distribution of school funds in rural states where local property tax redistribution has not been addressed in recent decades. Recent considerable concern in some rural states has led to identifying the inequities in education funding. In several states, such as New Hampshire and Vermont, the mechanism of funding schools has been found to be unconstitutional and the states have been directed to work out funding mechanisms that provide equal education for all children. Changes to the laws in these states have yet to be fully implemented and are controversial among the populace, despite mandates from state supreme courts.

Also of serious concern is that most children are taught nothing about agriculture or forestry in school, whether rural or urban. The result is that most adults in the United States are at least two generations removed from the reality of rural, agricultural-based life.

Team leaders in the EPIC project were determined to work out a mechanism for involving schools in various aspects of sustainable development, whether through leadership, seed grants, or any mechanism that teachers or school leaders could suggest, but we found that it was almost impossible to get teachers or schools interested. Teachers typically have little or no background in community interaction, or in environmental or ecological issues, and are thus afraid to get into a situation where they have no control. There were some exceptions, which will be discussed in Chapter Five, concerning seed grants. But in regard to leadership, we found that the best way to work with children was to approach the youth directly, working, for example, with a school-club teacher or parent leader; then it was relatively easy to find an interested and enthusiastic set of participants.

Taking an idea from Colorado, which hosted a well-received Youth Environmental Summit, students in Vermont developed a similar environmental summit under the leadership of an EPIC outreach person, a young, urban woman who was working on a recycling project. Not all schools were involved, but an effort was made to bring together some of the poorest rural towns with the more urban "better" schools. The results were hard to assess. It was easy to identify short-term inspiration, networking among schools, and improved self-esteem among those surveyed after the event, but substantial changes in attitudes toward environmental and conservation issues, or real leadership skills developed, were only minimally noted.

Nonetheless, some of the students did go on to request seed grants from EPIC to carry out local community efforts, and all found the summit inspirational. Certainly the idea of this youth environmental summit (which the students called YES!) can be used almost anywhere in the nation. One point made very clear was that the youth involved all wanted to learn much more than we could provide about leadership training (Photo 4.4).

To link the role of youth in rural communities back to some of the basic principles articulated in Chapter One, it must be emphasized that there is an urgent need, throughout the United States, to engage youth in rural community life. It is imperative that youth leadership and youth community involvement be built into the school curriculum or that local community workshops be established in rural communities and run by the local citizenry. Youth can and undoubtedly will be agents of change in their communities if given the chance. Such involvement will strengthen the democratic system of government.

Conservation Leadership: A Focus for Sustainable Communities

In assessing lessons learned from a wide diversity of rural leadership development efforts, there are several general observations that can be made:

- Communities often come together around a single issue. Moving them from this issue to a broader vision for the future often takes years of effort—literally as much as twenty years from the inception of the vision to its broad acceptance and use in the community.
- A single issue can be effectively used to rally community support for broader conservation goals if it was approached in a proactive, rather than a (crisis-driven) reactive, manner.
- Most communities can develop goals and a vision, but cannot integrate the social, economic, and cultural environments with the ecological infrastructure.
- When children and whole families are involved in the "visioning" of the future and in community planning, the community is less likely to polarize over single issues. Furthermore, children and youth often demonstrate a clear environmental ethic and can effectively be drawn into conservation activities.

- It is important for rural communities to keep community-based conservation efforts initially separate from traditional municipal-based land-use planning and zoning; the latter is often a bone of contention in rural settings. Zoning is perceived to be more closely associated with traditional economic development than with sustainable development.
- Communities will be more likely to accept ideas if they have seen them used effectively by neighbors or in neighboring communities (theory of innovation).
- Efforts to bring together people from neighboring communities will help to establish networks with a region.
- Good community stewardship will lead to a sense of local pride, formation of broad collaborative coalitions, and more action-oriented, nonconfrontational activities.

Conservation activities in a rural community can lead both directly and indirectly to leadership development, public policy formulation, and a strengthened democracy, meeting all the tests of the Key Principles for Sustainable Rural Development. Leadership activities that focus their discussions and community activities around issues of natural resources (such as forestry) will similarly meet these principles. Both approaches can be used to broaden the pool of community participants. The tasks for the rural developer are to work with communities to determine their collective priorities and figure out how to achieve them. Focused, community-based and community-driven, conservation-based leadership training can thus be one of the most effective mechanisms for meeting all the key principles of sustainable rural development.

Chapter Five

Seeding Rural Sustainable Development

The EPIC rural development model urges the community to encourage its citizens in systems thinking, to pay special attention to the linkages that connect parts, to empower women and youth, and to promote capacity building and innovation. This chapter discusses community-based and community-run seed grants, a component of a rural development model. As do conservation-based leadership programs, seed grants reflect the key principles of sustainable rural development introduced in Chapter One.

What Is Sustainable Rural Development?

This book explores sustainable rural development from a variety of perspectives. It is not easy to define, but its definitions need to be carefully considered if we are to accurately assess the ability of seed grants to increase sustainability in rural communities. The term perhaps first attracted attention in 1987 with the publication of the Brundtland Commission's Report *Our Common Future.* The commonly used definition from that report is as follows:

> Sustainable development is development that meets the needs of the present without compromising the ability of future generations to meet their own needs. (Brundtland 1987, 43)

This is a brief global definition that is helpful at the broadest level of public policy. I prefer, however, to look at sustainability in a more integrative manner that acknowledges the constant changes occurring locally and globally, which can be summed up by paraphrasing a definition of sustainable development found elsewhere in that landmark report:

> Sustainable development is a process of change in which the exploitation of resources, natural and human, the direction of investments, the orientation of technological development, and institutional changes are made consistent with future as well as present needs. Sustainable development is not a fixed state of harmony. (Brundtland 1987, 9)

Here, sustainable development is seen as a process, not an end in itself. It also captures some of the elements that must be present for sustainability to exist. Just as important is the last sentence of the definition. There are many who keep looking for a "sustainable community" as though it is a fixed state. But it is no more homeostatic than is the ecological fabric on which we depend. Perhaps even more useful to consider is the following, from *The Keystone National Policy Dialogue on Ecosystem Management*:

> Ecosystem management is a collaborative process that strives to reconcile the promotion of economic opportunities and livable communities with the conservation of ecological integrity and biodiversity. (Keystone Center 1996, 6)

The analogies between the definitions are obvious. What is particularly important about this latter definition is that it includes the concepts of collaboration and community, together with concepts of conservation. Collaborative conservation, as seen in the previous chapter, is a key mechanism for achieving sustainable rural communities. And these communities will not be static. They will change and must be encouraged to do so to meet changing global conditions. The romantically inclined person who moves to a rural area previously visited and sees that nothing has changed has either shut his or her eyes or is looking at a "dead" community. A good definition of sustainable rural development must combine elements of both definitions.

Rural development stands a better chance of protecting and enhancing resources of a community for future generations if it is managed by local citizens and grounded in both the history and the present knowledge of the community. Earlier chapters have discussed the threadbare nature of many rural communities in the United States. Some regions and some communities are in worse shape than others. Some may be so fragile that the local populations are unable to keep the community alive, let alone in a healthy condition. Even so, local knowledge must be tapped and mixed with knowledge and ideas from other rural communities and also with ideas from rural Canada, urban America, Europe, and elsewhere. Immigrant knowledge has always been a significant and typically positive aspect of rural development.

As discussed earlier, there has been a tendency to respond only when there's a crisis, such as a severe flood or the loss of major local industry. Money and expertise are sent in from outside the area to solve the problem, after which the outsiders move on to another crisis elsewhere. This may indeed resolve the immediate crisis, but rarely does it address or attempt to understand the underlying cause.

Communities are systems within systems, and approaches to rural development must be locally based, comprehensive, and integrative. In each community there will be limiting factors (factors that limit growth) and "leverage points" (key factors critical to a specific situation or community that can be used to build interest and possibly generate positive change) that influence what can be done. In addition, rural communities may be isolated in some sense, but all the communities in a region are interconnected in some way. The scale and strength of these interconnections will vary from the large, open, widely spaced communities in Nevada or the Dakotas, for example, to the close, evenly distributed pattern of villages in New England. Thus, in addition to identifying the leverage points in the local community, it is also necessary for different communities to learn from each other and to work together. This regional cooperation may be easier in the Plains states than in New England, where towns can be little kingdoms, but thinking globally and acting locally are good concepts worth trying everywhere.

Although one can generalize about rural America, provide data, and postulate about the grand scheme of things in the more obviously delineated regions of the South, the West, New England, or the Midwest, the reality is that no two rural communities are alike. Each has a different history, ecology, cultural makeup, and economic drivers. The geographic location of the community, its present socioeconomic status and trends, and internal and external factors will all influence the health of the community. The word "community" itself has many connotations. It can cover concepts as diverse as simply a group of like-minded people, a close-knit religious population, or the more commonly used idea of a governmental unit of township, village, or neighborhood. As used here, the concept of community, while including the intangible sense of camaraderie, is intended to cover the holistic, most complete sense of the word: the buildings, the people, their history and culture, the ecology, land use, and politics—everything that makes the community work. It is a system made up of diverse components, some easy to measure, some intangible and elusive.

How Long and How Much Money to Achieve a Sustainable Community?

How does a foundation or government body provide the right amount of help, to the right people, at the right time, in the right place, for the right number of years? One of the most important lessons that I have learned living in rural communities around the world is that it takes time to effect changes that will be long lasting and result in sustainable communities in the fullest sense of the word. Twenty years is not an unrealistic time frame for an innovative idea to become established. Theories of innovation support this assertion. Essentially, it takes a generation of time.

Given the single-issue approach taken to many rural problems, and the limited amount of time assistance is actually rendered, it is difficult to point to a rural town or community and say, "That's a sustainable community." A single problem may have been temporarily alleviated by an injection of funds or other resources, but the community as a system may not have been affected. As discussed at the opening of this chapter, the problem is made more complex because, although there is a *general* sense of what sustainable development means, there has been no real attempt to identify all the characteristics of the resultant "sustainable community." We can easily identify negative and positive "facts" about the community, but since so much of real sustainability results from a collaborative *process*, it is far more difficult to provide a clear list of characteristics.

If, however, we examine the elements of the EPIC rural development model and apply the key principles of rural development, we may identify a framework that helps the community ascertain how close it might be toward attaining sustainability. Both community leaders and funding agencies need to understand this perspective.

While conducting rural development work, it became apparent that I could identify certain factors that I came to call "Indicators of Stress" in a rural community. These are presented in Chapter Eight, using several towns as case studies. The EPIC elements and key principles are emphasized here in order to work toward community development from premises based on positive principles and goals rather than merely the identification of nasty problems and the difficult steps needed to seek long-term solutions. So, although the community and the outside funding organization of a rural development project will want some negative facts to support the need for funding, the communities should emphasize the positive foundation upon which they will build the project and thus maximize the money so generously provided. "Accentuate the positive," and be optimistic about success.

The typical time frame of funding for rural projects is two or three years, but this is not adequate. It takes a year to get up and running and known in the community, a year to build programs, and then, if the citizens know that resources are soon to be gone, the next eighteen months to explain to this hard-won audience why the program is now dormant. By the end of three years of creative community building through EPIC, we were beginning to see far more creative and sustainable projects being proposed, at the very time we had used up our funds. This time frame for action, "do as much as possible in a short period of time," flies in the face of our understanding that it takes a generation to effect substantive, beneficial change. A small amount of funding over a longer period of time will be more helpful than a large amount of money that must be expended within three years. Accordingly, it is my contention that funding must be provided for rural community-based projects for twenty years if permanent benefits are to be seen.

Short-term-funded rural development projects are common not only in the United States but also overseas. They usually involve retaining the services of "experts" (the traditional, "expert model" discussed in previous chapters), who draw expensive salaries. These funds could be used more effectively by the community to purchase short-term help (expert or otherwise) from a wider diversity of sources. Some may contend that this only leads to dependency: "The rural community members will just sit and wait for handouts." Not if you do it right. Not if it is based on principles and process rather than on stress factors. For example, having identified either a community leader or a specific factor or issue that can be used as a "leverage point" in the community, one can begin by giving small "seed" grants in the first year or two, followed by somewhat larger amounts as interest builds, and a diversity of interests and people are slowly but surely involved in various projects in the community and the surrounding region. Then you can gradually reduce funding to very low levels as the community fully invests in the changed direction of development and is shown how to seek funding from other sources.

One might counter this position by suggesting that that is, in effect, what the cooperative extension system set out to do decades ago. And there are certainly some analogies in that model. But the suggestions here are for community-initiated, community-run projects—not programs delivered by experts. The emphasis is on the process, not the crisis. These are different times. Furthermore, the extension system developed a vast and expensive bureaucracy and an institutional structure that became in many respects an end in itself. The rural development suggested here, with twenty years of funding, must take place from decentralized "virtual" centers rather than from large, well-funded government or university centers. In this manner, the rural development efforts will really belong to the local communities and to the individuals living and working in them. This is more economically efficient and more effective for the communities themselves. And it is far more likely to lead to sustainability than will short-term funding of expert-based development models. It will also permit more effective involvement of people in the communities that are most in need, most disenfranchised, and least likely to already be part of the community leadership.

Funding organizations, program partners, and universities should keep in mind that by endorsing short-term projects they are necessitating costly (money and personnel) start-up and shutdown efforts, leaving some of the richest fruits of their investment to wither on the vine just before harvest. Community projects need long-term commitment for long-term, sustainable changes to be realized.

Finding the Best People

Chapter Four looked at leadership and described several ways to find new leaders with new leadership styles among the many leadership training models available and how to further educate present leaders. Community seed grants discussed in that chapter were not separate from but rather were an integral part of the comprehensive EPIC model approach to rural development. Many who took part in the leadership series became seed grantees. In other rural development projects around the nation, such as in North and South Dakota, leadership and seed grants were deliberately linked. In developing community leadership programs, we had identified what other leadership programs (if any) were available or had been used in the past, locally and regionally. In the EPIC approach, leadership programs had been deliberately developed to meet the most basic needs of individuals in the communities, such as extension seminars for town officers, professional training for business people, and so forth. Townspeople frequently commented that the visible town leadership was often entrenched—the same old families who were not open to newcomers or new ideas or else were just tired. New leaders could be a welcome change.

In a similar manner, the community seed grant program identified those who were community volunteers with good ideas but were not town officers, members of nonprofit organizations, or someone with obvious leadership potential. (In fact, in most of the communities where seed grants were given, there were no nonprofit organizations.) We also wanted to draw in those individuals or groups that might have felt disenfranchised or unimportant for one reason or another. Therefore, we advertised our EPIC seed grants as being especially aimed at women, youth, senior citizens, and those in real need—needs not addressed by society.

It was my hope that the combination of community leadership with community seed grants would not only improve the lives of individuals and lead to community improvements, but also that it would bring an added understanding of what the environment means in the fullest sense of ecology and culture, resulting in truly sustainable communities. In the EPIC model, this goal is not forced on communities; we wanted townspeople to identify their own local issues and address their own needs. Facilitation can sometimes aid this process; once the right stakeholders are involved and the process is under way, it is possible to provide assistance when asked.

The hope that I had was that, in time, EPIC team leaders and community citizens both would come to a fuller understanding of sustainability, and I had hoped that there would be a much improved ability to see the community as a system, linked with other systems, and linked irrevocably with the ecological environment. In truth, very few of the EPIC staff coming in and out of the work over the four years ever understood the whole—not in the integrated nature of community and context, and not in the synergy resulting from harnessing diverse approaches to rural life and livelihoods. Their formal education, as with many rural community citizens, had been too fragmented. It was difficult to look at the whole from a different perspective. For a few, the system did seem more complex.

In the rural communities some seemed to understand the whole, or at least more of it. However, a full understanding was certainly not common during the core four-year period seed grants were dispensed to communities. There were too many pieces of the system broken. Too many basic needs had to be met first. It takes time. At least twenty years.

Community Seed Grants and Their Management

Seed grants are small amounts of money (usually between $50 and $2,000) awarded to individuals or ad hoc groups for some collaborative, community-based activity. The amount of money given is small enough so that established organizations and government are less likely to be interested, but enough to capture the attention of youth in the community and of those not typically involved in community activities. Among other things, seed grants are aimed at capacity building of individuals and the community.

Grant Application and Management

In beginning the EPIC model seed grants, I was able to find little written on the subject, except in occasional foundation and extension reports. Even these reports were sketchy (evaluation and ongoing assessment not having been a high priority in the need to expend limited funds over a limited time frame). My assistant and I therefore had to invent the process of applying, awarding, managing, and evaluating the seed grant program.

In Vermont, EPIC awarded several hundred seed grants over about four years, ending in 1996. The results are still being evaluated, and so the lessons learned and presented here must be considered preliminary. But they might, perhaps, provide some basic observations that others can use, whether community leaders, those funding activities, or those involved in the education of a wiser and more comprehensively educated generation of students and professionals.

These seed grants, which were based on the EPIC model elements and key principles, were not "seeds" broadcast over the entire state or region to fall on rough and stony ground with a limited chance of growing into anything (so to speak). Rather, the grants were focused in what were considered "important" rural geographic regions. These target areas were selected based on criteria (both negative and positive) such as areas with high levels of poverty; areas with known, active, community innovators; or areas with an intact rural infrastructure that included active agriculture and associated businesses and market towns. Preferred recipients were women, youth, and senior citizens, with an emphasis on women. Experience, intuition, and bias suggested to us that involving women was critical to community viability, a perspective validated by research in Missouri by David O'Brien and his colleagues on social networks (O'Brien 1991).

Within the designated counties, grants were "clustered" in groups of nearby towns/townships to promote possible synergistic effects. "Cluster granting" has also been successfully used by the Kellogg Foundation (Tom Thorburn, personal communication, 1996). We also built on earlier work by others wherever possible.

The seed grant application was a one-page form whose simplicity, combined with the assistance happily provided by EPIC staff, contributed to the success of the EPIC model approach and its goals of community revitalization.

We were offering seed monies, not a million dollars, and we wanted to attract applicants new to grant seeking, including people who could neither read nor write. Thus, every person applying was strongly encouraged, before submitting the application, to contact the EPIC office (one tiny room at the local university) to discuss the proposed project. This human element, on tap almost continuously, evenings and weekends, over the four years, was an absolutely critical factor. (Note: We received a three-year grant for EPIC, but we extended the spending time for seed grants by a year.)

By having applicants call the office and discuss the proposed activities, we were able to prescreen projects for their suitability. But, more importantly, the phone calls permitted discussion about how to strengthen the application, involve other people, and leverage other funding sources. Several times, we were able to help individuals (who were indeed illiterate, unemployed, and fairly desperate) to write their applications. These phone calls also permitted EPIC staff to learn about the needs of communities and to share what we knew in a relatively efficient and informal manner. We could thus redirect individuals to other potential funding sources or encourage them to apply to us and be fairly certain about a likely positive response. Grants were not normally given without a visit from either the EPIC Director or the person hired to coordinate the seed grants.

In addition, it is important note that this careful but simple approach allowed EPIC staff to redirect energies when necessary, and only rarely did we turn down a submitted grant. Community members saw it as a positive process. Again, the process was virtually as important and in many cases more important than the actual small sum of money provided. Even when turned down, the applicant typically felt that he or she had been handled with care and consideration.

The grant application process itself was found by many to be empowering. The director of Indian Education Programs in Franklin County, Vermont, found that the personal contact was very important to seed grant applicants from the economically depressed Abenaki community, saying, "Often people don't have any idea of how to write a grant. This process was painless. It's a couple of pages—you call, you'll be walked through it. It allowed a lot of people to become proficient at something they were afraid of."

When organizing the first ever Abenaki Heritage Festival, bringing in Canadian Abenaki and Wobenaki peoples, the Abenaki leader told us, "We did not have a clue [how to do it]." But he found that the friendly, approachable human help and professional support "gave us confidence to go out and find the rest of the money, call the governor, and get him to come." He told us that "we built partnerships with the grant-making people. . . . The EPIC seed grant money was just that, seeds, and it was only $2,000, but it gave us confidence in our abilities to go further."

One member of this tribe who became particularly good at fundraising used the friendly EPIC model to help him deal with other granting organizations, many of which can be unfriendly and overwhelming to approach. "As a Native American, I have heard 'no' all my life. EPIC gave me a 'yes'—and the expertise and confidence to get around the next few 'no's' and move on to the next 'yes.'" He often told a story of one community grant organization that required six copies of the application, each in its own binder. He observed that "communities who can afford to do that probably should not be asking for money."

We were always interested in learning how people heard about the availability of EPIC seed grants. It turned out that word of mouth was the primary means and that very few found out through the media or other established organizations.

Early in the program, EPIC staff spent many hours giving presentations about this new comprehensive approach to rural development at Rotary clubs, schools, churches, business groups, and municipal meetings by sending out mailings and by contacting local media (television, radio, and newspapers). But no grant requests appear to have originated from these presentations. Instead, most grantees heard of EPIC funding possibilities through one person telling another—a network.

As with other aspects of EPIC, however, the local newspaper was the next most important source for learning about how to get a grant. The seed grants were not large enough to attract most organizations but were large enough to attract the very people we wished to reach: budding leaders and their collaborating partners.

We also found that those communities that had gone through a participatory planning program such as the Take Charge program (discussed in Chapter Four) were fertile ground for interconnected seed grants. In a related manner, it was found to be beneficial to cluster the grants geographically where possible, in the hope of creating a synergy. Although this did happen in some areas, it was difficult to force a clustering. The change agents were either ready to go or not. Nonetheless, the EPIC model approach encourages such clustering in much the same manner as it clusters leadership programs in communities and between communities.

> Often people don't have any idea of how to write a grant. This process was painless. It's a couple of pages—you call, you'll be walked through it. It allowed a lot of people to become proficient at something they were afraid of.
> —The Director of Indian Education Programs, Franklin County, Vermont

The next critical factor was the personality type of the person hired to coordinate the seed grants. Such a person must be an outgoing, enthusiastic, patient "night person," willing to go to the numerous evening meetings, weekend retreats, fund-raisers, and building bees in far-flung rural communities often filled with local folks somewhat suspicious of "that young woman from the university." The coordinator should not be a "know-it-all," yet should have lived for at least several years in the rural area, be willing to learn and share lessons learned, be a consensus and community builder, be a generalist with networking and resource skills, and have excellent media, writing, and oral skills. Natural resource, environmental knowledge, and technical detail are less important than the human skills. These skills should complement the Director's leadership. I was fortunate to persuade someone to join me in this difficult-to-explain project. Susan Clark, a graduate student, proved just right for the challenge at hand. During her work with EPIC, she completed her master's degree on the subject of citizen participation (Clark 1996); following her work with EPIC, she has continued on to set up her own community-building organization in another rural region of New England. Her commitment and enthusiasm were crucial to the success of the seed grant program.

Another important aspect of the seed grant program was that grants were accepted and considered on a rolling basis as they came into the office. We also found it was necessary to offer funds as well as support for technical skills training and information resources at the right critical "learning moment"—when the community members were most needed and participants were most receptive. Thus, a quick response to a request for funding was very important.

It can take weeks, months, or years to eventually get the actual check from a granting source. The EPIC model of community-based rural development does not give large sums of money, and it typically provides funds to individuals or ad hoc groups that have no money. So time is of essence in many cases. If, following review, a proposal is deemed a fundable project, EPIC requires that the check be in the mail to the community within two weeks. For example, after several weeks of discussions, meetings, and efforts to bring more stakeholders into the group, an initial grant of $2,000 was made to fund a brand-new community center. A few months later, the new community-based organization realized that it did not have all the skills necessary among their membership to spend the money efficiently, run meetings, set up a nonprofit organization, and so forth. They also needed additional funding to be able to send citizens to a half-day workshop on fund-raising and board development offered by the cooperative extension service. Within two weeks, EPIC provided the funds to cover course registration and travel expenses for a small group of community members.

In another situation, a group of people wanted to use the community center facility to open an adult basic education center as a resource for locals needing to learn to read, write, or earn their GED (high school equivalency) diplomas. They wanted the education center to be independent, set up as a separate program in the new community center. Here was a perfect way for EPIC to empower a new group of people. We could quickly fund the new group because they were able to build their work into the new community center. The effort was thus synergistic. This group still runs the program, attracting many new people from surrounding towns. As the grant came into the office, it was reviewed by the EPIC Director and the seed grant coordinator.

As mentioned earlier, EPIC has a council of advisors that provide guidance on a range of matters, including review of seed grant applications. Individual council members provide advice by phone, depending on their area of expertise, about given proposal. These council members were scattered over a broad geographical area and represented as many diverse aspects of rural life as possible. Proposed projects were evaluated for broad community support that would empower individuals and improve the local community and—where possible—the environment. We did not encourage applications from municipalities or from groups with well-established funding sources, or for capital and equipment needs; we wanted to be able to give grants to individuals, to ad hoc groups, and to people who could not read or write, had no checkbooks, or were under the age of eighteen (and thus ineligible to sign contracts). We wanted to feel confident that the money we gave away based on a simple, one-page application would be put to good use.

The role of the University of Vermont was especially important in this endeavor. Foundation monies had been received by the university— the designated not-for-profit recipient organization. The university accounting department staff, who oversaw the distribution of these funds, had to feel comfortable that our activities met federal laws and that there was a chain of custody in place that could be reasonably tracked. This was not an easy task, and it required experienced financial managers at the university—and their trust—for this to work. We were fortunate to work with a supportive and experienced accounting staff. They were prepared to share this trust of the community and to work with all the successful seed grant applicants—from young children to senior citizens—and they demonstrated an understanding of the dilemmas facing rural communities. Checks were thus written to individuals based on trust, and reports from grantees could be either oral or written. We believed that we would get far more out of our small investments than the mere value of the money given, and we were not disappointed.

Once a grant was approved, the seed grant coordinator spent time with the grantees to encourage and guide the success of the projects. This included actively assisting and training the grantees in organizational and planning skills, troubleshooting projects, and often just lending a sympathetic ear. It also included connecting groups with appropriate training programs, consultants, and other seed grantees working on related projects or on other parts of the comprehensive EPIC endeavor.

Reaching the Needy and Starting Where the Community Wants to Start

Building on the W.K. Kellogg Foundation mission to "help people help themselves," the EPIC model makes a considerable effort to reach the needy and the often-hard-to-serve populations. As described above, the EPIC model aims to fund those who might not be able to read or write well, or who have little or no money, or who have no checkbook. This means that EPIC leaders must understand rural statistical data but work at the human level, getting to know people in the poorest areas. We observed that larger grants dispensed in the traditional expert-driven model of rural development tended to go to regional centers, with the expectation that the "needy" would go there for help. But, in fact, the complete lack of public transportation in New England makes this impossible for these people, just as it does in many other regions of the nation. The real need is for small, locally based projects and community centers that serve people in their own communities. In some regions, a community center might supply these needs; in other areas, a health center might be most important; in yet other areas, the school or farms might be most in need of attention.

> The fact that the more-elaborate grants often don't help those who most need them most was made clear by Pat Parsons, a resident of the very poor community of Richford, Vermont, who observed: "Organizations, the universities, and government have used [our town] for years. They need to have our [poverty] statistics to get their grants. But the money never gets here." EPIC funding for that town secured part-time staff to work with volunteers to revitalize a much-needed town health clinic. Pat went on to comment that the health clinic was "one of the first positive things that has happened here in years."

It is essential to build trust with those who feel disenfranchised, and seed grants can be one way to achieve this. The Abenaki leaders, as mentioned earlier, had no trust in "the system" and felt stigmatized by their low education levels and low income. The Abenaki average per capita income in Vermont is $7,000 per year, compared with the $13,500 average per capita income statewide.

EPIC funded the Abenaki Tribal Council leaders' Heritage Festival (the first of its kind ever in this region) not once, but three years in a row, in order to more firmly establish anticipation for the event in the broader community and to empower the burgeoning Abenaki tribe. By the third year, more people were feeling comfortable acknowledging their Native American heritage and trying to relearn their lost traditions. To aid this process, EPIC was happy to fund a proposal for language training. This grant, Alnobaodwa! (Speak Abenaki), supported travel and compensation for language classes taught by Cecile Wawanolet, a member of the Odenak Abenaki Reserve in Canada. We were also able to link this effort with a new education project that was later started at the local high school, under Title V, in which the Indian Education Office offered Abenaki language and culture classes and area youth were able to visit the Odenaki Reservation. In the fourth year of EPIC, we were able to fund the Abenaki Self-Help Association, allowing us to "institutionalize" a Native American perspective linking land and people with history and culture. The Heritage Festival is now a well-attended, annual festival with a powwow and has been a source of great pride (Photo 5.1).

Where seed grants are deliberately kept low (under $2,000) the money not only serves as a "jump-start," but also is more likely seen as a sign of confidence and support by the outsider funders. The money itself does not resolve the problem, but the cooperative endeavors of several individuals working together in a community might be able to do so. "We did it ourselves" was a common expression following completion of a project or the development of an organization that was "seeded" by EPIC funds.

Other seed grants to populations in need included funding a parttime staff person at a new health clinic and board development for sev-

Photo 5.1. Community must be inclusive. If the disenfranchised are encouraged to represent themselves and to rebuild their own sense of identity, all members of the community benefit. Here, Chief Homer St. Francis of the Abenaki Tribe enjoys the sun at a regional powwow. These powwows are uncommon in the Northeast. Growing out of small seed grants, this gathering has provided a positive image of a group of people who were often angry and often poor. The gatherings are inclusive of all in the region. As one Native American put it, "We are all indigenous to the Earth."

eral newly formed nonprofits; meeting costs for food and beverages to celebrate those who had completed GED classes and passed exams and for those who had learned to read (these folks insisted on returning the $10.20 that they had not expended out of the $100 grant); parent-to-parent support groups; an intergenerational meeting; and a mental health support group.

Seed grants often provide unexpected results for individuals and community. Some of the very smallest grants were found to be immeasurably significant. For example, one participant in an adult reading program supported in a remote rural community by a small EPIC grant reported that she had been afraid to attend parent-teacher conferences. By becoming a more confident reader, she found that she not only had the confidence to the meetings, but also that she could actually "go alone, without my husband."

Networks Can Be Built through Seed Grants

In as many grants as possible, we sought to encourage cross-fertilization of ideas between people. For example, in funding a "Conservation Congress," we were able to be the catalyst that brought together people from neighboring towns in a watershed area to discuss a broad range of conservation issues. It allowed people with many different perspectives to come together in a neutral forum. Although the event lasted one day and was limited to 200 persons, it was videotaped for cable access to reach broader audiences. A spin-off from this included the fact that an international conservation exchange group, hearing of the congress, sent the organizer of the event, a forester, to England to study European conservation mechanisms; upon his return, he helped to establish a new nonprofit organization that purchased a 600-acre tract of land for an education center.

EPIC funded a regional Conservation Congress for three years in a row, and one of the results was a flurry of grant requests for conservation-related activities such as for community-based citizen stream pollution and erosion monitoring; erosion-control projects; and several school-based projects for nature trails, wetland surveys, river walks, wildlife tracking, and natural resource inventory work for town planning commissions.

The networks built were based on watershed boundaries rather than on town boundaries and between communities rather than within single communities. This fostered collaboration between towns and linked schools with their communities in new ways.

Seed Grants Should Not Directly Fund Polarized Community Issues

Although conflict is inherent in discussions over use of natural resources, and indeed can be harnessed effectively, as we saw in the Conservation Congress described above, the EPIC model of seed grants had a specific policy to not fund issues that polarize communities. To do so would not meet the elements or key principles of the EPIC model. Sometimes, we found a way around a conflict. For example, despite antagonism over the Native American rights of the unrecognized Abenaki Nation, we were able to fund a cultural festival, which became a positive focal point for the tribe, and which, in the years since, has helped foster a positive relationship between Abenaki and European-origin peoples in the area. Conflict should not steer funders away, but the focus must be on positive broader long-term solutions.

Occasionally, there is just no way to bring the sides together, and funding cannot be provided. For example, a plan to build a huge Wal-Mart store in a rural community was perceived by some as a sensible way to attract Canadian shoppers to the poorer northern tier of towns in Vermont, to provide cheap goods readily available for businesses and households alike, and to use a piece of wasted land near the interstate highway. But others saw it as a nonsustainable aspect of rural develop-ment, environmentally destructive, and likely to destroy downtown community businesses. Other EPIC team leaders (notably, our interna-tionally known business expert) and EPIC advisory board members went to the community to determine if there was a project that could be funded that would help bring the community back together. We looked for creative, innovative, citizen-based solutions to fund, but, unfortunately, this conflict had "festered" to the point that we believed our funds would be more likely to increase polarization than to reweave the fabric of the community.

It Helps a Lot if You Pay the Volunteer Leader a Little

The following story illustrates several important aspects of volunteer work and seed grants: (1) It addresses a concern common in many rural regions of the nations—the need for improved, more-accessible health care; (2) it shows the critical role that nurses can play in improving rural health care delivery; and (3) it reminds us that all the volunteers burn out in about six months, but that providing a small honorarium to a volunteer for a few months or a year can make all the difference in providing a sustainable solution to a local or regional problem.

One community seed grant request came from a nurse whose goal was to help build a regional community-based health-care coalition. The health needs in the region were increasingly dispensed from centralized regional facilities, because amalgamated hospitals, like amalgamated schools, are considered to be more "cost effective." My experience worldwide over many decades suggests that this is not only simplistic, but also that such centralized school and hospital facilities are not conducive to sustainable rural development. In the instance at hand, the local hospitals in northwest Vermont had been amalgamated by the vote of the competing hospital boards, under pressure from the distant university hospital. The number of hospital nurses was reduced, and, with the goal of keeping all the beds full, outreach services were reduced.

Suggestions of rural, town-based clinics, well-child programs, senior checks, pregnancy checkups, and ambulatory care units proposed by the maverick on the hospital board in the late 1970s through the mid-1980s had been met with the fear of "socialized medicine." Home health nurses and physiotherapists began to see higher patient care loads as insurance coverage for hospital stays was reduced and more were sent home too soon.

The goal of the EPIC grant proposed in 1993 was for a coalition health-care organization that would bring together all the diverse groups of medical providers and consumers to work out a solution that would better address health care for the area. The nurse who requested the grant first served as a volunteer, and her efforts were astounding. Quiet and patient, she slowly built a small coalition, initially of women home health nurses and other nursing staff. Shortly after she began this effort, someone nominated her for the EPIC leadership training, which she completed, along with her husband. In the training, she learned how the quiet leader could work, with persistence, to build consensus around common goals. She also learned how to start a not-for-profit organization. After almost a year, physicians were drawn into the mix, especially the younger, newly arrived physicians.

The organization was struggling with a mix of people who had not typically worked as "equals," and the physiotherapist volunteer (with a builder husband and five children at home) was close to burning out. EPIC suggested that she be paid a part-time honorarium (salary) for a year or so until this complex project was relatively stable. Her fledgling board agreed. Two years after she started this project, there was a non-profit regional health-care coalition organization. Satellite rural health-care clinics were established for the first time in several rural towns and others revitalized. One of the new health-care clinics would soon go into the community center in Fairfield, Vermont, which is discussed in Chapter Eight.

Two important outcomes of this effort were improved communications and that decisions on regional health-care delivery were now made based on a broader view of the situation. One of the results was that the medical community applied for and received additional federal assistance.

Seed grants such as this one are also found to act as incubators for not one but several kinds of leaders. EPIC funded part-time volunteers in several Vermont communities, especially where we were aiming to cluster seed grants, such as in Fairfield and Hardwick, where a broader community renaissance was desired by the local people.

Building Community through Funding Rural Heritage Projects

The rural heritage of a region can be a critical factor in a future sustainable society. However, like most rural development projects, expensive capital campaigns to rebuild entire buildings or refurbish museums are not possible. EPIC was not able to rebuild historical barns, but we could reward those landowners who strove to renovate their barns and to keep them in farming or other rural uses. This project was called Barn Again! EPIC's concept of Barn Again! was to award owners of historic barns who voluntarily renovate or adapt the barn for a rural purpose. These awards were given at the annual state agricultural show in front of many people in order to motivate others. This was an offshoot of the national Barn Again! Project, headquartered in Colorado. We worked collaboratively with farmers, departments of agriculture, and state and federal historic preservation associations. The colorful poster and T-shirts were very popular (Photo 5.2). This project enables landowners to look at their old barns through new lenses (so to speak), to see them as valuable resources, and it also enabled the architecturally minded historic preservationists to realize that barns have cows and the like inside of them.

Other rural heritage projects funded by EPIC seed grants included providing timber to replace the floor of the only community meeting place in town (here was a clear connection between community needs to meet and a place to do so); helping several service center towns foster tourism by producing brochures for walking and driving tours to see historic buildings; and funding the compilation of a state database on historic structures in Vergennes, Vermont (the smallest city in America,

Photo 5.2. Barn Again! A project to encourage preservation of farm buildings used for agriculture and other rural functions.

so they claim). Here a local minister, working with a recent EPIC leadership graduate, was funded to develop community support to start a capital campaign to save the old opera house.

In a service center town on the Canadian border, EPIC funded the renovation of a boat dock on Lake Memphramegog, which straddles the international border—the focus of considerable attention in this poor region.

In all of these efforts, the goal has been to bring the community together around issues of common interest. We had never imagined that any of the seed monies would go to buying timber for floors and boat docks. But we knew we must accept the community where it was and use that to bring about a community renaissance.

It Pays to See Innovation in Agriculture

Innovation in agriculture is one of core ideas in the EPIC model. We therefore approached agriculture from many different perspectives: seed grants for linking farms directly with hotels and restaurants; bed-and-breakfast tourism projects complete with brochures and workshops; business plans for developing value-added products; a new rural cooperative bake shop; workshops on pasture management; 4-H Club demonstration projects; young farmer meetings; Hay Art (to build links between the urban "sophisticate" and the realities of rural landscapes); and school-farm transition workshops.

Other seed grant projects included helping reduce some of the risk for innovative farmers who wanted to experiment with a new type of fencing, spring calving, heifer pasture feeding, or sheep milking. The cost of borrowing money for a risky venture often puts farmers off, or they are pushed to borrow far more than they really need, and the losses can become too high.

EPIC also funded several projects that brought schoolchildren and farmers together, and Georgia Elementary School produced an excellent video about pasture grazing on the local farms. There were also school-farm projects to help students understand where their food actually comes from.

Tiny amounts of money could make enormous differences. For example, by EPIC providing funds for relief milkers, many more farmers and their families could attend town or regional meetings or celebrations, reducing their isolation considerably.

These many agricultural seed grants were in addition to the major funding we provided for intensive pasture management (which is discussed in detail in Chapter Six).

Not Every Community Seed Grant Will Be a Success

Rural development projects need to be tracked to ascertain which did not work and why. Nevertheless, risk taking is an important ingredient of good leadership and a vital part of seed grants. We should not be discouraged by failures. Several "unsuccessful" grants involved school-related projects. One involved taking rural school students on an exchange visit to Harlem in New York as part of a rural/urban learning exchange. The project had the potential for success but at the last minute the school administration pulled its support. Organizers learned the hard way about the need to maintain open lines of communication. In another school-related project, several schools around the state were funded to allow teachers to gain training in the REAL (Rural Entrepreneurial Action Leadership) project in which teenage students are trained to set up a business while in school and continue to run it after graduation. A state organization was set up to build on this process after we had provided grants to several teachers for national training in several schools. Some students succeeded, but the teachers receiving the funding could not adequately mesh their work with school administration and students.

Entrepreneurial Communities, Clustered Seed Grants, and a Role for the Expert

In Chapter Eight, several rural towns are profiled as sample case studies of whole towns. In particular, one town is profiled to demonstrate the affect of clustering seed grants in a town that had already undergone a Take Charge program (described in Chapter Four).

Hardwick, a town of 3,000 people in northeast Vermont, is located in the mountains at the confluence of three rivers. It is not easy to get to and is regularly cut off by roads washed out in floods. It is a service center for an extensive rural area that supports small, upland farms, logging, and quarrying. For the last thirty years it had been described as a depressed area.

In 1991, the initial Forestry Leadership Program was offered to community members in the Northeast Kingdom of Vermont, a nickname that began in the 1960s for three isolated rural counties: Essex, Orleans, and Caledonia. Several residents of Hardwick who participated in the Forestry Leadership Program considered it valuable and requested that the program be repeated in the Hardwick area during the fall of 1992. Eleven Hardwick residents graduated from this program, creating a corps of potential leaders to guide a renaissance in Hardwick.

Its population has steadily increased, once again reaching its peak population last seen around the turn of the century. Since the early 1900s, Hardwick had been the granite capital of the world, exporting building-grade granite until the early 1960s. The local economy is presently a mix of dairy and organic vegetable farming, logging, and related industries, with employment opportunities beyond its boundaries, requiring a daily commute for many. Hardwick began its renaissance in the early 1980s with a downtown revitalization effort. By the end of the decade, it had fizzled out, giving the community its nickname of "Hard Luck Hardwick," complete with Hardwick jokes and a lack of community spirit. In January 1992, while a local committee was planning to initiate a Take Charge (community assessment) program, a fire destroyed two blocks of the downtown. At the same time, the local "old-boy network" was split up after the arrest of several local bankers. A cadre of enthusiastic, newly trained community leaders to replace them was just what was needed in Hardwick.

With renewed leadership and motivation, Hardwick citizens began the work to improve its economic base and were successful in securing an Enhancing Community Awareness grant and also support from EPIC. A cluster of EPIC seed grants was provided to the town and to the high school. One of these included a grant to assist in the operating of a small cafe in the town center to serve as a coffee shop and meeting place. As in other towns, we found that this was a much-needed function. Here, book club meetings, youth meetings, town officer meetings, and just general chance meetings took place (and still do) at what was eventually called the Renaissance Cafe. Citizens also established a Hardwick Area Adult Learning Center from which they are targeting projects to empower adults to improve their employment options.

The town leaders were successful in pulling together assistance from a variety of sources to fund numerous community events and projects. One project was a comprehensive marketing survey designed by two University of Vermont faculty members of EPIC. This project assessed the shopping patterns of residents in nine surrounding towns. The survey results were then used by Hardwick merchants to guide their future expansion and advertising, as well as to provide information for prospective businesses and industries. Hardwick merchants formed an informal association and are cooperating with local service organizations to host community events such as an annual Fall Foliage Festival and a Memorial Day celebration. The colocation committee, which acted on its vision to provide a central location for community social services sustainable on a long-term basis, conducted a survey of agencies to determine if interest existed for colocation. The results indicate that a number of agencies are interested. Joining a newly formed "patch" group, which has opened an office in downtown Hardwick, several social service offices relocated to this office, including mental health and vocational rehabilitation; clinics for the Women, Infants, and Children program; and teen and family mediation services. Such "wellness" efforts are enormously important in all the rural areas where I have worked.

Today, because of the synergy of these diverse but collaborative approaches to rural development, Hardwick feels like a vibrant community again. This can be captured in the comments of one Hardwick resident, a graduate of one of the forestry leadership programs:

> What seems to be important is a commitment by the leadership of the community to learn how to lead in a fashion that involves community on all levels, a commitment by outside agencies to work together to provide opportunities without telling people what to do or vying for ownership or glory, and a desire by a large group of community members to make a better community.
>
> —Jim, a resident of Hardwick, Vermont

It is community leaders throughout rural areas who must deal with change in the economy, the environment, and the social structure in their communities. Hardwick is just one example of how leadership skills, combined with seed grants, can contribute to positive change for communities in transition.

Ronald Savitt, professor of business administration at the University of Vermont, one of the EPIC core team leaders, was one of the professors who provided external support through ongoing discussion, research, and analysis with town leaders in Hardwick. He found that it was possible to stimulate what appears to be sustainable rural economic development in the town, because many residents had taken part in various leadership development seminars and workshops, and several town leaders had gone on to request seed grants clustered in and around the town. The depressed period had pushed the community to the bottom, and humility set in. These town leaders were determined to work together rather than fight and compete with each other.

Ronald Savitt adds the following:

> In Hardwick, not willing to wait for the government or some other savior, they began to take hold of their own actions. The participants had to discover new ways to assert their strengths. They had to break down competitive individualism and their own attitudes about the market as well as the stereotype of being rural. They actively sought methods to improve their lives. Seeking a "little help from their friends," they soon realized that cooperation not competition was an important means of exerting their own strengths and developing unknown resources. They soon learned that without a community, they were their own worst enemies. And, the market they blamed for all too many ills was an important instrument in developing solutions. For example, inn keepers, manufacturers, and merchants of all stripes came together to develop a marketing strategy that served to identify what their community was to all of its citizens and what it could be to outsiders who might want to do business there.
>
> They learned that by cooperation they could enjoy the economies of advertising and promoting the community and, as a result, draw more customers there

than anyone could do alone. They learned that as they know more about one another's business, they could do what they did best and in the end provide more reason for locals to shop and to attract others from far and wide. They saw the results in people once again becoming aware and then proud of their community. They saw young people having more economic opportunities and they saw pride across the board.

Given that sustainability is measured by adaptation of the community to change, one question (rhetorical) must be raised here: Can Hardwick or other similar rural service center towns continue to change in positive ways without a continuous process of deliberately developing leadership to assure expanding community roles needed to strengthen the community and sustain it in the long term?

Communities are powerful elements in economic development. Once able to put aside the selfishness of individuals, they use the market not simply to improve the well being of the immediate participants but everyone they involve. It is all based on a vision that individuals working together can use the market and all the technology it offers to enhance their own freedom and opportunities. (Savitt, personal communication, June 1998)

The Hardwick example, where numerous *citizen-driven* initiatives were used to address the need for integrated modern rural development, can be seen to meet EPIC's Key Principles of Sustainable Rural Development. In the Hardwick case study, all the elements of the EPIC model can be identified. Grants were clustered in and around a rural service center, providing several different groups of community people with assistance, technical and financial, over a period of several years.

The role of Ron Savitt provides an interesting and significant lesson. Here is an outside "expert" in rural marketing strategies, not only in America, but also in Europe. He did not arrive in Hardwick with all the data and an answer—as would have been the case in the traditional expert-driven model of rural development. Instead, he came when invited by the community, as one of several experts. His role as facilitator, leader, teacher, expert, and coach was collaborative rather than competitive. He worked by example. He was a critical factor, a catalyst as an individual. But he could not have had such success without the earlier activities of Hardwick's citizen leaders. They had undertaken the community-based Take Charge program a few years earlier, and they were ready and able to use Savitt's expertise.

There was a synergy in Hardwick that evolved over a period of about ten years. Savitt's ability to draw on his work in Europe provided him with ideas to share that had been used elsewhere. This also enabled him to avoid possible failed methods. Savitt also clearly exhibits the ability to use diverse leadership styles, from assertive, to gentle and persuasive, to fully collaborative. He is comfortable "giving away" his ideas and quietly leaving town.

The types of grants clustered in Hardwick included marketing surveys; support for renovating a small, old store on Main Street so that it could become a meeting place/coffee shop (the Renaissance Cafe); a community-building holiday open house; a community newsletter and part-time coordinator; a chamber of commerce brochure and information booth; meetings for area businesses; and a community theater evening.

By contrast, there were two other "depressed" rural service centers where, as director of the overall EPIC project, I had tried to encourage deployment of Savitt's expertise, but the rural marketing strategy could not be used there. These other two communities had not undergone an earlier Take Charge type community assessment and were therefore not ready for Savitt's expert help; we had to step back, instead funding other more basic projects in those communities.

Sustainable "Green Region" Development and Focused Seed Grants

Rural communities are systems, and they function within the context of ecological systems. As discussed in previous chapters, there is a need to interconnect the natural environment with the human desire for development in the region. The need for conservation and economic development must be harnessed and worked together if sustainability is to be the outcome. Although different in many ways, there are lessons that can be learned from mechanisms successfully used in Britain for a generation (since they reached rural crises earlier than in America).

One of the EPIC goals is that all those involved with rural development should come to understand that sustainable rural development must include an appreciation of the interconnected nature of everything and mesh with the needs of the environment. But this cannot be forced on people. We tried to demonstrate, by our support of a wide array of community projects, that "environment" was indeed everything and that no matter if it were a school project on recycling, a new community center, a rural health clinic, or a cultural heritage festival, all aspects of rural communities mattered and were part of the whole.

I knew from experience that to be sustainable, service center towns like Hardwick could not be funded in isolation from the surrounding communities that it served, nor was the town separate from the farms and farm families in the region. I also knew that a large "block" grant delivered and administered from "outside" would take too long and would probably not meet the real needs of the local populations. I recalled the range of efforts at rural development that had been deployed in my earlier years in northern England, which was declared a depressed area, with economic collapse, loss of rural transportation, rural depopulation, and a generally demoralized atmosphere. We were too far from the capital, London, to be of much importance (it seemed). As with Hardwick, the rural service center of Hexham, on the river Tyne, and its rural hinterlands where I grew up demonstrated characteristics of economic, social, and environmental stress. In rural Northumberland, on the Scottish border, with industry long gone, rural revitalization of the poor rural areas and dying rural towns during the late 1950s and early 1960s developed out of the regional planning efforts at county and local district level. These efforts involved many diverse groups, including schoolchildren like myself, in an analysis of what was needed to revitalize the town of Hexham and the surrounding areas. We worked on rural development plans for the urban service center and for the rural landscape and communities. These plans were then presented to government officials for their consideration. Steps forward were slow, because bureaucracies do not move fast. But by the 1970s, rural revitalization appeared to have taken place in a manner that was integrated and comprehensive. Revitalization included then, and still includes, grants and tax incentives. Grants such as these are often called "subsidies" and disparaged by those who oppose this means of rural revitalization. In England, however, these grants were handled in a bureaucratic manner that would be unacceptable in America, and they are not often truly community driven, but the long-term impact of this has conserved rural Northumberland and transformed its economic base to some extent. Activities involved developing farm tours and bed-and-breakfast places, working cooperatively in a region—an idea that was one of the measurable outcomes of the EPIC project. Reforestation was important for that region, essentially deforested with no hope of natural regeneration. There had also been planning support to provide assistance to "growth towns" (service centers) such as Hexham and assistance to "no-growth" areas such as small, attractive rural villages, country houses, and castles to conserve the environment and the working landscape.

Today there is a vibrant town, with a fine regional heritage museum for tourists and for local education, a network of farm tourist amenities and forestry tours, and many other aspects of a conserved working rural landscape. For Northumberland, this also includes a national park. Unlike those in the United States, such parks are multiple-use regions with farms and related activities but with restricted development opportunities. The focus has been on conservation with economic development only in designated growth towns, but with funding to ensure that no-growth areas can also flourish and meet the changing global markets.

Green planning like this varies from region to region throughout Western Europe, but there are some templates that might work in parts of rural America. In the United States, we had to do it using small seed grants from a generous foundation and investing in the local population.

Thus, in addition to funding a cluster of seed grants in the Hardwick town service center, EPIC seed grants were also directed into specific communities and to farmers in the rural area around the town, to stimulate a regional network. One early seed grant (1993) involved bringing together hotel owners and operators (these are all small in this part of the nation) and operators of bed-and-breakfast inns (often farm wives) to build cooperation rather than competition. The effort resulted in a regional marketing brochure in which all places offering accommodation in the region advertised together. Spin-offs from this have included attracting the attention of the state tourism staff to buy in to these ideas, and the concept is now "institutionalized" by the state and various chambers of commerce. In this case, the chamber, not always an environmentally friendly partner, could understand the conservation and landscape aspect of rural marketing.

This first EPIC regional farm/business alliance grant in our first year stimulated many other requests, which we able to meet not only in the same region but also throughout the state during the following two years. These involved making links between farm producers and restaurants, as well as bed-and-breakfast places, often new to farm families, with tourist visits to farms. Today there is a stable, sustainable, and strong official link between farmer producers and restaurants, not only in the Hardwick region, but all around the state. Through this system, farmers producing a commodity such as vegetables, milk, or maple syrup agree to provide fresh produce to restaurants and to offer farm tours to visitors. This has in turn stimulated interest in more value-added farm and rural products. Other seed grants linked with these were made to local schools—especially elementary and junior high—to develop school community gardens for produce for the poor and needy or to sell. Some schools in Vermont, like Georgia Elementary, were more open to innovative ideas than other schools and were able to take advantage of many seed grants.

Today, when visitors come to Jay Peak Ski Area on the Canadian border, they can take farm tours when the snow is not great, or, when they need a change of activity, they can find bed-and-breakfast inns, and the food in all the best restaurants will probably be local. Jay Peak is a small ski mountain, often on the verge of bankruptcy, in the heart of a poor rural area on both sides of the border.

The Conservation Congress described previously was also a focused, collaborative grant. In addition, several grants were made to children who wanted to plant trees in a community, refurbish housing for senior citizens, and develop a community recycling system; others funded regional meetings for teachers interested in environmental education, conservation commissions, or just grants for food and beverages for a lunchtime gathering. Every little bit helps.

The Role of Assessment in Improving Seed Grant Effectiveness

As discussed in Chapter Three, we found that ongoing evaluation was useful in several ways: it helped us to understand what others saw happening in their communities (as compared with what the EPIC staff saw); provided us with ideas that we could use to modify or guide us in the seed grant and other EPIC programs, regarding both substance and process; and provided an ongoing mechanism for capturing lessons learned, and not merely a retrospective analysis but also lessons learned at many different stages in the seed grant activities.

Assessment took place in several ways, informal and formal, including ongoing phone calls and visits to grantees on site; informal discussions; meetings of local boards where relevant analysis of community meeting minutes took place; regular discussion of seed grants with EPIC staff and with various individuals on the council of advisors; a simple, written evaluation form distributed to grantees upon completion of their project; an in-depth interview process involving a cross section of seed-grant participants; focus-group meetings; and written evaluations and discussions with the external evaluator. The informal information was particularly easy to obtain, building as it did on the trust that existed between EPIC staff and the community members. It was not seen as "evaluating or assessing" and thus was not threatening. Community members felt equally at ease telling us about the things that were going wrong and the things going right. The informal information also allowed us to change our methods and to modify guidance and advice, not just to the group activity being evaluated, but also to other groups. We also used this informal information to place groups in contact with others in the same or other communities. As a result, it became another way to build networks.

The written evaluation (Appendix B3) sent as follow-up was not particularly helpful because although some of those who received the hundreds of grants given over the four years did fill it out in detail, there were far more who did not return it, even after written reminders.

The interview process, using an interview guide, was a very productive albeit time-consuming process. Each interview took about one and a half hours on average, plus the travel time to the grantees' work or home location and phone time to set a mutually convenient time for two busy people. Some of the interviews were of small groups rather than of one individual. Interviews were not selected randomly but were determined by looking at the clusters of seed grants given. This allowed us to assess the cluster impacts of the seed grants rather than single impacts of individual grants. Given time and money it would be informative to continue this evaluation process indefinitely. Suffice it to say that, based on these interviews, some common factors, patterns, and lessons learned were identified, and the process was very useful.

At the beginning of the EPIC rural development project, an external evaluator (an independent reviewer) was invited to undertake periodic assessment of our activities, in all of the diverse (but hopefully integrated) parts. This was useful for providing annual report information but not for improving our work. It did allow us to identify some areas where there were misconceptions by individuals in institutions touched by our work. One of the problems found by the external evaluator was that despite all efforts to find a person who really understood the holistic nature of the comprehensive approach needed in rural development, we were never entirely successful. However, we wanted to leave the external evaluator to work without being influenced by us. This external evaluator did attend one or two of the EPIC staff meetings each year, however, and overall this was felt to be an important part of our assessment efforts.

Evaluation and assessment were thus internal and external, formal and informal, and always ongoing.

Spin-Offs from Rural Community Seed Grants

It is not possible to present here many of the individual spin-offs recorded during the last few years of EPIC-funded seed grants. Some have been discussed earlier in the chapter, so only a few more examples are added here.

The initial funding source can quickly become obscured in future activities. Most of the organizations begun with EPIC seed grants have gone on to expand their funding bases, in some cases dramatically. A community center started in 1992, in Fairfield, Vermont, with a $2,000 seed grant, had a $30,000 annual budget by 1995 and continues to thrive. A lead safety project started with a $2,000 grant by three mothers of lead-poisoned children in Vermont received $70,000 in grants and other sources and now has a full-time staff.

Other spin-offs include the ever-expanding network of farm linkages with businesses and bed-and-breakfast places and farm-product direct sales to restaurants. All of these are now a major aspect of Vermont's agricultural tourism industry. I am sure that no one knows that these were first seeded by EPIC grants during the period of 1992 to 1995.

Another project was the environmental quality indicator (EQI) in which citizen-based perspectives on the quality of their land, air, water, forests, and so forth triggered an official state initiative. This permitted EPIC to redirect funds marked for another two years of EQI to other seed grants.

A small grant to a few people can lead to major changes in society. The lead safety seed grant proved remarkable in that Leslie Wright, despite being shy, was willing to take the leadership role in a complex political issue. She set up a series of educational forums for other mothers, which quickly caught the attention of the governor and the state legislature. Her work began in October 1991, when her children were found to have elevated lead levels in their bodies. She joined forces with a group of mothers and founded a nonprofit organization aimed at teaching other mothers of small children the hazards of lead poisoning. Vermont, like many rural states, has a very high level of old housing stock covered in lead paint. This small group of mothers was quietly persistent, and their results included pushing the state legislature to enact new laws and a sustained effort by the state to address the serious health impacts for children. Her efforts involved forming a coalition, called the Conservation Law Foundation, with the state department of health and several groups in Washington, D.C., and running several news and media events to raise awareness.

Serendipity plays an important role. Unexpected spin-offs occurred in many cases, spreading the activities to neighboring towns. For example, two women requested an EPIC seed grant to work with junior high and high school students to connect the town's burgeoning bed-and-breakfast establishments with the neighboring farms, nature trails, and related rural activities. This involved creating interpretive pamphlets to place in the bed-and-breakfasts, driving around to make the connections, and building a network. After three years, the effort had garnered broad town support, spawned an incorporated organization, inspired similar efforts in neighboring towns, and even connected with a cross-state trail used by hikers and snowmobilers. In addition, these activities brought together environmentalists with snowmobilers in a positive manner.

Lessons Learned from Rural Community Seed Grants

Seed grant programs were effective in inspiring leadership behaviors in previously uninvolved citizens and can thus be considered incubators for leaders. EPIC tried to reach a new set of change agents. Many seed grantees built self-confidence and gained new skills and knowledge. Running the grant was like leadership training, and most grantees were entering public life for the first time. In making the seed grants, efforts were made to cluster grants in various community areas so that they could learn from each other. In addition, several potential leaders from these same communities were nominated to take the EPIC leadership courses that were being held at the same time. A number of seed grantees went on to run for public office and got elected: one woman became a senator; others took volunteer or part-time positions in the town, such as zoning administrator.

Seed grants provide models. Good ideas catch on. Although EPIC did not fund the Native American heritage festival held in New Hampshire, we were told that its organizers had come to the Abenaki heritage festival held on the Vermont/Canadian border and talked to the organizers about how they did it. So this local idea became the stimulus for the idea that an important cultural event could take place elsewhere.

Participation increases. Consistent with adult-learning theory, participation itself is one of the most effective enhancers of citizen behavior.

There is a sequence of leadership. The person who is the visionary leader, who gets something off the ground, is very often not the person who will then lead and manage the organization in its next phase of development. For example, Vanessa Madden, the nurse volunteer who envisaged and began the regional health-care coalition, stepped aside once the coalition was established to allow new leaders to take the organization to its next step.

Seed grants can build connections between major sectors of society. One grant of $2,000 was given to bring together artists and farmers around the role of hay in the landscape beloved by rural and urban resident alike. The goal was to hold a summer-long series of demonstrations of "hay art" in the fields, with artists and farmers collaborating and with daylong farm exhibits at a very large farm. The vision of one woman artist proved to be enormously successful.

Civic responsibility can be engendered through seed grants. Many grantees felt a new pride in their community, an absolutely vital ingredient for sustainable rural development. This pride took many forms. In one elementary school in a poor town, students planned and implemented a schoolwide recycling program. This involved one dedicated teacher over a three-year period. The program, in turn, pressured town officials to develop municipal recycling. And, eventually, the school felt inspired to do more service learning.

Rural community-based seed grants are an effective process for meeting the Key Principles of Sustainable Rural Community Development. In sum, ideas from Europe and elsewhere have been both deliberately and intuitively introduced through development and management of seed grants as part of the EPIC approach to rural development. These ideas, seen and used elsewhere, have stimulated and helped refine an interconnected set of community ideas adaptable to rural communities in America. These ideas have spread and been further refined by the active community-collaborating partners. Ideas have been successfully transferred and modified by individuals and local communities. EPIC personnel have long since left, allowing the real players to go forward and further modify the ideas to fit changing local circumstances. Few people know the role played by the integrated rural development effort known as EPIC. Anonymity should be accepted as a given for those who choose to be involved as catalysts in rural community development that is most likely to be truly sustainable.

Seed grants are one very effective mechanism for moving a community toward a more sustainable future according to the definitions of sustainable rural development presented at the beginning of the chapter. We clearly see that a sustainable community is not a fixed state of harmony, but a dynamic and changing community.

Chapter Six

Innovation and Renovation in Farming Communities: Rural Space, Natural Resources, and Property Ownership

In many parts of the United States there is a joke among farmers that goes something like this: "What would you do if you won a million dollars?" The answer: "Why, I'd just go on farming 'til it's all used up!" The vagaries of weather and climate (perhaps even climate change) combined with cash-flow problems and high capital investments on the farm, plus changing market demands, make this flippant joke all too real in rural America. And, although farmers feel isolated from urban America in some respects, the impact of urban and global demands adds fuel to challenges that are already more than some can bear. Many farms have been abandoned, and not just those in marginal ecological areas but also those on prime growing land, because of other ecological, economic, and social reasons. The total number of farms has fallen from about 7 million in 1930 to about 5 million in 1950, and to about 2.5 million today. Yet we Americans have some of the richest agricultural soils in the world, and we can and do generate vast quantities of food and fiber.

Agriculture is the principal land use in many rural regions. Since the first days of agriculture, the evolution of humans from mere hunters and gatherers has been marked by the establishment of permanent settlements. These family groups gave rise to rural communities that continue to be the hallmark of rural society, rich in local history, and reflecting human successes and failures. This rural society has made an imprint on the American landscape, from Kahokia and the Mound Builders of the Mississippi valley, to the cotton fields and plantations of the Old South, to the wheat and cornfields of the Midwest. To a large extent, the physical/biological landscapes have been transformed into cultural landscapes that reflect not only varying components of the vegetation of America before human settlement but also show the impacts (positive and negative) of thousands of years of human use. They show the fields that replaced the forests and grasslands, for example. They show the pattern of roads crisscrossing the vast interior of America and the rivers dammed and reservoirs built to quench the thirst of urban society and irrigate farmlands. These landscapes show us the patterns of earlier cultures and of the present. Although these cultural landscapes are not as manicured as the English countryside, many of the concepts raised by Hoskins, in his book *The Making of the English Landscape* (1970), are applicable to them as well; the analogies and application of the history are important. Knowledge of the past, including resource use and present trends, is essential to making decisions now that will affect future resource use and the rural communities that provide society's sustenance. Sustaining rural life and livelihoods is thus important ecologically and socioeconomically for the entire country.

The key principles of sustainable rural community development, when applied to agriculture and forestry, must focus efforts on conservation and innovation: encourage youth to more wisely use natural resources and devise better agricultural practices; strengthen the role of women, and learn from them; and foster strong and mutually beneficial links between urban and rural communities. The focus in this chapter is thus to provide, in a brief overview, a context of major land uses, including forest and agricultural production, and then to discuss examples of rural development mechanisms that may be transferable from one region of the country to another, or from which useful concepts can be derived. First, however, there are several major social and political realities that must be addressed.

Major Dilemmas in the Perception of Rural Resources

The 2 percent of our population engaged in food and fiber production does so with great efficiency. The urban dweller in America is accustomed to cheap food. As a high-tech, developed nation, about 98 percent of our population is distanced from agriculture by a minimum of one generation and most by many more. Although some immigrants came from poor rural regions of Europe, many emigrated from urban centers and became urban settlers. Many of these families have not lived in rural settings for five generations so that, although their voting strength is great, their understanding of rural society and of agriculture and forestry is minimal. How can the rural few share their knowledge and influence the urban many?

Most Americans do not consider agriculture and forestry to be the major economic forces today that they were in the eighteenth and early nineteenth centuries. This, however, does not make today's rural economics any less important. We must all eat and have wood for building and for paper, and we all need rural landscapes for their natural ecosystems, biodiversity, wildlife, and recreation. Rural regions still represent 83 percent of America.

In Chapter One, many of the problems associated with rural regions were introduced. How can we better communicate the challenges of rural America to the urban populations? How can we persuade policy makers and corporate leaders to invest in rural regions? These regions need, for example, economically and environmentally sustainable businesses that process commodities locally rather than shipping the raw materials to sources of cheaper labor. The traditional industrial location factors—raw materials, energy, labor, transport, and market—have always included politics. A values-laden set of policies is needed in the renovation of rural America.

But once engaged, how can we sustain urban America's interest in rural communities? And at the same time, how can we empower more and stronger rural leadership that can carry a clear message to state and national policy makers? How can we take innovative ideas and changing consumer values and apply these in a manner that cultivates more sustainable rural communities, including more sustainable agriculture? Those involved in sustainable agriculture, together with forward-thinking environmentalists, ask us to apply criteria other than economics to decision making in rural development. And, another dilemma exists in the fragmentation of opinions and approaches within agricultural and environmental circles: both groups are in some chaos, each having at least two schools of thought concerning rural development. In the agricultural camp, some contend that increased efficiency is the answer, with megafarms, agribusiness, high levels of technology, and few employees—as though production of cows and carrots is similar to an auto assembly plant in Detroit. Others believe that agriculture integrated with the living ecosystems will be more sustainable—this is also a belief shared by many environmentalists. Extreme environmentalists apparently prefer that forests and landscapes be allowed to revert to their "natural" states—with little room for humans and their livelihoods. But out of this chaos, as Margaret Wheatley (1992) suggests in her ideas on chaos theory, can come a reinvigorated society.

Then there is the dilemma (if such is the correct term here) of private property ownership, a core value and a political reality of American life—urban or rural. This core value is one of the primary reasons why immigrants continue to come, seeking the American Dream. Although it is easy to add the implied doctrine that "private property must be subservient to the public good," the dilemma is to balance those critical private rights against the public interests of future generations. To add to the private property issue is the complication of an increasingly fragmented pattern of private property ownerships nationwide. This increase in numbers of parcels of land is seen not only in urban-rural fringe areas, but also in abandoned forest and farmlands in almost all rural sectors of the nation. How can the United States Department of Agriculture (USDA), the U.S. Forest Service, land grant universities, and the extension system best address this changed ownership, with its changed values and perceptions of agriculture and forestry?

How can we best address the needs of this vast rural area with its scattered communities, ignored by most Americans? Given that these dilemmas must be addressed by a society that is, in fact, urban, and unlikely to read books about agriculture and forestry, the next three sections of this chapter attempt to synthesize some basic data and concepts concerning the natural resources base of rural regions. These sections provide a sketch of resource productivity and trends. The remainder of the chapter discusses some examples in which changed use of resources has been shown to positively affect other components of rural life and move us closer to more sustainable rural communities.

Forest Resources

The forested lands of the United States have been in transition since European settlement (Cox et al. 1985). Initially, the "Great Eastern Forest" was replaced by open agricultural landscapes, but it is now returning to forest cover in many areas, this time far more fragmented in ownership (see Reidel [1995] for a discussion of this trend). A similar story is found in the Great Lakes region, where the cultural landscapes today show little of the remnant mixed hardwood forests of the not-so-distant past (Flader 1983). Rural development has not typically

addressed the combination of forests and agriculture, let alone the fragmented patterns of private ownership that exist in most of the East or
the changes now taking place in other regions of the United States.
The context within which agriculture takes place includes other
major land uses that greatly influence the range of farming activities
and that, in turn, are influenced by changing trends in agricultural productivity and products as farmers react to national and global consumer demands. In terms of general land-use categories in the United
States, approximately 32 percent of the land area is in forests (about 13
percent of the world's forest cover); 26 percent is in grass (mostly native
grasses in the West and introduced grasses in the East); 21 percent is
cultivated cropland of nonnative species; and the remaining 21 percent
is composed of urban land, "wasteland," and mountains. Some of the
latter may also be considered part of the rural landscapes in regions
such as the Rocky Mountains, where communities depend on "nature"
as a major natural resource in the local economy.

The vast areas of forest cover are, roughly, evenly distributed
between the western and the eastern states. Europeans visiting the
United States are still astounded that New York State, for example, is
largely forests and rural agricultural areas with a concentrated area of
urban settlement and are amazed at how tall and fast-growing the trees
are compared with Europe, where forest cover is very limited, trees are
small, and forests are low in species diversity. Indeed, the naturally high
species diversity and resilience of forests in the northeastern United
States is a surprise to visiting foresters from the western states.

Of the total U.S. forested land area, 66 percent is classified as commercial forestland (likely to used for commercial wood production).
However, of the total forestland in the West, only about 38 percent is
in potentially commercial forest because so much of the Rocky Mountains and southwest regions are pinyon-juniper and so much of Alaska
is muskeg. Those regions have intrinsic beauty and value as scenic
recreational areas, but not as commercial timberland. In contrast,
almost 94 percent of the total forest cover in the East is in commercial
timberland (Perry Hagenstein, personal communication, 1999) (Figure
6.1 and Photo 6.1). Communities based on forestry are not wealthy,
and livelihoods can be cyclical in a given geographic area. Community
stability is more fragile in forestry communities than in most agricultural communities.

Land ownership is of critical importance. Of the land area that is
forested, one-third is in federal ownership. Of those federal forests, 87

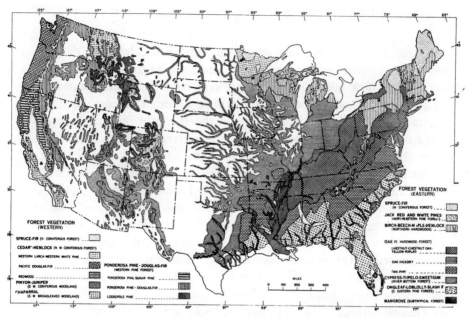

Figure 6.1. Natural forest vegetation of the United States. (U.S. Forest Service)

Photo 6.1. Forest cover in the East is increasing in acreage again as second-growth forests replace agriculture. This new forest is fragmented into millions of small private parcels, providing a very real challenge for managers of these lands to manage for many uses, including sustainable timber production.

percent lie in the West. Nearly 10 million people own America's private forestlands, and 85 percent of these are parcels of less than 50 acres. In the East, regional differences in natural forest cover types, along with their historical uses, have resulted in fragmented forests today. Thus most eastern U.S. commercial timberlands are highly fragmented blocks, and most privately owned forestland is composed of very small holdings. This is one of the many criteria that make the eastern and western United States quite different. Furthermore, it is estimated that private ownership in the East has increased by more than 2 million (parcels) since 1978, with a doubling of small parcels (under 50 acres) to about 77 million such parcels. It is also important to note that there is a large increase in the acreage of forestland owned by retired and "white-collar" owners and a corresponding decrease in the acreage of forests owned by farmers.

Forest-related issues in rural communities are thus quite different in the western and eastern states. Forests, both timber-producing and natural second growth, are very much part of rural agricultural communities in the East (less so in the West). Western commercial timberlands are more often found on federally owned land or in large corporate holdings. Forest management activities often take place at a considerable distance from viable farming activities and traditional rural communities. Concerns with forests in the West tend to be at the federal level and less locally and community-based. Although the U.S. Forest Service is under the jurisdiction of the United States Department of Agriculture, there appears to be little coordination of their mutual activities or databases. Despite our American love of statistics, land data are not always accurate or up to date in terms of land-use categories, acreage, and maps. Forests and forestry have typically been handled separately from agriculture, and yet the need to work cooperatively is of great importance, especially given the enormous holdings in forests and the increasing rate of forest cover spreading over eastern states as arable farmland and pastures are abandoned or sold for higher-profit development.

Data on forest ownership also influence the socioeconomic makeup of land ownership in rural communities, likely bringing more traditionally "urban" perspectives to the agro-forestry mix of land uses in rural communities. New forest owners may be retired dentists rather than farmers or foresters, and an increasing percentage of women now own small forest tracts. Combined agro-forestry approaches in the East are unfortunately not common at present.

The continued trend toward small ownerships, especially in the East, provides a challenge to forest policy makers and program administrators. This was aggravated by the difficulty in developing a collaborative model of modern forest management. Most of these owners lack the knowledge to ask the right questions, and they lack access to technical assistance when they have land-management questions. Many parcels are actually so small that management options are limited. There is an urgent need to help these land owners work together in cooperative and multidisciplinary collaborative groups to come up with a more community-based or regional-based set of management objectives. Burgeoning efforts at "green" forest management, forest certification, and related activities may provide some assistance in this area, although the path is presently strewn with political potholes. With care, these lands can be managed for timber production as well as for wildlife habitat, recreation, scenic beauty, critically needed environmental and ecological restoration, and community benefit. There are certainly examples of family forests and certified small forest tracts of land that are doing so. There is also a project called the Coverts Project, which is spreading around the nation. (Useful texts for help with forestry at community level or for the individual land owner can be found in Mollie Beattie's *Working with Your Woodland: A Landowners' Guide* [1993] and Thom McEvoy's works [1984, 1985, 1998].)

McEvoy's coverts project (a covert is habitat suitable for food and nesting for game species such as grouse and partridge) is particularly important because it is landowner- and community-driven and leads to a network of training. It evolved in response to a request by some local landowners for forest management practices to be applied that allowed habitat suitable for grouse hunting. McEvoy trained a number of people, typically landowners, on how to use a more comprehensive approach to managing forested land. He soon realized, however, that as an extension forester he should be teaching others to teach others. (See, especially, "A Preliminary Approach to Improve the Effectiveness of Extension Wildlife Habitat Education," an 1984 article he wrote with several others.) So, he agreed to work with landowners to improve grouse habitat only if they in turn agreed to teach others. From this collaboration, a network of teachers has built up. Although this was not a direct aspect of the EPIC model as applied during the last seven years, it contains all of the EPIC elements and meets its key principles and can easily be adapted in other areas. The coverts project demonstrates how extension foresters, too, can play a key role in engaging the community.

As it turned out, it was—for many reasons—extremely difficult to weave forestry operations and forestland management into projects using the EPIC model for sustainable rural community development. First, much of the land had been totally deforested by the mid-nineteenth century and then reforested in this century (especially since World War II) as agricultural land decreased in acreage. Second, many new forestland owners have not been trained in any form of land management. Third, there are fewer trained forestry professionals to assist these new landowners, and many long-time foresters are not conversant with newer, comprehensive approaches to forestry practices on small rural parcels. Fourth, some antagonism exists between environmentalists and professional foresters. Fifth, rural development has only recently begun to incorporate the idea of forest management. Land-use conflicts are increasing as more farmers sell off their "unproductive" forestlands and instead specialize in one or two major food products, further changing the balance of forests and agricultural land. Many farmers tend to ignore their own "woodlots" and abnegate responsibility for these forests to someone else. This further fragments decision making about the management of natural resources in rural areas. Efforts to develop urban forestry projects, forestry leadership programs, watershed conservation activities, and related collaborative efforts are even more vital in almost all rural areas where sustainable rural communities are the goal.

Interconnected Ecological and Agricultural Resources

The United States land area is large—about 920 million hectares (372 million acres)—highly diverse in its geological and ecological makeup, and blessed with a wide array of natural resources. Those interested in rural development must carefully assess the ecological context of their activities, with an eye to its geographical and historical contexts as well. Before humans grew corn crops in the rich, Midwest soils, tall-grass prairies grew for thousands of years. Wheat now replaces short-grass prairies on the best soils; in marginal soils, domestic cattle and sheep graze, replacing the native antelope and buffalo. From the tops of mountains to the river valleys, all regions of the United States have been subject to change, reducing species diversity and accelerating soil erosion. In all ecotone zones (margins between major ecological regions) and in fragile ecosystems, the negative impacts of human disturbance have been especially marked. The Dust Bowl erosion of the 1930s provides the most extreme example of agriculture at the margins of ecological regions. During that time, an extended drought caused severe erosion over thousands of acres of land that had been plowed and planted with grain crops, especially wheat. Harvests had been fine for a few years, but the region was only marginally adequate for growing such crops. In addition, virtually all the land area was plowed, leaving no buffer zones to reduce the impact of erosion. Dust from Kansas and Oklahoma blew all the way to the streets of New York. Most undergraduate students today, even in environmental studies classes, have never heard of the Dust Bowl. History is likely to repeat itself unless we teach youth about the mistakes that were made in the past.

Most Americans learn little or nothing about agriculture, forestry, or mining in school, except with a quick social-science brush stroke at some point in time. Yet, not only do we all eat every day, but also the United States is a major world exporter of food, fiber, wood products, and value-added products from these industries. For development in rural areas to be sustainable, the citizen leader must have a basic understanding about regional agriculture and forestry practices, and of production trends, in order to assess the development in a natural resources context. Every American, rural or urban, should be taught about agriculture.

Citizen leaders and would-be developers (rural and urban alike) should examine closely the locations and production trends of major crops grown in the United States today (Figures 6.2 and 6.3). A review of major agricultural and forestry trends will permit a global perspective on how farming and forestry communities are affected. Based on this discussion, some selected innovations can then be presented.

Major Agricultural Products, from Corn to Organic Spinach

This section presents a quick overview of crop species commonly grown in rural America, in part because so many new settlers in rural America have little farming or agricultural knowledge, and because decisions about rural areas are often made by people in urban areas with scant farming experience. I offer my apologies to readers already familiar with this basic information.

Corn, a crop first domesticated in Central America, flourishes on the rich tall-grass prairie soils of the Midwest. Corn has proved to be a major staple in the New Word and is a farm staple throughout the eastern United States. *Soybeans,* recently introduced from Asia, are grown in the core areas of corn production in the Midwest and down the Mississippi valley. *Barley* and *wheat* still come from the northern Great Plains, growing on the natural short-grass prairie soils in vast unfenced

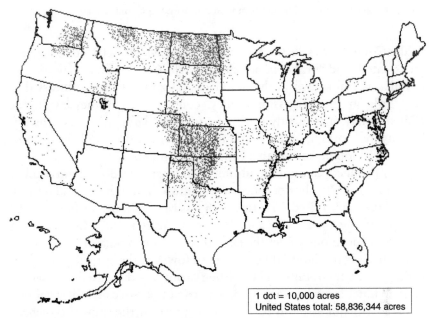

Figure 6.2. Wheat production, 1997.
(Source: www.nass.usda.gov/census/census97/atlas97/map234.htm)

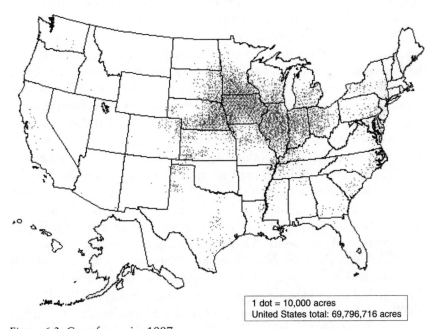

Figure 6.3. Corn for grain, 1997.
(Source: www.nass.usda.gov/census/census97/atlas97/map225.htm)

fields. Communities in the Great Plains are widely separated, farmers are isolated, and rural depopulation is high. *Cotton,* first domesticated in India, is still grown in the old Piedmont zone of the Southeast (but very little in the Mississippi valley, compared to its heyday in the 1950s); today, it is mostly grown on irrigated lands in the Southwest. For anyone working in the South, the story of cotton is still very important to developing sustainable rural development.

Beef production, after an all-time high of about 130 million head of cattle in the 1970s, has declined to about 34 million head, and 64 percent of these are raised on farms with less than 500 head of cattle. The number of *hog farms,* once a major part of farming in the Cornbelt, has decreased enormously over the last 20 years from a high of 700,000 pig farms in 1979 to about 100,000 today. However, the critical factor here is that, while the total number of hog farms has decreased, the size of an individual farm has increased. The rise of large-scale industrial hog farms is a major issue in rural areas because of the impact on small-scale hog farmers and because of the serious negative environmental impacts they cause. For example, USDA figures show that 54 percent of all pork slaughtered is now handled by only four large firms, and 42 percent of all hog production is from the 2,000 largest operations. The 62,000 smallest hog farms produce only 2 percent of the total.

Sheep production, primarily a western mountains and Plains product, has also declined from about 11 million on 120,000 farms in 1985 to 8 million sheep on 70,000 farms today. There is, however, a renaissance of sheep production on small farms in the East, with newer high-tensile electric fences and moveable polywire fences using New Zealand fence chargers making it easier to keep roving bands of domestic dogs and native coyotes away from the breeding ewes and lambs. Specialty Easter/Passover *lamb* and value-added commodities such as sheep and goat cheeses are popular in the Eastern urban markets and are increasingly popular elsewhere as well.

Animal fat intake, however, has decreased among many Americans as they become aware of the health impacts of excessive fat intake. Environmentally conscious Americans are also minimizing fat intake in response to studies that show bioaccumulation of toxics, such as PCBs, mercury, and dioxin, in animal fat. Research on "good" and "bad" fats has also led to an increase in use of vegetable oils, especially olive and the newer canola oils. The dioxin in oil added to chicken feed in Belgium in April 1999, which resulted in high levels of contamination of human food, has had serious repercussions throughout Europe. Consumers there are concerned not only about animal fat but also about the potential for bioaccumulation of toxics in animal fats that are subsequently consumed by humans. This trend of consumer demand for more information on food and beverages will undoubtedly continue.

Health warnings have led to a change in dietary preferences from marbled beefsteaks to low-fat meats and fish. In response, *chicken* and *turkey* production have increased phenomenally, as well as *fish* production in fish farms. *Turkey*, a native species, has made a major comeback in the wild as land reverts from farmlands to scrub or forest, but also commercial turkey production has increased from negligible production in 1950 to over 300 million head in 1998. Turkeys are produced in almost every state, but top producers are North Carolina, Minnesota, Arkansas, Virginia, Missouri, California, Pennsylvania, and Indiana. In the Northeast, as farmland is replaced by second-growth forests and scrubland, and with years of restricted hunting laws, wild turkey populations have increased phenomenally.

Eggs, produced throughout the nation, have also become a far more important part of our diet since World War II, despite scares over high cholesterol, with production going from about 40 billion in 1940 to almost 80 billion in 1998. Egg and chicken production techniques, however, have come under considerable criticism for the inhumane methods used in factory-scale production of both eggs and chicken for meat that carry a high potential for diseases such as salmonella. This industry will undoubtedly be one of those affected by changed regulations over the next decade. Human health will most assuredly be a critical component of agricultural production, marketing, and consumption in the next millennium, with growing interest in natural and organic foods by consumers.

Fruits and nuts are grown throughout the nation, although most commercial nut production is concentrated in the West. *Pecans,* probably the only domesticated agricultural crop native only to the United States, is harvested in its wild range in the Mississippi bottomlands, into Texas, and in the Southeast (where it is grown in orchards) and in its "seedling" range, where it has spread naturally. Pecans are a nice example of a native tree with many uses, from summer shade, to nuts, to wood for furniture (Richardson 1970). The history of pecans in the renaissance of nineteenth-century southern towns and villages will be important in sustainable rural development, built on an understanding of rural heritage, in those areas where it is both planted and native.

Most *apples,* an early colonial introduction from Europe, are still produced in Washington State, with Michigan, New York, and California each producing about 10 percent of the nation's supply. But international competition is presently having a negative impact on the apple industry, and apple orchards may well decrease over the next decade. *Oranges,* a Mediterranean native, have become, through brilliant marketing over the last 20 years, a staple breakfast drink for a vast number of Americans. Today the trend is toward orange juice with added calcium, "fresh squeezed" into cartons (even for rural supermarkets), and frozen or concentrates; it has become a high-priced commodity for the diet-conscious American. This trend in diet consciousness, coupled with medicinal herbs and other health "alternatives" for a more holistic approach to health, will undoubtedly continue. There is also a trend toward more home canning and gardening, with national sales of bedding plants on the rise in most regions. Such market gardening activity represents only a tiny percent of farming, but it is a fast-growing sector of mostly small farms, often run by women—a return to traditional roles of the past. Women still constitute the majority of farmers worldwide, although they are far from the majority in land ownership.

Farmers caught in the production modes and techniques of the 1950s and 1960s will find it hard to meet the increasingly sophisticated rural and urban consumer demands of the twenty-first century. There are many market opportunities here for the rural entrepreneur. What are now specialty crops, like *ginseng,* and varieties of herbs grown by innovators will, like *Echinacea,* become mainstream, while *tobacco,* once a major staple of the Southeast, has fallen farther into disrepute as an unhealthy product.

Other specialty crops such as *hops, peppermint, mushrooms,* and *sunflower seeds* are on the rise. The acreage devoted to hops, for example, has risen considerably over the past decade as more local breweries have been built in many parts of the nation. The "romance" of microbreweries is both an urban and a rural phenomenon and is likely to increase. Washington and Oregon presently account for majority of the nation's hop production, and also, together with Wisconsin, produce most of the peppermint. Mushrooms have also become part of our diet in recent years, from negligible production in 1960 to almost 700 million pounds in 1998. Increased crop diversity in high-value specialty crops will likely increase in the twenty-first century.

Sustainable rural development requires that we understand the natural and agricultural ecosystems, changes that have taken place, and trends. The ecosystems that underlie and support these land uses have always been in a state of change, responding to climate shifts from the retreating ice of the last ice age (which, for example, left Wisconsin as recently as about 10,000 years ago) to the present climatic instability all over the country. But the rate of change to which ecosystems have had to adapt have not only increased in the last 150 years, but also have involved far more complex effects, reaching into many of the interconnected biological cycles in ways hitherto unsuspected. Since 1950, ecosystems have had to deal with far more toxic pollutants than at any time in the past. Indeed, some of the worst air and water pollutants were knowingly discharged into the environment in the 1970s, after the passage of the National Environmental Policy Act (NEPA) in 1969, and hundreds of toxic pollutants remain unregulated. Lakes, watersheds, and croplands all face this pollutant mix in water and air.

Human Resources

Given the urban nature of the U.S. population, and the fact that it has been many generations since most Americans grew food crops, there is an enormous gap in understanding between those people who are in daily contact with food and fiber production and the average city dweller who isn't. The intent here is not to romanticize the lives of our farming ancestors, bemoan the loss of the family farm, worry about environmental damage, and the like. But, rather, it is to gain perspective on the changing face of farming and forestry communities, present some selected innovations as examples, and discuss some stumbling blocks, with a mind to determining what role society could or should play in ensuring sustainable agriculture and forestry (Figure 6.4).

Who are the people living in agricultural communities today? To repeat some of the data presented in Chapter One: On January 1, 1999, only about 2 percent of the employed population in the United States was engaged in agricultural production, with an additional 0.3 percent engaged in forestry and mining (these numbers do not include workers employed by state or federal governments). As pointed out earlier, the total number of farms of all types decreased rapidly following World War II, from about 5 million farms in 1950 to about 2.5 million today, about half of which would be considered commercial farms. However, at least 21 percent (about 51 million) of the U.S. population lives in rural areas. Four decades ago, 15 percent of all Americans lived in rural areas, and of that population, almost one-third worked directly in agriculture. The gap between hourly wages of farm and nonfarm workers

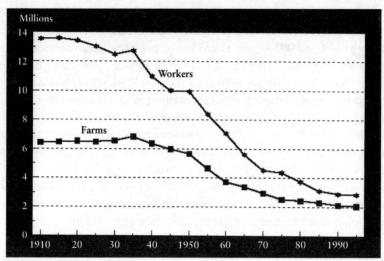

Figure 6.4. Number of farms and all farm workers, 1910–1995, in the United States. Source: USDA National Agricultural Statistics (www.usda.gov/nass/aggraphs/fl_frmwk.htm).

has increased over the last few decades to the point where the farm worker wage is typically half that of the nonfarm worker. This means that there are distinct socioeconomic classes in rural areas. There is a major social and economic gap between those who work the land for their primary income—farmers—and the vast majority of rural dwellers who derive their income from nonfarm sources.

Several additional factors should also be noted: most farm families do not place themselves on a payroll; hence husbands, wives, and children do not show up on employment rolls, nor do they qualify for unemployment benefits. Modern farm families do not often join groups, and the older organizations such as the Farm Bureau and the Grange are no longer as relevant in most areas. And farmers often have (or choose to have) a limited voice in major land-use decisions until there is a crisis to be averted. Many nonfarm rural dwellers must subsist outside the system for one reason or another, and in the declining farm, mining, and mountain communities, there is a great deal of hidden poverty: in this land of plenty, many children in rural communities go hungry, despite their proximity to agricultural production. There are also many disenfranchised rural dwellers. African-American farmers have endured generations of discrimination, such as well-documented evidence of the USDA refusing farm loans to African Americans, thereby creating an underclass. The many diverse tribal groups that compose the loosely designated Native American population are also largely disenfranchised, especially because of their systematic removal from tribal lands in the not-so-distant past.

These historical problems are exacerbated by newly arrived urban immigrants and by the seasonal visitors who prefer the romantic vision of rural landscapes with farmers and choose to ignore the harsher realities these communities must themselves face. Many immigrants, however, bring innovative ideas into rural communities and are major role players in the sustainable changes that eventually take place.

All of these populations exist side by side in rural communities, their children typically attending the same schools. Rural land-use decisions do not rest solely in the hands of the rural residents, who are subject to the political dictates of the state capitals and Washington, D.C., to the impacts of the national and international marketplaces, and to the whims of absentee owners of large tracts of land with valuable natural resources to be extracted and sold. Rural residents have remarkably little say in rural development over the long term, a trend that could significantly limit options for community-based rural development.

Life Support Systems

As humans, we have many needs that must be satisfied in order to survive in our preferred habitats. The list can be long, but the basics generally entail water, food, air, fiber, housing, waste management, clothing, energy, transportation, communication, and materials. Rural areas provide us with many of these items, which means that care of rural areas is the responsibility of all Americans, urban and rural.

Past generations supplied these life support items for themselves, but with increased technology that has changed; unfortunately, it has also meant that very few know any longer how items such as food are produced, where they are produced, and how they reach market. The closeness to the land felt by those in centuries past has continually dwindled as we have become more specialized in our career pathways and not so dependent on small geographical areas.

Tom Jorling (1982) evaluated the geographical distances required to meet basic living requirements in Albany, New York, for the years 1850 and 1975. For example, to derive the geographic distance required for meeting housing needs he calculated the distance between place of origin and place of use for each of the basic materials used in housing

Table 6.1. Geographic Distance and
Community Needs

	1850 (miles)	1975 (miles)
Food	0–5	1,300
Water	0–5	50
Housing	20	750
Clothing	20	1,000
Sewer/Waste	0	200
Materials	30	1,000
Transport	10	500
Energy	30	500

(concrete, lumber, wallboard, pipe, wiring, roofing, and the like) and averaged their sum. The comparison, shown in Table 6.1, is striking.

Technological distance, perhaps of greater significance today, is more difficult to measure than the geographical distance of commodity production. For example, the automobile we drive may be Japanese, and the computer software used to feed cows on a dairy farm in Wisconsin may be designed in California, manufactured in China, but distributed through farming organizations and serviced and technically supported by someone in Boston who is twenty years old and knows nothing about daily life in a milking parlor. There is a complicated, risky dependency in this chain of custody and care, where the user of the product likely knows little about the manufacturing process or the products needed to make the software in the first place. And the designer of the software may know little of the ecology of agriculture. Our systems function because cheap energy sources facilitate the movement of goods great distances at minimal cost.

These two aspects of geography and technology greatly affect the sense of security that people have in the support they need to function. Such a dependent relationship leaves the rural consumer vulnerable, because the rural community today is tied to a megasystem over which the consumer has little control.

Concern over the Trend toward "Big Business"

During the opening legislative session in January 1999 in Vermont, a rural politician expressed concern that residents of rural areas are divided between those who are doing extremely well, often with jobs tied to urban America, and those who are being left behind. If that trend continues, rural America as we now know it will be lost forever. He described the gathering of his family around the Thanksgiving table. It included the cousin with a successful business and no money worries (at present); the single-mom sister wondering if she will be pushed into "early retirement" at her high-tech place of employment before she qualifies for a pension; two relatives fearful of being laid off (one because of a local bank merger and the other—a nurse—because of a hospital merger); a mother-in-law who lost her sales clerk job because a Wal-Mart store displaced several smaller businesses in the community; and an older cousin who wanted to retire from running an "inefficient" 150-cow dairy farm—he was being forced to sell his farm to urban speculative developers to cover necessary health-care and retirement costs for his ailing wife and himself. He would have preferred to pass the farm to his daughter or son, but they could not afford to pay him enough money to support him and pay his medical costs.

Many rural residents are overwhelmed by the ever-increasing trend toward "big-box" development, big-box banks, big-box stockholders, big-box ski mountains and hotels, big-box hospitals, and big-box managed health care. In conversations around the country I find that while some will feel these changes work to their benefit, many will not. We know that most of the wealth in the United States lies in the hands of a tiny percentage of people. For the rest of rural Americans—the loyal rural residents—there is fear that these changes will mean lower wages, lost job security, and evaporating pension plans and health-care benefits.

Sustainability cannot exist under such conditions. As long as we accept our dependency on these systems, there will be increasing centralization and increased vulnerability. Low-input systems such as intensive pasture management (discussed later) are part of the trend toward greater sustainability, but they are not readily accepted by a society trained to conform to bigger and more "efficient" systems and resistant to learning about the alternatives.

Life support systems, however, need to be reviewed at the community level and new plans devised that address the consumption of goods, life-cycle costs, and replacement-and-maintenance costs in ways that demonstrate greater understanding of linked cycles and systems. No society, anywhere, has ever deliberately set out to understand these connections. Earlier societies may have temporarily had "stable" life support systems, but this was by chance and not by choice.

The United States is still the world's major consumer of natural resources and producer of the most waste per capita. As more information becomes available concerning the toxic effects of our waste on human health, and as more communities attempt to address waste issues in rural communities, it will become more apparent that we are at a serious transition point in the history of the United States. Changes are needed at all levels, and actions taken in rural communities—the most local level—can highlight the larger picture. In many ways, life in rural communities is a microcosm of the urban and national picture. Rural communities have the opportunity to become national models of sustainable human-ecosystem systems, and its citizens, national leaders.

Using the Rural Heritage

How people acquired their land and resources, what the chain of ownership has been over the decades or centuries, how long they have owned it, how the land has been used, and who was disinherited all affect local and national land policies. In an agricultural society, access to the land conveyed security, an identity, and a territory to be managed and defended from neighbors. Settlers from Great Britain in particular were drawn to the New World, where the opportunities for landless urban and rural people to own land in fee simple was a fabulous dream for those brave enough to leave one home to start another. Not everyone owns land in the United States today; however, good management of the resources handed down to us or development issues to be voted on at the zoning board or development meeting require a sensitive understanding of the history of the land and its inhabitants.

Each settled region developed its own character that was influenced in part by the underlying soils, rocks, forests, grasslands, and the dominant cultural imprint. The "sense of place" that Rene Dubos (1972) and others have talked about is a very real thing. We have a concept of territoriality that, according to historians like Ben Labaree (1982), derives from the "castle and border" behavior observed among most creatures. Border areas are rarely well defined, yet are often in dispute. The Not-in-My-Back-Yard (NIMBY) syndrome is also well rooted in our collective psyche. If children in schools are taught to observe and to understand the history of the community, then their ability to make the right decisions in the decades ahead will be greater. Their education must include learning what we have kept hidden about the settlers in the New World, and about the Native American peoples, with their own diverse cultures.

Nineteenth-century settlement began in the East with mixed farming, but the farming methods used were never as sustainable as those used at the time in Britain and Western Europe. To begin with, forests were seen as a nuisance, a hindrance to crop production, to be cleared as fast as possible. Europe had been deforested for hundreds of years because of the same way of thinking, and likewise in the New World these "bad habits" became ingrained as commodity production became the norm and there seemed no end to land's abundance.

Land ownership, from its Anglo-Saxon origins, has always played a significant role in land policy. Land provides a home location, a means of life support close to home, security, and the ability to feel close to land and community. But of even greater significance is the role of taxation, which requires in many areas that landowners pay taxes on property for maintaining the schools and the rural infrastructure. Land owners—private, state, and federal—fight over who can develop what, bring nuisance suits for air and water pollution, and lobby heavily over natural resource use.

But the disenfranchised, including rural poor, Native Americans, and African Americans, were effectively segregated from mainstream decision making about natural resources. Others have immigrated more recently, and while many have settled in urban centers, others have moved to rural areas, such as the Hispanic populations in the Southwest and Chinese from Hong Kong in the Northwest. Immigrants have always played an important role in rural life, bringing innovative ideas that are adapted and assimilated locally.

Children have the important role of asking the naive and pointed questions, such as, "If the waste is hazardous, why do you allow it to leak into the water at all?" In all cases, it is necessary to somehow reconnect people with their rural heritage and bring back a sense of belonging to the whole.

A sustainable rural land-use plan, for example, must be built on the local history and the planning document used as policy to inform decisions on zoning issues. Another project that can help in rural areas is called Barn Again! It originated in Colorado but is now used all over the nation, typically as a part of state and regional historic preservation programs. In Barn Again! farmers are awarded for having conserved a barn rather than let it fall down. Rural heritage has also been used to build new markets and strengthen old ones as tourists interested in rural areas and American history are increasingly attracted to parts of the nation heretofore bypassed.

Moving to an Ecosystem Approach from Commodity-Based Thinking

If we can accept that there is a need for a more comprehensive and integrated approach to agriculture, then we need to identify successful examples where divergent perspectives on natural resources have been reassessed by communities in a more positive light. It is especially important to identify projects that result in "win-win" solutions that improve our understanding of the biological, agricultural, and (changing) cultural contexts.

Farmers and Environmentalists Cooperating

It is not easy to find common ground between farmers and environmentalists, but it can be done. One such example is in Ohio and involves a river watershed. Farmers in the Darby Creek Watershed were alarmed when environmentalists looking at the river sought to have an 88-mile stretch classified as a Scenic River. Farmers relied on the river for watering cattle and for discharging farm wastes. Environmentalists saw that agricultural runoff is typically the major source of water pollution in rural areas. Farmers observed that a lead environmental group invited twenty-five different organizations to meet to discuss what should be done, but neglected to include the farmers, even though they owned most of the land. Farmers fought to stop the scenic designation on the grounds that it would have a negative impact on their ability to make a living. Farming practices included direct and indirect discharge of agricultural effluent into the river. Initially, they won. Then The Nature Conservancy named the Darby as one of six "Last Great Places in the Western Hemisphere," and farmers and extension agents gathered to determine what to do. They formed Operation Future Association composed of 140 of the 1,100 farmers in the watershed. This new nonprofit organization was funded by the W.K. Kellogg Foundation as part of a cluster of grants under the Integrated Farming Systems (IFS) program. The farmers reported that they did more listening than talking and in the process learned that The Nature Conservancy was not so threatening to farmers after all. It paid landowners for development rights and for outright ownership of land—an approach farmers preferred over zoning and other regulatory approaches.

The Nature Conservancy saw farming as the best use of the land, but it wanted farmers to use conservation approaches to farming. It was difficult to reach the farmers as a community because there was no single organization. Operation Future Association, a local organization, provided a way to work with the farmers. The farmer who took the leadership role agreed that until then no one had really looked at the history of settlement of the area, or even identified humans as part of a watershed. Ecology had not been part of their training; farmers identified with county-level government, not with river basins. And few farmers realized that farming at the top of a watershed could be different from farming at the bottom.

Canoe trips, organized by Operation Future, became an important educational tool; the trips often included local environmentalists, farmers, and biologists from the Ohio State University and the state Department of Natural Resources. They would move in a flotilla of several canoes, with periodic stops to look at fish, snails, and midges and to interact with the aquatic ecosystem. This inventive solution allowed the farmers to learn firsthand the impact of agricultural runoff. "In the process, our fear turned into pride," said one farmer—pride that they still had a pretty good river, and pride in their history. It also introduced the farmers to a new network of advisors, whom they began to call on a regular basis. The growth of "no-till" farming rose dramatically; some farmers fenced off the river from grazing, and others planted buffer strips. Farmers from this group are now available to help other farmers in other watersheds.

Thus the farmers moved from working as individuals to working as a group, and the results were synergistic, building confidence and leadership skills. The Nature Conservancy considers this a model for other projects. There is now a relatively united group of farmers and environmentalists who regularly work together. As a group, they see urban encroachment as the next big threat, but instead of viewing this as a confrontation, they hope to work out a collaborative approach with developers.

The words of Justice Douglas in *Sierra v. Morton* (1972) are particularly relevant here: "The river . . . speaks for the ecological unit that is part of it. Those people who have a meaningful relation to the body of water— whether it is as fishermen, a canoeist, a zoologist, or logger—must be able to speak for the values which the river represents and which are threatened by destruction."

Small-Scale Farming, Local Produce, and New Markets

Although there is still a perception that large farms are the most efficient, a great deal of data collected over many decades suggest that in fact smaller farms can be more sustainable and that yields on carefully farmed units can be higher by several measurements, including that of economic efficiency. At present in the United States, there are 60 million acres in wheat and soybeans, 80 million acres in corn, and millions more in large-scale meat production. A group in Wisconsin, the Wisconsin Integrated Cropping System Trials (WICST), has been working to farm "for profit and a clean environment." The group, with leadership by both farmers and researchers at the University of Wisconsin, wanted to see if more complex systems with fewer purchased inputs could be productive and profitable while at the same time reduce negative environmental effects. A collaborative team was built that included conventional and organic farmers as well as extension agents and environmental activists. The goal was to change farm practices. Usually, university research takes place under scientifically controlled laboratory settings and does not involve applied research on farms with farmers as active partners. But in this venture, farmers work collaboratively with the researchers, and discussion groups are important in sharing lessons learned. This work is a twelve-year trial, now about half completed. So far, profitability per acre has increased, while input of fertilizer, pesticides, and herbicides is down.

Purchase of Development Rights

One mechanism increasingly used in some parts of the country to conserve ecosystem integrity is the setting aside of development rights and the establishment of so-called conservation easements. Typically development rights are held by a local land trust, and carefully selected corridors of forests, open land, or watersheds, each with their native animal species, are bought, piece by piece, permitting long-term and large-area opportunities for sustainable ecosystem conservation. Here, forest and farmland conservation must come face to face with private property rights.

To understand land activities in the United States, one must also understand the importance of private property. Private property can only be regulated by government under very specific conditions, such as for public health and welfare. The parcel of land that a person owns in the United States is typically owned in "fee simple" on a warranty deed. This is a mechanism in property law that comes to us from English heritage and was adopted with the foundation of the United States. To the landowner, it means that he or she has ownership of a "bundle of rights," including air above rights, ground and below-ground rights, water rights (which are relatively straightforward in the East but can vary enormously in West), and so forth. Normally, when land is sold, all of these rights go in fee simple to the next owner who purchases the land. However, the bundle of rights can be broken up. Some parts (sticks in the bundle) can be sold or leased separately to someone other than the primary owner. Hence, in the West one may have land but no water rights or no mineral rights. By selling off certain rights to the land, the value of the overall property is typically diminished and certain kinds of development are prohibited. Property taxes may also be reduced. Consequently, if one sells or leases the development rights, depending on how the agreement is written, such an act can prevent building of any kind on a parcel of land. As a mechanism for conserving farmland, this is becoming a strong tool in sustainable rural development.

Zoning, regional plans, transfer of development rights, and a wide range of planning tools have been available for a long time to guide land-use development in an area. Urban sprawl has nonetheless covered many thousands of acres of fertile soils around cities, replacing farmland with urban and suburban settlements and associated shopping malls and industry. Meanwhile, inner-city residents may have limited access to economical, local fresh food. Most farmers have little invested in pension plans and few or no health benefits, yet their property taxes increase each year in the borders around growing towns and cities. As a result, the generous money offered by speculating developers is often felt by farm families to be the best solution for them. However, as more urban migrants develop greater sensitivity to the requirements for maintaining the rural areas that they love—the areas to which they migrated—there has been a marked shift toward purchase of development rights. This is a mechanism that keeps the farms in active farmland by removing the development rights: the farmer receives a large sum of money and the property taxes are greatly reduced.

Here again, as in the models above, new collaborative partnerships have to be forged to make this work. In Michigan, Pennsylvania, and Vermont, there are many examples of the successful purchase of development rights. In Michigan, the Potowatomi Land Trust began the process of seeking public and private funds to separate the development value of farmland from its agricultural value. The fund would be used to buy development rights from farmers, leaving them to farm the land. A coalition was formed with the county Farm Bureau, the Michigan chapter of The Nature Conservancy, the Huron River Watershed Council, the Michigan Environmental Council, the Ecology Center of Ann

Arbor, the local Sierra Club chapters, the League of Women Voters, three land conservancy groups, and others. The group became the Citizen Task Force for Farmland and Open Space Preservation. In Vermont, the governor has taken a major leadership role in the purchase of development rights. Working with a legislative fund, the Housing, Conservation Trust Fund, and the Vermont Land Trust, other land trusts in the state, and many major private donors, he has been able to broker major purchases of both farm and forest land over the last six years. The results of some of these will be discussed in Chapter Seven.

From Milk Production to Grass Production

The basic premise in this section is that agriculture that is conducted in harmony with ecological principles and more closely approximates the original "natural" ecology is more likely to be sustainable. Agriculture that "mimics" the natural ecosystem has the potential to produce more food and fiber than agriculture that is less ecologically based. Sustainable agriculture leads to sustainable communities through improved daily life for farm families, increased time for community interaction, and increased profit margins. All parts of the system must be seen as living and connected.

For those familiar with intensive pasture management, this section may seem overly detailed. However, for the recent rural resident, urban person or rural planner, and those less familiar with hands-on agriculture, the details provide contextual insight into the daily life of farm families. Milk has become a staple of American society, consumed in many forms throughout the lives of most Americans. The technology of milk production over the last fifty years provides us with a story that reflects the decline in rural communities, while recent trends in grass management give hope for a future rural community renaissance. In the past, milk was produced at home, or a few neighbors would share a milk cow. With the growth of rural communities, specialization and mutual support meant that only some would produce milk. Liquid milk production typically meant that around all growing urban communities there would be farms producing milk. With industrial expansion came the production of cheeses and butter, which could stand longer storage and greater transportation distances to market.

Milk Production

Milk cow operations nationwide have decreased 46 percent over the last ten years. There are now only about 120,000 dairy farms in the

United States, with major producing areas located in California (where dairying is supported through redistributed water in a nonsustainable manner) and in Wisconsin and Florida (where climate extremes are compensated for by proximity to major areas of feed-crop production). Dairying in the Northeast, where traditional production close to the market continues despite extremes of climate, is protected by regional pricing compacts such as the New England Dairy Compact, which was approved by Congress in the mid-1990s and hard fought for in periodic political battles in Washington.

What is interesting about the dairy industry, however, is that while the number of dairy farms has declined by 46 percent over the last ten years, milk production overall has increased by almost 20 percent, with much of that increase attributable to an increase in milk production per cow.

Management-Intensive Grazing as an Alternative to High-Input Milk Production

Smaller farms with less than 200 cows per farm still account for 60 percent of dairy farms, but there is a trend toward larger farms, with ever-increasing amounts of milk produced per cow. Milk production is affected by many factors, but careful genetic breeding, feed rations with high concentrates, and in some cases the injection of bovine growth hormones have all contributed to the incredibly high milk production per cow that we see today.

Dairy farmers by tradition and training see themselves as producers of milk. Researchers have worked hard to develop genetic breeds that produce large amounts of milk, with a complex of feeds from a combination of forages, hay, haylage, silage, corn, feed concentrates, barley, cottonseed, fat, soybean meal, canola oil, and so forth. Confinement of cows in barns over most of the United States has been the norm for several decades now. Most cows are thus milked and fed in a barn and rarely spend time grazing, although they may go outside for a short walk in a paddock near the barn once or twice a day. This form of dairy farming means that the animals are essentially held in place, and all the feed is brought to them. All the manure, of course, then has to be hauled away and during the winter stored or spread on the lands where crops are being raised to feed the cows. Storage and handling of manure is expensive, and pollution runoff into streams negatively impacts aquatic ecosystems.

However, the system can be highly mechanized and carefully controlled for feed input and high milk output. Milk cows thus have a very short productive life—perhaps five years of milking—before slaughter. Land on the dairy farm can be minimal in size, with most of the feed purchased elsewhere, or produced on the farm, and farmed with heavy equipment and a limited diversity of crops. These farmers often have high capital investment in equipment, and the work is enormously time consuming and hard on families who never seem to get out from under long-term debt.

Many dairy and other farms using innovative grazing methods are now radically changing their animal feed management. A new concept emerged about two decades ago known by several names: intensive pasture management, rotational grazing, or rational grazing. Under this method, farmers are asked to view themselves more as producers of grass, with milk a secondary product. In an ecological sense, these farmers are capturing solar energy in the grass produced. This modern intensive grazing system is not the standardized pasture rotations of forty years ago. Then, the cows were turned out of the barn after milking, grazed selectively on the pastures, eating only what they liked. The result was high growth of thistles and weeds, low quality of feed, and low milk production. Hence, this method was abandoned in favor of crop and high-quality hay forage production and feed concentrates.

Intensive grazing today is quite different in concept and practice, but it is more complicated and is an art as well as a science. It was introduced into several locations in the United States in the mid- to late 1970s and met with a great deal of resistance from traditional farmers and extension agents alike; it was seen as an example of an idea by environmentally and ecologically minded people who understood neither agriculture nor business economics. In line with the innovation theories discussed earlier in the book, these ideas had to first be tried by the pioneering innovative leaders and before slowly spreading to others in the community. In some states, such as Vermont, where the idea arrived about 1977, there is now a 12- to 15-percent dairy farm usage, so the practice has become mainstream. Grazing work in Vermont was tried first on sheep farms, such as our small farm in northern Vermont, and in the Tunbridge area in southern Vermont. In both locations, we used sheep to clear out scrubland and rebuild new pastures on old dairy farm lands that were reverting to forest and scrubland. The work on these pioneer farms led them to share their ideas, discussing and modifying the new system of intensive grazing methods with each other. Their work would not have been possible without modern New Zealand and the English electric fence systems that kept out stray domestic dogs and the ever-present coyotes and permitted easy-to-build permanent and temporary pasture areas. Hitherto barbed wire fences and crumbling stone walls had been the norm. The barbed wire fences were typically rusty and difficult to work with effectively, especially in combination with electric fencing, because the old barbed wire fences cause electrical shorts that can take days to locate.

It took about fifteen years before dairy farmers, seeing the beautiful new sheep pastures, could be persuaded that it would work for cows. Many cow farmers told us that cows really could not eat much fresh grass, because these farmers had become so accustomed to feeding the cows grains and other supplements with dried hay and silage in the barns.

About twenty years after the first intensive pasturing in Vermont, the concepts are now widely applied by people keeping horses, goats, other ruminants, and even chickens. Meanwhile, other innovators in other states had been experimenting over the same period in Wisconsin, Pennsylvania, Virginia, and some areas out West. Intensive grazing concepts are moving more into the mainstream.

Stimulus for the grazing efforts in recent years has come from supportive grants for the necessary research and collaboration from private foundations, such as W.K. Kellogg, more than from universities or the government. This support has been essential to the successes now seen. Once there was a database of field research (which is far more difficult to do than in laboratories), government funding has been forthcoming to support ongoing research, such as federal SARE (Sustainable Agriculture and Rural Education) grants for raising sheep on grass. It is still difficult to find funding to undertake extensive research on low-input systems such as grazing. These do not seem as "high tech" as other farming systems, especially given the parallel trend toward enormous factory farms. Low-input farming research must use traditional scientific approaches to demonstrate scientific results. At the same time, intuition is needed because each farm has a slightly different ecology, and each flock or herd of animals has a different behavioral makeup.

Management-intensive grazing might sound simple at first glance, but it is actually quite a complex ecosystem approach to farming that requires discussion with other farmers. The farmer and family are asked to look with new eyes at the entire farm and its natural resources. This may or may not involve the kind of holistic resource management (HRM) approach advocated by New Mexico rancher Allan Savory

(1998), but it should involve a careful look at the soils, hills, slopes, forests, available water on the farm, farm layout, and, last but not least, farm family economic and social goals (Murphy et al. 1994, 1997, 1998). The goals are that the cows should go out to the pastures to eat their feed and come into the barn or milking parlor for milking only. Manure thus does not accumulate in the barn or barnyard to anywhere near the same level as in confinement farming but instead is spread by the animals as they move across the pastures. Far less supplemental feeds are provided to the cows in the barn. Some farms use no added feeds, with the exception of winter forage during the season when the grass is dormant. It is important to note that good pasturing will lead to better pastures and can extend the outdoor grazing season by another month, even in northern climates such as Vermont where cows can still be grazing in December.

The management-intensive grazing farm is divided into managed grazing fields, or paddocks. There may be twenty-five or more such paddocks on the farm. The subdivisions do not need to be permanent but can be single- or double-strand electric wires for cows and polywire mesh fencing or seven-strand for sheep. Fences are often most easily operated by the use of low-impedance energizers (the New Zealand Gallagher fence chargers, for example). Milk cows are turned into a new paddock after each milking, which is typically twice a day. The size and location of the paddock will depend on many factors, such as underlying ecological history, soils, quality of forage, time of year, number of cows, stage of lactation, and so forth. Cows are forced to eat pretty much everything in the paddock, not to bare earth but enough that the species diversity of the pasture becomes high in biomass, with changed species composition that includes an increase in white clover (Flack 1995). The pasture will thus be grazed down from about four or five inches in average height to about two inches. After the twelve-hour period of grazing, the cow is milked again and moved to a new pasture, and the grazed pasture is rested for about twenty-one days. The timing depends on many ecological and climatic factors at the specific farm, how long intensive grazing has been practiced, what the previous species diversity was, what breeds of animals are being used—here is where shared experience in the community is so helpful. There is not a "one size fits all" approach. Pastures are typically four or five inches deep in new grass when the cows are moved into a new pasture, and the cows soon get the idea and can be seen hanging about near the electric fence waiting for the greener grass (Photo 6.2).

Photo 6.2. Management-intensive grazing in Vermont, on the Canadian border. Here cows wait by the single-strand, moveable electric fence. Cows soon learn that a new pasture becomes available every day. The pasture on the right is eaten down to about two to three inches, indicating time to move to the next pasture.

Grazing farmers must learn many new things to change to this system, such as animal behavior, the vegetative and reproductive cycles of pasture species, and how to counter the variable effects of wet seasons and droughts. The farmer must reassess the kinds of crops grown on the farm, how to manage crop fertility, how to manage the distribution of drinking water, and how to manage the alleyways for cow paths across the farm. In some cases, the breed of cattle will be changed because some breeds may adapt to grazing better than others. (There is no clear proof of this at this time.) Holsteins, the black-and-white breed now common on farms, are able to produce vast amounts of milk on high-feed concentrates in TMR (total mixed rations) and may not do as well on the pasture-only diet. Some farmers believe that a smaller breed such as a Jersey cross-breed will produce more milk on less feed than a Holstein will. Also, cows are social animals, and the herd has a complex set of behaviors. The dominant cow is actually in the middle of the herd, but a grazing herd needs to have a leader out front who leads the cows to feed in the pasture and knows the way to good feed. Thus, identifying the kind of lead cow you want for your herd is important.

So why do farmers take on such a complex system? It greatly decreases the labor they spend on gathering feed, serving it to the cows, and hauling away the waste; it increases profitability per cow and per acre of land (Dick Lehnert 1996); it reduces cash expenses and investment in feed storage, forage harvesting, and manure-handling equipment, fuel, and electricity; it reduces costs to veterinarians for care of animals, because the animals are more healthy (the result of being outdoors, moving around, producing less milk, and perhaps even because the cows are happier). With improved animal health, longevity increases, which in turn extends an animal's economically productive life; the environment also benefits considerably, because the cows become the feed harvesters and manure spreaders, reducing the need for tractors. Agricultural runoff decreases and stream quality improves.

For the farm family there are even more benefits because the daily chores are reduced, allowing more time for family affairs, social life, and activity in the community. This is the most profound aspect of these changing farming practices.

> I soon found myself with time on my hands when I was usually spreading manure, so now I could go fishing with my kids, and go on farm pasture walks, and not feel so isolated. Of course, I had to start paying taxes with the increased profits, but I could at last fix up the house a bit.
>
> —Farmer Mike Hanson

Although cows produce less milk on pasture, the inputs are lower and thus profits can be higher. It can therefore become possible to move toward seasonal dairying, the system in which all cows calve in the same month or two each year, so that all cows can be in their dry period simultaneously, also saving labor and seasonal feed costs. Again, some breeds may be moved to such a lactation cycle more successfully than others. This style of dairy farming is common in New Zealand, and since the EPIC pasture management program was started, considerable exchange of expertise has taken place between New Zealand and the eastern United States.

Seasonal milking means that in regions where purchased feed costs are high, such as New England, this is an attractive proposition that may lead to a considerable improvement in lifestyles for farmers and their families. In other states where feed is cheaper, such as Pennsylvania, seasonal dairy farming may prove attractive for a range of other reasons, including seasonal shifts in milk prices and feed costs (Ford 1994).

The Importance of Farm Walks

Such changes do not come about by individual farmers just reading books, however. Farmers, like most of us, learn best through experience, by doing and seeing things. In all cases where farmers have entered into grazing farm walks, grazing clubs, sustainable farming organizations, and the like, their joining in has permitted participatory research, reduced the isolation that sustainable farming pioneers feel, and stimulated information exchange and mutual encouragement. One of the primary mechanisms used—brought to us from northern England and New Zealand—are farm walks. These are regularly scheduled gatherings of farmers and their families on one farm one week, another on another week. During these sessions, they share lessons learned about grazing but also about total farm management, home veterinarian care, farm economic systems, water management, conservation mechanisms, grants, and available funding help. Just as important is the fact that the whole family is encouraged to be involved, so that school issues, family needs, and other social interaction can take place in the pasture, in the farm kitchen, or in the barn. The experience of hosting a farm walk helps farmers to become more active and effective as innovators of this and other ideas and more confident as leaders. Younger farmers are more likely to be drawn into farming when it looks more attractive rather than just more of the same.

In the state of Vermont, where the EPIC model was used, dairying is the dominant agriculture by economic worth and by landscape impact. This is dairy farming where the price of cheese in Wisconsin (a national policy mechanism used to set dairy prices), the weather in California, and grain purchases in Asia determine the price of milk in Vermont. Dairying needs to be conducted within that global construct. The pasture management outreach program was central to EPIC's goal to be a catalyst for more sustainable rural development, with sustainable agriculture central to that framework. The Pasture Management Outreach Program (PMOP) involved the training of four field technicians at the graduate level. This took place under the leadership of Professor Bill Murphy, in the Plant and Soil Science Department at the University of Vermont. Murphy is an expert accustomed to working in the expert-driven style of land grant outreach. But he had also been an "early adopter" of the pasture idea and was able to work as an EPIC core team leader, taking an active part in pasture walks. The technicians, pasture team leader, and EPIC director, working with farmers and extension staff, identified 100 demonstration farms in a set of geographical clusters in the primary agricultural counties. Some farmers were new to the idea and willing to try; other farmers were the "early pioneers" and could bring some expertise to the learning.

The pasture technicians were each assigned about twenty-five farms, and it was their job over the next three to four years to work collaboratively with the farmers to establish a core of farms using intensive pasture management. Farm visits included pasture testing, economic analysis, holistic resource management, layout of farm for water and cow lanes, herd care, ration balancing, and other related activities.

Unexpected requests included how to manage winter depression and other issues related to isolation, and we found that women pasture technical staff were more effective in making the farmers feel at ease in a shared conversation. The women were perceived as less threatening when introducing new ideas and more willing to listen, share, and be flexible in their approaches to agriculture. The women technicians also demonstrated an ability to see family and community issues as an integral part of the roles as "farm" technicians (Photo 6.3).

Photo 6.3. Women play a significant role in changing the nature of farming in America. In New England, we found that technical advice was more likely to be received positively by farmers if provided by a knowledgeable *female* technician than if by the same aged equivalent *male* technician. Similarly, if the support provided was shared with the farm *wife*, then it was more likely that those new ideas would be adopted early and farm life would improve overall. Farm pasture technician Sarah Flack and a woman farmer in partnership with her husband check the fields.

Pasture Management in Vermont and Neighboring States

Guest essay by Sarah Flack, pasture management consultant

Before the EPIC project, there were only a handful of dedicated grazing farmers scattered across the northeastern United States—one or two in Vermont—and supportive individuals in only a few of the state agencies and universities. EPIC staff carefully worked to move the innovators into leadership positions, creating a more supportive community for a more ecologically sustainable form of agriculture.

The two most important things that the EPIC Pasture Management Outreach Program did for Vermont farmers were (1) to find and train a group of farmers, consultants, and agency personnel to have the technical knowledge of pasture management and of other types of management changes that occur on farms that make the transition from confinement to pasture and (2) to build a community of grazing farmers throughout the state, because the technical knowledge of grazing alone would not have been enough to maintain long-term support and success of Vermont grazing farmers. By contrast, grazing farmers in other states in the Northeast are still struggling to find technical (and social) support for themselves.

The EPIC pasture project provided frequent visits to new grazing farms by a trained pasture consultant. This technical and moral support allowed farmers to risk switching to a completely different farming system, because potential problems were discovered and fixed promptly before they could lead to serious problems. These frequent visits also helped these farmers become confident in their grazing skills and to develop confidence in the pasture system as a whole. In addition, there were the frequently held pasture walks. These were held during farm workshops attended by grazing farmers, pasture consultants, and agency personnel. Pasture workshops helped farmers learn from each other, but perhaps more importantly they helped to develop the strong sense of community. These pasture walks also helped researchers and outreach personnel in Vermont universities and state agencies to recognize pasture as a valuable part of Vermont agriculture. The new community was also strengthened and a knowledge base was built through monthly newsletters, annual grazing conferences, and research, all of which began with EPIC.

At the completion of the EPIC pasture project, there was considerable concern that support for grazing in Vermont would decline. However, this proved not to be the case. In the summer following the end of the EPIC project, a large group of grazing farmers (most of whom participated in the EPIC pasture project) met on a sheep farm in central Vermont and formed the Vermont Grass Farmers Association (VGFA). We wrote bylaws, elected a board of directors, and set priorities to help grazing farmers in Vermont continue to be successful. During the next few months, VGFA worked with the University Center for Sustainable Agriculture and the Natural Resources Conservation Service (NRCS) to

(continues)

Pasture Management in Vermont and Neighboring
States (continued)

develop a cooperative agreement, in the fall of 1996, to continue support
for grass farming with funding from the NRCS Grazing Lands Conservation Initiative and from annual member dues. This innovative agreement
between two agencies and a farmer association has allowed continued
support of grazing in Vermont on a relatively small budget. Building on
the strong grazing community in Vermont and on the priorities set by the
VGFA, this cooperative agreement has organized an annual grazing conference, continued pasture walks during summer months, distributed
quarterly newsletters to the 200 VGFA members, and developed farmer
discussion groups.

These farmer discussion groups are the most innovative and perhaps
most important continuation of the EPIC pasture projects, strengthening
the farmer family community. The type of farmer discussion groups developed in Vermont bears some similarity to the discussion groups that many
Australian farmers belong to. They are small groups (six to twelve farms)
that meet regularly (every two to four weeks) on each other's farms.
Because the same farmers attend each meeting, and there is a relatively
low turnover rate, the farmers and their families get to know each other
and each other's farms well. This, when combined with the high level of
trust that develops within these groups, allows the farmers to really be
helpful to each other in problem solving and in fine-tuning their grazing
operations to be more successful.

The Vermont model of how to support grazing farmers has given Vermont a distinct advantage over many other states. At meetings throughout the Northeast, farmers from other states talk about Vermont as the
"Mecca" of grazing. Not because our grass grows greener or our cows
graze better, but because of the grazing community and expertise that
EPIC helped to create. At a recent meeting of grazing farmers and
researchers from throughout the Northeast, a Vermont farmer commented, "After hearing farmers from other states describe the lack of support for grazing, I realize that we really have it pretty good in Vermont!"

Pasture walks have become common practice now; farmers are
moving away from their dependency on university/EPIC staff and are
setting up their own nonprofit organization and running their own pasture walks, year round, and are holding an annual meeting at which
many other innovative ideas including farm diversification and value-
added products are featured. There is also a Vermont Pasturelands
Network. These organizations have been able to find funding from

diverse sources to operate, including the National Resource Conservation Service.

The EPIC Pasture Management Outreach Project lasted four years, but in that time it built and strengthened a grazing community in Vermont in ways that will last long into the future. Having built a strong foundation in Vermont rural communities, it now allows grazers to thrive and multiply.

Measuring Success

Not everything is perfect, however; there is still continued resistance to grazing within the community of university researchers, extension service, the USDA, and state agencies. Obtaining funding for pasture research and education is not easy, since the main beneficiaries of this effort are farmers and not institutions or businesses. However, the EPIC pasture project helped recognize existing leaders in the field of grazing in all the agencies and universities and established grazing firmly enough in our community that it will continue to remain a significant aspect of agriculture and land use in our region.

Long-term success of the EPIC pasture project is measured in many ways:

- The environmental benefits of hundreds of acres of cornfields being planted to permanent pasture sod include less soil erosion, more wildlife habitat, improved water quality, more carbon dioxide removed from the atmosphere, and decreased fuel consumption.
- The animal health benefits include cows living longer and perhaps happier lives and decreased use of antibiotics and other drugs.
- The decreased fuel consumption on farms reduces overall energy needs and capital investment by farm families.

The human and community benefits are perhaps the most important measure of success. These are not easy to count in terms of dollars earned or pounds of soil saved, but they are easily counted in terms of the stories people tell of more time they can spend with their family instead of on their tractor; being able to take their children with them when they are moving the cows to a new pasture; and the son or daughter who decides to move back to the family farm because the profitability and quality of life has improved so much that it begins, for the first time, to look like something she or he might want to do for the rest of her or his life.

The Forgues family farm is in northwest Vermont, right on the border with Canada. This farm was once a 220-cow (where more often than not the cows were kept in the barn) confinement dairy farm that produced corn and alfalfa as cattle feed. After 17 years of operation, the enterprise fell into debt. The family joined the EPIC demonstration pasture group, stopped corn production, sold all of their farm equipment, and planted perennial grasses and legumes on the entire farm. In only one year they reported a dramatic improvement both financially and ecologically. Their son, who had left the farm to study psychology at university, regained his interest in farming and returned to run the farm as it became profitable enough to support not one but two families. The Forgues family then sold the development rights to the Vermont Land Trust. They then became a registered organic farm and have increased their margin of profitability. They are very active as a family in farmer-run pasture walks and meetings and always claim that it was the EPIC pasture technician who saved their lives.

Details of all aspects of the rural community are vital if the whole system is to be understood by all who dwell there. The urban newcomers and the present farmers need to more accurately assess the whole. What are the inputs that go into farming, and what are the outputs and impacts of the different ways to farm? The urban influence in rural areas needs to be more effectively assessed and harnessed.

Blending Urban with Rural

There are many other trends taking place on a small scale in rural areas, especially those close to urban markets or where urbanites have moved into the rural community; these include chicken tractors, where chickens are raised in moveable trailers, grazing old pastures and spreading a thin veneer of high-nitrate manure, organic vegetable farms, milk, cheese, eggs, and other products (Photos 6.4 and 6.5). These changes can be seen on a much larger scale in Western Europe, where regulations have changed radically over the last ten years to meet consumer demands for more "pure" products.

One of the demands made by the modern urban and suburban populations and also by many rural residents is the trend toward home gardening, both for food and for flowers (Photo 6.6). Many such gardeners like to use "natural" fertilizers, and one innovative dairy farmer in Vermont found a way to make money out of the cow manure produced on his dairy farm. The Foster brothers of Middlebury, Vermont, hit with increased energy costs, decided to take the piles of manure and biodigest them to produce methane. This in turn would run the gener-

Photo 6.4. The chicken tractor method of "grazing" chickens permits production of both meat and eggs in a manner attractive to the urban consumer and profitable for the farmer.

Photo 6.5. A nationwide increase in demand for "natural" or "organic" foods has resulted in farm stands and downtown farmers' markets for both rural and urban consumers.

Photo 6.6. Intensive greenhouse production of herbs and vegetables for the home garden, as shown here, has become increasingly popular in urban, suburban, and rural communities.

ator, supply power for the farm and reduce electricity costs for them. They have been "off the grid" ever since, saving over $30,000 per year. They soon discovered that there was an added use for the residual manure. The brothers formed a subsidiary called Vermont Natural Agricultural Products, made a substantial investment in composting technology, and began producing an all-organic fertilizer made totally from farm and forestry waste. This *Moo Doo* is sold to farms and retailed at many hardware stores.

Where farmers can sense the urban trends and work with them, they may be able to find new markets for their by-products as well as for their products. Such innovation and renovation on farms will increase in the future if children can be involved through such activities as 4-H Clubs, and where barriers between urban-oriented children and adults and the realities of farming are broken down through such activities as open days on farms, farm "museums," harvest festivals, farm and wilderness camps, and celebrations such as Hay Art, which can bring together such unlikely bedfellows as artists and farmers with tourism. In the 1950s, over 85 million people were expected to attend the state agricultural fairs—before television and the Internet lead to the increased isolation of individuals and families. Agricultural fairs are not as common today, but love of celebration, as discussed elsewhere in the book, is an important part of the human psyche. All these activities help to bridge the gaps that have opened as society became more industrialized and even more as we have moved into a postindustrial economy. Not only are we not an agricultural society anymore, but also we are no longer a nation of heavy industry. This postindustrial phase, already in place in Western Europe, is more of a service society, where reassessment of values is changing the structure and function of rural areas and the expectations of urban populations.

Lessons Learned from a Sampling of Forestry and Agricultural Issues and Projects

This chapter has addressed some aspects of rural land use, agriculture, and forestry, suggesting some mechanisms that can be used to move communities in the direction of sustainability. There are clear linkages with the community leadership programs in conservation and forestry, which were discussed in Chapter Four. Lessons learned in agriculture and forestry are more than techniques that can be used by those in agriculture and more than processes for community empowerment: they reflect the interconnections between the parts of a rural community. Working to build interconnections is critical, especially when they may also provide the leverage points that lead to positive changes in a community. The following list is somewhat repetitive but builds on lessons presented in other chapters. This list prioritizes important factors to consider if we are to ensure sustainable rural development:

- There needs to be adequate and affordable health care for everyone and an increase in rural investment to raise rural standards of living. If family farms are to remain viable, the serious problem of health-care cost and availability in rural communities, and the serious lack of investment in business in rural regions, must be addressed. Rural communities are not as wealthy as urban communities, and if we Americans are to be able to continue to purchase whatever we want to eat, grow all the forests that we want for fiber, and have clean surface and ground water and scenic recreation areas, we will have to develop policies that provide for sustainable rural communities with a higher standard of living, and this will take ongoing financial investment in rural environments in all aspects of infrastructure and support systems.

- We need to increase knowledge about the "natural" ecology and linkages with production of food and forest products. This is of critical importance. One needs to understand the local and regional ecology to be able to make ecological decisions. Agriculture that is ecologically based will be sustainable. We must change education from kindergarten through the university level and change our thinking from commodity production orientation to one of care for ecosystems and their by-products sold as commodities on the market.
- There needs to be less farm family isolation and more support of local "family" farms. A changed local agriculture with a high percentage of farms in sustainable production practices will involve greater community interaction and reduce some aspects of isolation. However, rural public transportation will always be a problem. Local farm support can take place directly through state-based marketing incentives and support, through assistance in opening up more global markets, and through fostering an atmosphere in the state and region that encourages purchase and consumption of locally produced food and fiber, even if higher prices are required to do this. This will also involve building trust and collaboration locally between diverse stakeholders. Such activities need to take place within rural communities, between communities, and between rural areas and urban fringes. Buying locally will mean that there will be increased prices for foods seasonally in many parts of the nation. This requires changing attitudes about food purchases.
- There is a need to strengthen rural leadership capacity to foster a strong voice for rural communities, locally, regionally, and nationally. Rural residents cannot wait until the urban majority is better informed. Rural leadership training, as described in Chapter Four, is needed for farmers and for those involved in forestry, with an emphasis on empowering women key to rural leadership.
- We need to pay close attention to trends in rural and urban Europe, identify new markets in the changing nature and demands of consumers, and be prepared to pay more for food and fiber products. Animal rights, "natural" and organic foods, ecolabeling, and related issues have made a major difference in the lives and landscapes of everyone in Western Europe over the last ten years. This has taken place despite the fact that Europeans are limited in their access to data on human health impacts of various chemical inputs into agri-

culture. Factory farming and excessive use of pesticides and herbicides and related activities will soon be under the same scrutiny as the level of sophistication of the average American increases in the global marketplace. Anyone listening to the story of how cheaply Purdue chickens are produced, or anyone spending time working on a typical confinement dairy farm, will soon be demanding far more humane care in the growing and processing of the meat and milk that they buy. The March 1999 issue of *Consumer Reports* magazine did not provide a comforting picture regarding pesticide residues in American fruits and vegetables. And we need to pay attention to the recent headlines in Britain and Western Europe that expressed serious reservations about "GM" (genetically manipulated) foods. Genetically modified crops such as much of the corn and soybeans in the United States are not likely to be accepted for import into Europe if the pattern of concern increases. Farmers who have chosen to use such crops because they have permitted less use of pesticides and herbicides will be caught in a difficult situation under such circumstances. But quality over quantity seems to be the new consumer message. Meanwhile, food prices in the American supermarket continue to be some of the lowest in the world per capita relative to income levels, and family farm income is not increasing. Rural protection, conservation, and sustainable development will require that farmers receive higher prices for the higher-quality food they need to produce.

• There needs to be a modern assessment of forestry that recognizes the critical and changing role of forests in each region. Despite all the databases and our love of statistics there is an inadequate understanding of how many people are engaged in forestry either in the field or in the forest products industry, or how much forestland is being well managed, if at all. It also difficult to ascertain how many government employees may be available to provide assistance in the field for individual forest owners or rural communities. Given the changed, fragmented land ownership patterns of forest parcels, government and universities need to reassess how they should teach and serve the public in regard to forest management.

• Develop regional thinking for all land-use planning. Not all solutions to rural problems will be found locally or nationally. As in Western Europe, there is a need to provide local, regional, and national tax incentives and loans that permit identification of both "growth" and "no-growth" areas in rural America, recognizing that both need tax incentives to be sustainable. This could include designation of special rural zones with both restrictions on development and special financial incentives for sustainable forestry and farming practices. Federal policies could facilitate the necessary regional and community-level policies.

- We must also stop being led down the path of "economic efficiency" as a primary goal of development and avoid the megatrends. Although the USDA and others have provided research that shows that small farms, when measuring all inputs and outputs, are actually very efficient, the perception is that there are economies of scale in all things. If rural communities are to be sustainable, we will need to avoid amalgamations of rural schools, rural hospitals, rural banks, and other institutions serving rural regions. We will need to avoid the "big-box" dilemma and avoid being drawn down the path of thinking that larger farms are the wave of the future.
- We need to support stronger downtowns in rural service centers. A sustainable rural economy requires a relatively stable infrastructure, a market center, a place to buy materials and equipment, and a place to send children to school. Dispersed giant shopping malls may be more efficient in a global sense but where they replace a diversity of local businesses they destroy the necessary fabric of rural regions. Both nationally owned malls and smaller local-owned businesses are needed, but a balance must be deliberately sought.
- We must teach more about the local rural heritage, including history of land use and culture. The more that people can learn about the local history of their communities all the way back to the natural vegetative cover that existed before European settlement and even before the presence of native Americans and begin to build pride in the complex threads of local history, the more they will be able to avoid the mistakes in land use and mistakes leading to the rise and fall of rural communities of the past and plan for a better, more sustainable future.

Chapter Seven

Information Sharing and Celebration

As a rural development model, EPIC seeks to reach those not already leaders with established organizations or representatives of large organizations with well-established funding sources or other means of providing rural assistance. EPIC tries to reach the innovative person, the younger person just starting in community life, the recently retired person who could look at life and the community anew, the disenfranchised, the new rural resident, and so forth. There are other programs those already in networks can take advantage of. But this model seeks out community members with budding public lives—individuals who are only just beginning to be part of an active network. This makes reaching them a challenge.

The EPIC model of rural development assumes that communities are made up of people who live in various forms of the modern family. The idealized and much-romanticized nuclear family of two parents (one male and one female) with two children, typically with the mother at home all the time, existed for less than one generation in the United States during the period following World War II. The small nuclear family is not the norm. Modern families are far more complex, but the myth is hard to break, and society struggles to deal with the realities of modern rural and urban life. It is these new, extended families that make up the communities. Extended families may have parents who are remarried, living as a single parent with several children (perhaps from more than one family), or living with friends or other relatives. There may be family relationships between stepchildren and their spouse's families, and the grandchildren may have numerous grandparents to keep track of. It is these complex families that will determine the sustainability of the rural community, and so EPIC hopes to reach as many as possible.

To do so, the rural development effort must use a variety of mechanisms to get the word out, including newspaper articles; word of mouth; radio spots with interviews; television interviews; phone calls and flyers; and presentations at schools, community meetings, church groups, civic organizations, chambers of commerce, Rotary clubs, and established nonprofit organizations.

It is important to note that during the development stage of our efforts, the Director (who for almost a year was the only staff person) laid the groundwork by meeting with community leaders throughout the region in order to assess their interests and to develop a plan for next four or five years. The goal of these meetings was to allay unhealthy competitive fears and determine the community niche in which the EPIC model would operate. In turn, the newly established organizations that EPIC helped to found and that now carry on its work in New England could keep us apprised of their progress ·and offer assistance to former EPIC grantees and collaborators as their abilities to do so increase. The EPIC model is thus to work collaboratively and in a synergistic manner with other organizations and programs. The only area of unnecessary stress and unhealthy "turf protection" was within the university. While this acrimony did not affect rural communities directly or negatively, when the leadership of the various colleges (such as agriculture, natural resources, education, and liberal arts), along with the School of Business and the extension service and related programs, were able to cooperate, the communities benefited far more. Happily, some individual faculty were able to overcome the territorial tendencies of their administrations and became EPIC core team leaders, as described in Chapter Two.

Of all the mechanisms for getting the word out and for sharing lessons learned, three stand out: (1) word of mouth, (2) the local newspaper, and (3) community gatherings.

Word of Mouth

We kept track of every person who contacted the EPIC office and as many as possible of those who contacted the various team leaders in the field or on campus. Some of these contacts were in writing but many were phone calls. (We chose not to use e-mail at that period in the region.) Because we were trying to reach the beginning community leaders, the telephone was very important. Many of these folks were shy or nervous, not sure of what to say or what they could ask for. A quick phone call to our friendly secretary, Sue Bean, or to the coordinator of seed grants, or even the Director, was easier than writing a formal letter (although it was easier for those worked for nonprofits or who were already in business to write letters). Regardless of how they reached us, everyone received a personal phone call in response. We found when talking with people that "word of mouth" was by far the most common way they had learned about EPIC. The list of contacts quickly reached well over a thousand and became our core matrix of names and contacts for a large rural region. Something as basic as a friendly, helpful secretary can contribute to the success of rural development work.

The Print Media

The role of the newspapers in getting out the word was very interesting. Several newspapers—dailies and weeklies—took on the EPIC cause, reporting almost everything that we did or wanted to do. One newspaper stands out: *The St. Albans Messenger*. This daily newspaper serves the major rural agricultural counties in north and northwest Vermont. Embracing the concept of civic journalism, *The St. Albans Messenger* took its role seriously as a shaper of public opinion with the potential to empower the citizenry. Its owner, management, and staff were committed to reporting local programs and successes—not just the murder and mayhem, court appearances, latest Washington scandals, and other unpleasant news. They chose to serve as a conduit for information and publicity regarding local events and programs and solicited community opinion and debate from EPIC citizen leaders and others.

It is important to note here that *The Messenger* is locally owned and operated. It is not a "big-box" chain paper like the other regional papers, most of which are owned by the Gannett Company, a national chain press. Most of the articles in Gannett-owned newspapers are fed from other Gannett papers, including *USA Today*; only a few of its reporters have much local experience.

The role of the locally owned and managed newspaper was, in retrospect, absolutely critical to the success of the rural development model in that part of the state. *The Messenger*'s regular front page and editorial coverage speeded our efforts to attract community leaders and encouraged additional community collaboration. These articles, editorials, interviews, and stories of citizens "doing good" inspired others, allowing for an important synergy among networks. The editor and owner of the newspaper, Emerson Lynn, is a person whom I had known for many years through my civic presentations and other volunteer work. Having a contact made access to the newspaper relatively easy during EPIC's start-up. Following a phone call from an EPIC staff member regarding a particular event in the community, he would assign a reporter and photographer to write a story. Even more importantly, a day or two after the article appeared, Emerson Lynn himself would write a lead editorial about the article's topic.

Informing educators, local leaders, and activists about this integrated approach to rural development in its many diverse facets was an important first step in EPIC work. Both the media connections and the hard-won, long-term investment of the EPIC Director (having lived, worked, and volunteered in the region for twenty years) meant that there was a high level of personal, community trust in the EPIC project. After the first newspaper articles about the rural development grant and its Director were published, the story spread by word of mouth from one community to another. People knew that the leadership of EPIC was flexible in approach and open to new ideas. They understood that many of the EPIC leaders knew what it was like to raise a family, run a family farm, serve as a volunteer, and work several jobs. In other words, they understood the reality of rural life. The funding organization, the W.K. Kellogg Foundation, had put their trust in an established community leader who could in turn work to provide opportunities for others just starting. The task for others leading similar rural development efforts in other communities is to find similar dedicated volunteers.

Community Gatherings

Community gatherings at which information and ideas can be shared is vital for endeavors to be successful. This issue is covered in more detail later in this chapter.

Environmental Indicators

There are several aspects of the EPIC approach to sustainable rural community development that can be easily accomplished by a community, involving everyone from schoolchildren to seniors, and that can be a focal point for community renewal. One is the use of environmental indicators. Because these will no doubt be of great use to many rural community leaders, I will discuss them here in detail (copies of the Environmental Quality Index of Vermont, 1993, can also be requested from EPIC).

Many Americans prefer to think of rural areas as relatively pristine environments with clean air and water and perhaps also as "working" landscapes that can provide a brief respite for the weary urban dweller. Most rural economies are, to varying extents, dependent on fostering this image. Where data indicate environmental problems, those in leadership positions must enforce laws or otherwise establish policies to deal with these problems. There is the additional perception among Americans that most rural dwellers are not well educated, lack the political clout of those in urban centers, and live amid "all that rural space out there" that is seemingly ideal for dumping urban-generated waste. Perhaps they feel that using the large open areas of the United States with low population density for purposes such as this will affect fewer people.

Because of this, rural areas suffer environmental degradation, whether from insidious nonpoint sources of pollution from generations of agriculture and poorly sited industries or from severe degradation caused by dump sites of various forms of human-derived garbage. Any community seeking an "environmental scorecard" for its town or region should explore the Web site of the Environmental Defense Fund, which allows you to determine the environmental conditions prevailing in your region and describes related implications for effects on human health (http://www.scorecard.org). Another site worth viewing is the Environmental Protection Agency site on green communities (http://www.epa.gov/region3/greenkit).

Environmental indicators for a community or a state do not have to be all negative, of course. Wherever possible, communities should undergo an assessment, indexing or setting a baseline that describes the condition of the natural resources in their area. This may take place as part of the planning process for land-use planning and development opportunities in the community, or it may be a process conducted by the conservation commission or equivalent organization.

In 1992, EPIC developed a pilot program to provide a simple environmental quality index for the state of Vermont, intended to be educational in nature. The report was published in January of 1993. The plan was to publish the report for three years, encouraging communities to undertake their own simple survey, working with local elementary or high schools. It was hoped that after three years the state would take over the project. Some towns did in fact undertake an analysis of their town, normally as part of the planning process, but many towns were too poor or had too many other pressing concerns. The interesting result, however, was that it was only necessary to publish the index once before the state took it over. "We had always planned to do this," we were told.

Rural residents of other regions of the nation might laugh that Vermonters felt the need to establish an environmental quality index because of the common perception that Vermont is essentially pristine. But in fact, even though Vermont is a small state, and cleaner than many, it has plenty of environmental problems, including seven or eight Superfund sites and a large number of hazardous waste sites. Southern Vermont has ozone levels that frequently exceed acceptable EPA standards, and arsenic pollutes the air in winds blowing down from Canada. There are also advisories for mercury in fish in the majority of streams and lakes (including Lake Champlain). But data on many factors were not adequately collected or presented to the public, and enforcement of laws, and development of new policies to address problems, was not at the forefront of the state's political agenda. For example, lead in paint in old houses puts thousands of children at risk. This, as discussed in Chapter Five, was a serious health issue that needed to be addressed, and in 1992 it was taken on by a group of mothers with young children. Jobs, the economy, and school education seem to take precedence on the state agenda over environmental problems and their effects on human health.

The story of the environmental quality index is quite interesting. The goal was to provide a nontechnical, educational publication in newspaper format for wide distribution to schools and communities. The hope was that it would be a catalyst in schools, in communities, and at the state level. Several broad-brush natural resource categories were identified, such as water, air, agriculture, forests, waste generation and disposal, and energy (the "life support factors" discussed in Chapter 6 and listed in Table 6.1).

A team of undergraduate students working with the EPIC Director assembled data for each category from an array of sources, including focus-group discussions and one-on-one interviews with experts. Experts included not only state and university personnel, but also local citizens, including foresters, loggers, fishermen, hunters, farmers, bird watchers, seniors, physicians, and so forth. We sought their expert opinions as well as old photographs they might possess that could be used to document the changes occurring over time in a community. The data and information were then presented in simple narrative form with minimal numerical information. In addition, a "grade" was assigned to each category or topic area (Excellent, Getting Better, Getting Worse, Poor), using a half clock face with an arrow pointing to left or right of center. (Some of these ideas were adapted from those used by the National Wildlife Federation during the late 1980s.) For each category, we tried to identify communities in the state that were successfully addressing a similar issue and described how they were doing it: in other words, we presented "good news" stories.

The state agency that oversees air quality and forestry practices, the Agency of Natural Resources, was not happy with our endeavors. When assembling data for the "air" category, we were unable to locate an adequate database, because not enough data on the subject were being collected in Vermont. But without the data, it would be hard to prove our suspicions that air quality in certain areas of Vermont was poor. For example, southern Vermont has periods when levels of ozone exceed EPA standards for human health, and air toxics are continually deposited from out-of-state and out-of-country sites, posing potential health hazards for Vermont residents. The Agency of Natural Resources staff, while somewhat uncooperative with our data gatherers, showed us their data, but also pointed out that they did not have the right equipment to gather adequate data and didn't want EPIC to publish conclusions that state air quality is worsening without supporting data. I explained to them that they could use EPIC's conclusions to press legislators to provide the monitoring and measuring equipment needed to gather better scientific data. Meanwhile, children were coming home from school with the Index as part of their homework assignments, an important opportunity for them to be engaged with the community. In some ways, it is one of the more important elements of a successful environmental quality indicator project in that, often, the data are less important than the process itself. But the knowledge derived or the perceptions changed can also have policy implications. For example, following the publication of the Index, the state agency that oversees air quality standards did successfully approach the legislature for further funding to monitor air pollution, and I was able to work with the agency scientists on some regional air pollution research on dioxin in dairy milk in 1997.

In the "forestry" category of the Index, we simply put a big question mark. We could find no solid data from any source, government or private, that really helped us to understand the status of the state's forests. The state had been 90 percent deforested in the mid-nineteenth century; today 85 percent of the state is covered in second-growth forest, primarily in highly fragmented private holdings, as discussed in Chapter Six. EPIC received many differing opinions from forestry professionals at the state level, but there was little consensus among the various state agency divisions that handle forests about the state of Vermont's forests. Forestry leadership courses, classes in urban stewardship (such as those discussed in Chapter Four), and considerable political efforts at forestland conservation have taken place since the Index was published, but whether this was linked to our work is hard to say.

What we can say is that the state contacted us to let us know that it was not happy with the question mark about forests, or the poor grade for air, and that *it* would take on this Indicator project. Sure enough, the following year, state consultants, working out of the Vermont Law School (a free-standing private law school not affiliated with a university) and using *only* state-derived data, produced a biased, public-relations-oriented report on the State of the Environment. But with encouragement from many sources, the annual report that comes out each year since has become more accurate and much more useful. The State Agency of Natural Resources staff credit EPIC as the catalyst in all their talks about the report.

But the political reality of such an environmental quality index is that once there is official acknowledgment backed by scientific data that problems exist, then the government must take action to rectify the unhealthy situation. Vermont's economy, like so many rural states, depends heavily on tourism, and there is little incentive for the state to fully describe environmental problems more than it must.

This concept of a simple environmental index, or perhaps a natural resources index (to reduce anti-environmentalist reaction), is a transferable model applicable at community, regional, or state levels. It can be effective as an educational tool or as a catalyst for change in an institution. It builds community, involves children and youth, makes connections between diverse parts of the rural systems, and empowers many—building grassroots leadership ability. As an activity, it meets EPIC's Key Principles of Sustainable Development.

Here, too, is another lesson for those engaged in rural development. It is important to take risks and take the lead on solving important issues at all levels, whether state, regional, or community. Good ideas do often get picked up by others. When this happens, it is okay to step back and let it happen and let others take up the work.

Annual Meetings, Exhibitions, and the Role of Celebration

Once a year, the EPIC project invited all participants and their families to its annual meeting. Costs were covered by EPIC, and it was money well spent. Shared food had become a key component of all our community meetings (and pasture walks as well). Even the meeting location—the university—was important. The idea that everyone taking part in an EPIC project, or anyone who wanted to learn about what EPIC participants and their friends had been doing, would be invited to spend an afternoon and evening at the university was really important, because most participants had not received a university education, and others who had, had not been back since they were graduated. The format was always social as well as educational. Along with participants and their families, we invited other individuals and groups active in some innovative fashion in rural communities of New England, upstate New York, and lower Quebec in Canada—further extending our networks.

In rural areas, certain times of year are better than others for bringing a large group of farmers and others to a regional meeting. The time of year selected for the annual gathering was a Friday in April or May, after the snow and bad road conditions ended but before serious haying had started or the schools were out. Fine detail in planning was needed to ensure that the citizens felt at ease. We were careful to explain in the invitation where to park (prevention of parking tickets by the ever-zealous campus police was vital). Invitations were personally addressed to each participant and stressed that it was a family event. Attendees were encouraged to bring pictures or other materials to exhibit their work (Photo 7.1). In addition, the day provided us with an opportunity to run several short workshops for up to twenty-four people each. These covered topics such as fund-raising, pasture management, holistic resource management, starting a small rural business, and so forth. They also provided opportunities for people to share lessons learned, to network, and to find out about new ideas and resources. Workshops ran from 2 to 4 p.m., between milking, and toward the end of the school day for those with children.

Exhibits were open from 4 to 7, at which time dinner began. Some

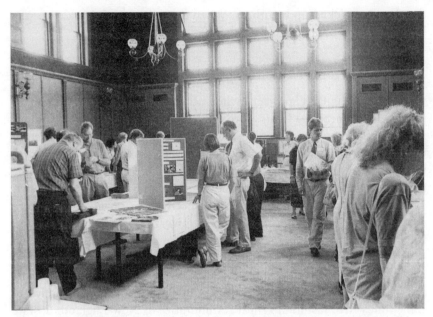

Photo 7.1. Exhibits like this, set up in a large, sunlit room, provided an excellent opportunity for sharing lessons learned and for networking. This exhibit is part of an annual rural development project gathering.

dairy farmers came early in the afternoon and went home to milk. However, we had invited dairy farmers to take the day off, and we had, at our cost, provided relief milkers for as many farm families as we could persuade to leave the cows in good hands for one milking. In the evening, during dessert, there was an opportunity to share lessons learned and to encourage people to talk in front of a large group. Seed grantees were able to hear firsthand the experiences of those in other communities.

The ongoing evaluation, discussed in Chapter Three, guided the selection of who might wish to talk, or who we could encourage to share activities and ideas with the broader regional group. The EPIC model celebration is designed to do what EPIC teaches: build networks, develop coalitions, and make connections.

A final and especially important purpose of the annual EPIC celebration is to acknowledge and praise the efforts of all the participants—seed grantees, innovative farmers, and community leaders—all of whom are volunteers.

The celebration and sharing at the university is thus an opportunity for the university president and other "important" people to thank local leaders for their work. Children have the opportunity to hear their parents praised and to see the respect in which they are held not just in the home community but also in the broader rural region.

Food is a surprisingly important community-participation builder. The food served by EPIC at the annual meeting permitted people with very different backgrounds and interests to find common ground. In the same way, we encouraged serving food, especially local favorites, at all community events and meetings. In fact, when seed grant coordinator Susan Clark and I sat down to review grant proposals, we joked that the "P" in EPIC really stood for Pizza.

After the first community building efforts were launched, EPIC team members began to notice that grant proposals often included requests for money for food for a meeting.

The importance of food in bringing people together is a serious matter. Rural communities frequently hold meetings or gatherings that are "potluck suppers," and they can be fine for some events (although they get pretty tiring for parents and others who work full time outside the home). One often gets invited to "brown-bag lunches" where you bring your own food, and perhaps your own agenda. But where simple, nutritious, locally produced food is provided for all to share, then somehow more people are attracted to the meeting, and many barriers can be broken down. The offering of food also sets a casual, friendly tone and can diffuse potentially tense situations. Seed grantee David Brynn, a county forester holding a major one-day event to bring together environmental, forestry, and agricultural representatives, commented, "Our meetings have been surprisingly cordial between people who have polar-opposite views of the world. . . . Sharing food with people goes back to our basic instincts. When you break bread with someone it takes the steam out of things."

Critical factors at work here are networking, sharing accomplishments, eating together, and having fun. The element of "fun" is essential if a community is to be sustainable. As has been suggested by many studies on volunteerism, participants must feel needed, get engaged, and see results of their volunteer efforts. In addition, however, participants are more likely to stick with a project if they not only believe in it but also enjoy it. In their varied descriptions of efforts to build community and work with others, many seed grantees mention, often to their surprise, that the process is fun. Similar comments come from the farmers who take an active and regular part in the farm walks that occur on each other's farms in the region. The fund-raising community events, Native American gatherings, and farm open house days for new rural residents and visiting urban residents are all very important traditions that can enhance rural development projects (Photos 7.2, 7.3, 7.4, and 7.5).

In follow-up questions to grantees after their projects were complete, we asked about ways in which the project differed from expectations, and the organizer of the annual regional watershed-based Conservation Congress noted in one of her answers, "I am always amazed at how good a time people have. They call and ask when it is going to be so that they can be sure to schedule it."

Many of the seed grants included funds for the purchase of food, and many communities took time to hold gatherings, some for fund-raising, others simply to celebrate the work of the community and individual participants.

Photo 7.2. The fund-raiser barbeque, using local bands for entertainment, can be a good way to bring everyone together in a positive way rather than limiting interaction only to those times when there is likely to be heated debate over some local issue.

Photo 7.3. Local fund-raisers also provide an excellent opportunity to "show off" children's work. This exhibit of school crafts made parents, grandparents, and children feel good about themselves and the community.

Photo 7.4. Urban children, and those many rural children who do not live on a farm, can easily become estranged from agricultural life. It is important that all children learn about farming and about the side of rural life that they never see. Here a rural farm demonstration project is part of an ongoing farm education project open to schools and communities.

Photo 7.5. Celebration of community and the land was behind this Native American powwow. Each region has a many diverse cultural groups, and cultural celebrations provide an opportunity for learning by all attending and taking part.

Lessons Learned about Sharing Ideas

Key principles of sustainable rural development include community empowerment, encouragement of innovation, fostering linkages, and strengthening democracy. Careful attention to dissemination of ideas, lessons learned, projects under way, and celebration of these activities must be key activities for a rural development effort. The following synthesizes some of the lessons learned:

• Ideas and information are spread most quickly by word of mouth.
• The media, especially the local daily or weekly newspaper, can be a key catalyst for change.
• Environmental quality indicators or the equivalent can be a catalyst for gaining community interest, community involvement (including youth), and community rejuvenation.
• Face-to-face meetings, with stories about the things that are closest to our hearts, love, kindness, generosity to neighbors, and the safety and happiness of our children and grandchildren are important to everyone.

- The complexities of communities, cultures, and families need to be identified and appropriately addressed at several levels: personal, face-to-face meetings, media messages, and policy application at local, regional, state, and national levels.
- It is important to involve the children.
- Volunteers need to be praised and, where necessary, small honoraria provided to help keep an active volunteer through the "burn-out" phase.
- Celebration is very important in rural community development, especially where people can tell their stories and exhibit evidence of their accomplishments to others. Money spent on local and regional community gatherings is money well spent.

Chapter Eight

Small Towns with Renewed Community Spirit

When we see land as a community to which we belong, we may begin to use it with love and respect. . . . That land is a community is the basic concept of ecology, but that land is to be loved and respected is an extension of ethics.

—Aldo Leopold, *A Sand County Almanac and Sketches Here and There*

In the first chapter, there was discussion about some of the problems facing rural regions. The next several chapters presented various components of rural communities and some specific model examples for addressing problems in these components. This chapter seeks to draw together those diverse, interconnected elements that make a rural community viable. Accordingly, rather than look at the "threads" of the rural fabric as in earlier chapters, I will take a more holistic perspective here and look at several individual communities as case studies. At the same time, I will bring into focus some of the individual visionary leaders who provide the spirit in the communities that, when connected with others, can provide the necessary renewal of community spirit.

Rural Community Indicators of Stress

Before describing some of the rural development approaches used in three rural communities, I would like discuss indicators of rural problems and then demonstrate how different communities can identify and address the range of rural stressors in their geographical region. As the EPIC work progressed, it became apparent that there are identifiable characteristics of rural towns under stress, examples of towns that have addressed some of these stress points and others that have not. It is thus possible to identify factors in rural communities that might indicate the need for some type of rural development assistance.

In Chapter Seven, I discussed environmental indicators as useful tools for school and community education and as a possible catalyst for community renewal activities. The indicators discussed in this chapter are far more complex, dealing with a linked combination of social, economic, and natural resource factors and political issues. The criteria presented here do not comprise a complete list. Stress indicators will vary somewhat from region to region across the nation. The ability to identify factors and where possible to provide supporting data can, however, allow policy makers and local leaders to identify the direction of change for the community, making it easier to determine the most appropriate mechanisms to apply for rural renewal to take place in their local area. Indicators of stress should not be confused with a needs assessment, which is a far more focused effort that takes place at a later stage (if at all) in the community revitalization process.

In Western Europe, regional development in the 1970s involved, among other things, defining "problem" areas. Those regions were identified at the international European Economic Community (EEC) level by the combined efforts of the leadership of several nations meeting together. Once identified, these regions could then be deemed in need of help such as tax incentives, planning grants, transportation grants, and so forth. Some of the criteria used in 1973 included (1) more workers in farming than the community (EEC) average; (2) at least 20 percent of the workforce in declining industries, and (3) persistently high unemployment, or annual out-migration of population in excess of 1 percent over a long period of time (Clout 1981), but communities did not need to have all characteristics to receive aid. Using these criteria, areas such as the Highlands and Islands of Scotland and the Mezzogiorno in Italy were able to benefit regionally and at the most local level by a concerted effort to focus technical and financial assistance into rural development areas. Policy makers recognized that this could be a long-term need. The Scottish, English, and European countrysides that so many visitors from overseas admire are thus a cultural landscape maintained in a very complex manner, based on a desire to conserve agriculture and the "natural" landscape *and* to ensure that rural inhabitants will gain a higher standard of living. There are many local, regional, national, and EEC policies that have been adopted in a relatively integrated manner since World War II to provide for sustainable landscapes and sustainable communities. These range from national parks, which are multiple use, to new towns, to the establishment of Areas of Outstanding Beauty, to agricultural policies. The agricultural policies have been particularly contentious, but are identified as vital to the overall needs of rural landscapes and the lives of the inhabitants. The power of farmers as a political force has been used particularly regularly and effectively in France.

The European system is far from perfect, and the degree of control over private property exerted by European governments would not be tolerated in America. However, in the modern global economy, both Europe and America are affected by such global institutions as the World Trade Organization, the North American Free Trade Agreement, and the evolving Euro-based trading partnerships. There can be no doubt that rural and agricultural areas and the lives of the rural people have benefited enormously from the diverse but integrated approaches to rural development in Western Europe. The use of criteria to measure rural problems and some of the mechanisms for addressing them can be learned from both the successes and the failures of rural projects carried out in there over the last fifty years.

In retrospective analysis, considering the mechanisms used to develop rural criteria in Europe, and in looking at rural America today, I have identified several indicators of stress that may affect the structure and function of rural communities. Some use of the concepts of "degrees of rurality" (Cloke 1977) as discussed in Chapter One should be used as a contextual addition given the wide range of differences between rural areas in America, especially regarding the degrees of community isolation.

I suggest that Rural Community Indicators of Stress include the following: small and/or decreasing percentage of population engaged in agriculture; higher-than-average levels of unemployment and underemployment; school amalgamation; consolidated and centralized healthcare facilities; farm loss and increase in large "factory" farm businesses; limited or completely lacking public transportation; regional rural depopulation; changed structure of rural population in economic and social aspects; loss of a sense of community; feelings of isolation in many sectors of rural population (here one should apply the local feelings of isolation against the geographical, regional determination of degree of rurality); loss of local history; loss of children moving to the bigger centers; tendency for the community to become the dumping ground for environmentally damaging waste; high property taxes relative to farm income; and other factors that are locally specific.

One or two of these factors alone could be more than enough to push a rural community over the brink into extinction or to becoming totally urbanized with new, nonrural settlement. It is important to examine the range and scope of environmental stressors locally and regionally in preparing a rural development project. Which factors do the community members see as most critical? (These may be quite different from those perceived or even measured by the outside expert.) From a set of possible mechanisms for approaching the rural problems, which ones are most appropriate at that time and place as determined by the local community?

There is no "one-size-fits-all" approach to revitalizing rural America that can address these factors. In this next section, I will mention three approaches: one that is economic-development oriented, one that is linked to leadership development and seed grants, and one that is less structured but more comprehensive.

Economic Development in North Dakota: Gackle and Minot

"In the 1950s," writes Rollie Henkes about Gackle, "this small town in southern North Dakota had three grocery stores, three car dealerships, five implement dealerships, a hardware store, a clothing store, and a bowling alley among many other businesses" (Henkes 1998). Gackle has a population of about 500. Henkes points out that there are no longer any farms close by. Given the loss of farms, it is not surprising that the entire agriculturally related infrastructure is now gone and that all of the car and implement dealerships have closed, together with the clothing store and bowling alley. The hardware store closed in the fall of 1997, and only one grocery store remains. This region shows most of the stress indicators listed above, with farm consolidation, rural depopulation, lack of transportation, and isolation exacerbated by the loss of the railroad in the 1970s. The hospital that the town raised the money to build in the 1950s has closed for of lack of doctors, although it has turned the building into a care center.

The role of the bank in Gackle may be critical. The bank, First State, is local, started by the grandfather of the present president. The bank and the president/owner provide community-based leadership for economic-based rural development. The town formed an economic development corporation that has been purchasing and renovating vacant buildings and renting them out to new businesses. The town has prepared a promotional booklet about the area, aimed at business investment. The combined physical renovation and economic renewal of downtown areas has been known for decades, both in America and in Europe, to be a critical factor in rural and in urban revitalization. (We saw a similar but even more comprehensive effort in the Hardwick case study discussed in depth in Chapter Five.) What is interesting in the North Dakota story, however, is the collaborative nature of the several towns in the area helping each other rather than competing. This is an element that Ron Savitt (discussed in Chapter Five) identified as critical to long-term rural economic development. The high degree of rurality of the Plains region makes the decision to emphasize intertown collaboration even more critical.

The community goal in Gackle is to determine how best its efforts will complement the other towns on the Plains and not just compete against each other for the full market share. Small towns like this cannot exist in isolation. There is synergy in such an approach to economic development.

All towns, large and small, have geographical "spheres of influence" that overlap and lie within those of larger towns whose spheres of influence are, fittingly, much larger. The economic health of each can be enhanced by a more regional context for development opportunities.

Churches in the Plains region seem to play a more critical leadership role than in the past. One example that Henkes (1998) cites is that of Gackle's United Church of Christ, which spearheaded the building of a house for a needy person. The activist role appears to be a shift in the thinking of the congregation. Another example of church leadership is seen in the work of the Congregation and Community Services for Lutheran Social Services in North Dakota.

"About the biggest victory for any small town is keeping its school. The average class size in Gackle stands at twenty in the town's modern school building, which houses kindergarten through twelfth grade" (Henkes 1998). In schools like this, everyone can be on the sports teams, in the band, and in leadership roles. The leadership and confidence building that children get at home and at school will determine what future leaders will be available as adults.

Minot, a city of some 35,000 in north-central North Dakota, is trying to build such a regional network by giving area towns economic-development grants. The funds for this come from a special 1 percent local sales tax. There are also examples of new businesses, such as the pasta plant in Carrington, North Dakota, which is a locally owned and operated cooperative.

Every rural town that I have visited around the world talks about its schools and children as a key impetus to getting rural development off the ground. The problems of school size and structure are highly complicated given the ever-increasing scope of problems that schools must address, from providing breakfast to mainstreaming the handicapped and learning disabled. Policy makers must, however, look at the large, theoretically "efficient" schools with hundreds and in many cases thousands of children and make some changes in school and class size if the rural and urban issues facing youth are to be resolved. There are many things that economic efficiencies cannot buy. Rural communities cannot survive if the children continue to be "sent away" to be educated.

A recent article in *High Country News* (Solberg 1999) provides an eloquent analysis of life on the Great Plains. In interviewing people in Leeds, North Dakota, Solberg poses the question of the role of modern cooperatives as a way out of the loss of a strong economy and rural depopulation of the Heartland. This paper urges again the need for leadership education to bridge the cultures on the Plains, citing work in South Dakota's Rosebud reservation, where Lakota educators are working to reduce isolation and build community partnerships. Gary Greff, a visionary artist, decided to attract tourism dollars through construction of giant folk art, such as a forty-foot grasshopper in Regent, North Dakota. This motif and grand scale of art are in keeping with the scale of the landscape.

In each region of the nation, there will be innovators who have the potential to spark change that may permit a renewed economic and, especially, community revival, hopefully ameliorating the present severe challenges facing family farms.

Superior, Nebraska—A Small Town in Transition

Family farms are difficult to maintain anywhere in the nation, especially in the face of the national and global realities of agribusiness that are in effect "supply chains" developed to "ensure high-quality consumer products, capture economies of scale, and minimize risk" (Mark

Drabenstott, Kansas City Federal Reserve Bank, report to Senate Agricultural Committee, February 1999). It is not easy for small farms to flourish in the face of a trend toward agricultural supply chain monopolies. Low wheat and grain prices in the northern Plains and the Cornbelt in 1998, for example, combined with disastrous hog prices have resulted in many bankruptcies among independent producers that year. Only a handful of corporate entities control this cheap food supply. Our food is the cheapest in the world, and yet there exists the paradox that some rural families live below the poverty line and cannot afford to eat well.

To revitalize a farming community in regions like the Great Plains and to build capacity for development, leaders must be proactive, seek innovative ideas, find the change agents, and help community leaders of all ages and walks of life. Several areas in North and South Dakota and Nebraska have used leadership development as the key leverage for rural community development. Some model approaches for leadership development programs in the Dakotas were discussed in Chapter Four.

Other towns, such as Superior, Nebraska, have used rural heritage plus traditional economic development approaches as leverage points to their rural development. Superior uses socioeconomic indicators to address its needs. Leverage is an EPIC key principle. Superior provides an example of a small town working to meet the changed nature of its township in the Great Plains. Superior, population 2,400, is still very much a farming community, with traditional agriculture. It is larger than Gackle and its economic and social geographical sphere of influence is wider. Local leaders recognized that they are in a rapid transition closely tied to the global economy.

The town lies in a bend of the Republican River near the Kansas border. It is 60 miles to the nearest interstate highway. The nearest large town, with 23,000 people and a new Wal-Mart store, is almost an hour's drive away. Superior, however, has a large sphere of influence, being the only service center to a large geographical area. It has a modern medical facility and good retail businesses serving locals and also tourists who come in from recreation areas in Kansas and Nebraska. There are two banks and two grocery stores. And the locals like the competition within the town, which they see as healthy.

Superior focused its rural development around the history of the region and around its own community in particular. There are a number of lovely Victorian-style homes in the town, and it claims the title of "Victorian Capital of Nebraska." "The theme is reinforced with the new 'Lady Vestey Festival,' named for a turn-of-the-century native who made a fortune working in the meat-packing industry after she moved to Chicago and then married into English Royalty" (Luther and Wall 1991). The idea for this focus came from a community strategic planning exercise that followed the closure of both a cement factory and a meatpacking plant in the late 1980s and the loss of its largest retail store, J.C. Penney. The hospital is debt-free today but has operating losses that its managers ascribe to smaller reimbursements made to rural health providers through Medicare. The population is also aging, and the hospital has adapted to these new service needs.

Businesses in Superior have become more varied, and, thanks to the local banks, economic development has taken place in many ways. Townspeople believe that the strategic planning effort in the community, START (an acronym for the state economic development program that fostered it), was the key turning point in the community. START included leadership development and the heritage program that gave rise to the Lady Vestey idea.

Farming has not changed radically in the area around Superior, but there is innovation in low-input agriculture that minimizes tillage (discussed in Chapter Six), and some farmers have put their land into "special protection areas" to monitor nitrate pollution in ground water. The local farmers see environmental protection as essential both to their success and probably to their survival.

New residents and returning old residents seeking a quiet rural life for raising their families are also bringing new ideas to Superior and are entering into the community spirit with enthusiasm. One of the returning individuals was a physician who had grown up in Superior and was returning to open a family practice. In the early 1980s, the town had lost all its physicians, but the count is back up to four (Luther and Wall 1991).

Leadership by individuals has made all the difference in the renewed community spirit and sense of hope that the residents feel. However, Luther and Wall (1991) make an important point: Outsiders, researchers, and government officials consider the area "severely stressed." Their data show population decline, little new construction, an aging population, and rural isolation. The locals, on the other hand, see their hometown much more positively. They see a brighter future for those who can handle and adapt to change in the global economy that affects them all.

This caveat is thus added in regard to the use of "indicators" such as those presented at the beginning of this chapter. They should be used judiciously by those who do not reside in the communities and reviewed carefully by those who do, so that the *community* can best decide for itself how to use these indicators for the benefit of their own town and for future generations.

As a Vermont governor commented during the Great Depression, when he turned down federal aid for his state (which had been designated a stressed area), "You just don't understand the quality of our poverty." Rural community development must be community-based and community-driven to be sustainable.

A Farm Wife

Before leaving the Great Plains, however, it is important to again remind ourselves of the context within which towns like Superior exist—the vast richness of the land and the stoic nature of those who work it.

We need to remind ourselves that rural communities are composed of individuals and families with strengths, frailties, and a unique sense of place. Those involved in rural development must be able to put themselves in the shoes of the people in the community: farmer, shopkeeper, or teacher. In the fall of 1998, there was a public television special, *The Farmer's Wife* (available from PBS on video). This six-hour film documentary was made over a three-year period and profiles the lives of Nebraska farm couple Darrel and Juanita Buschkoetter as they faced seemingly insurmountable economic hardship, only to confront the even-greater challenge of saving their marriage. They agreed to be filmed because they believe that most Americans have little understanding of the realities of farm life.

The couple has three children and lives in a town of 300 on the border of Kansas and Nebraska. Corn is the primary crop. The story of their battle to keep their farm, their land, their equipment, their lifestyle, and their family intact is truly heart wrenching. They had overcapitalized their farm investment in machinery and buildings, a relatively common phenomenon in agriculture over the last thirty years. With the vagaries of weather and only a slim profit margin, their ability to borrow (in anticipation of income later in the year) varied over the three-year period, which was recorded in fine detail around the breakfast table and in the fields. They went through a period of having to work off the farm and then recovered later. They want urban America to understand the farm crisis and to understand the rural Heartland. The Buschkoetters are independent and hardworking. They do not seek handouts. They want farms, towns, and schools to be small and human-scale, and they are willing to fight to make it work. But they cannot do it alone; they wonder if America has forgotten them.

Fairfield, Vermont—An EPIC Model for Community Renewal

In another part of the nation, the concerns in rural communities are not necessarily that people have forgotten them but that they are too popular. Urban Americans want to visit Vermont and have it be the way they imagine it: where hardy visitors might settle. The land is not the vast Great Plains but rather rough valleys, hills, and mountains. Fairfield, population about 1,680, is presented here as a case study of sustainable rural community-based development. It is not a service center town like Superior, Nebraska, or Hardwick Vermont, but rather it is a very small township with two small village centers. It serves as a reminder that effective rural development is more likely to occur in regions that are large enough for efficiency and able to stand up to central government, yet small enough to preserve local values, a spirit of place, and a sense of neighborhood, and where individuals in the community have been encouraged to work collaboratively for local change.

The first task for the reader of this case study is to try to set aside the myths of Vermont and see the state realistically. (Otherwise, there may be a tendency to dismiss this case study, because it is from Vermont, where all is "perfect.") Certainly Vermont does have a unique sense of place. Some say that it is important just to know that Vermont exists as a place you can always go to. And the state has many fine attributes, including a relatively healthy economy. There is, however, another reality. Vermont is a postindustrial, declining dairy-farm state with many of the same environmental, economic, and social problems that the rest of the nation faces. Vermont's problems are smaller scale, but they are subject to the same external forces of world markets and politics. It is the most rural state in the United States in terms of the percentage of its population living in urban areas over 100,000.

Although the landscapes in Vermont's rural towns might appear to the visitor or newcomer unchanged for decades, the state is now 85 percent forested after being virtually deforested in the mid-nineteenth century. Abandoned farms soon turn into "puckerbrush" scrub and then grow back to mixed deciduous/coniferous forest as suburbanites buy up parcels of land for summer-home sites. These lots are often ten acres or more, because that allows developers to avoid the permitting process, septic regulations, or large-lot zoning (locally known as Act 250). Ten acres are more than most people want or need, and they soon grows back to a secondary forest. Few would deny that the underlying economic and social structures of Vermont have changed radically in the last two decades; today most rural villages in the primary agricultural towns are, in reality, bedroom communities. State policy directly affects how communities develop.

Although in 1998 Vermonters could claim to have the one of the best states in which to raise children, there are also less-positive statistical data: Vermont ranks thirty-sixth (with 1 being the best and 50 being the worst) in the United States in terms of average annual wage. It is an expensive place to live. Despite efforts to ameliorate the situation, there is little low-income housing available; Vermont is forty-seventh in average rent as a percentage of per capita income, and much of the housing stock is old and covered in lead paint.

Agriculture and related industries account for a large percentage of Vermont's income and provide a vital foundation for the state's economic base and the "working landscape" that attracts tourists and new residents and businesses. However, Vermont loses dairy farms every year. In 1981, there were 3,356 dairy farms; today there are less than 2,000. And those that remain are more isolated than they once were.

Within the national context of a strong economy, data concerning the economic well being of rural regions are conflicting. Between 1979 and 1993, the U.S. Census reported that incomes for the bottom 20 percent of families, adjusted for inflation, dropped by 17 percent. Overall, 60 percent of American families were worse off in 1993 than they were in 1979, while the income of the top 20 percent grew in real terms by 18 percent. Take Vermont, not the worst rural state economically by far, but with data worth looking at more closely. The average annual wage in Vermont is less than 85 percent of the national average and is dropping. Eighty-three percent of single-parent families with two children do not earn a livable income, and 21 percent of two-worker households are not making enough to cover basic costs. There are a record number of bankruptcies, and both public and social capitals of Vermont communities are eroding rapidly. Generally, projected jobs in Vermont over the next decade will be characterized by low wages, lack of benefits, and limited opportunities for advancement. This may perhaps represent full employment, but many will be underpaid and underemployed. Each rural region will have its own statistics that are equally—if not more—worrying.

The town of Fairfield was selected by EPIC as a possible "demonstration" town. I let folks there know about EPIC early in 1992, and consequently they were able to work with EPIC for the entire five years; even now, the community remains in close contact with former EPIC staff. Fairfield is not the picturesque New England village featured on postcards; rather, it is a small, rural, agricultural town in the uplands, with a lot of old, run-down housing stock and a changing population facing the challenges of tomorrow. Small seed grants, leadership development workshops, pasture management programs, and other stimuli were clustered in and around the community in a low-key manner. As part of the EPIC approach, towns close by were also provided with small seed grants, leadership workshops, and so forth, so that a regional network could develop. Additionally, 100 intensive pasture management demonstration farms are located across the county and neighboring counties, further increasing opportunities for developing new contacts and enlarging networks.

"Fairfield" as used here means the legal, political unit and includes two "villages," which are unincorporated hamlets. (In Vermont, there are only two levels of government: state and town. All land lies within a town. The county functions only as a subdivision of the court system and is not a unit of governance.) One village has two grocery stores; the other has one. Each village has a small gas station, and there is always someone who will fix your car. There are three churches in town, but Roman Catholicism predominates; its church is in Fairfield Center village. The elementary school, housing grades kindergarten through eight, is now located in Fairfield Center village. The school in East Fairfield village had housed first through third grades until the schools were amalgamated in the mid-1980s. The last of about fifteen one-room schoolhouses closed in the 1960s. High school for most children is about twenty miles away, down in the valley on the main north–south interstate. There are several home-operated businesses in town, but, apart from farming and the school, there are no large employers. Most of the roads are unpaved gravel or dirt. As an aside, it should be noted that the town leaders, Selectmen, retain the dirt roads for several reasons, one of which is to slow the likelihood of subdivisions and non-adaptive newcomers. People who complain that the mud is too deep in spring mudseason or that the snow is not plowed fast enough or that the dust is intolerable in summer or that the manure dropped during spreading is too smelly are encouraged to return to the city from which they came.

Photo 8.1. Knowledge of the history of a town, its early settlers, and its links to families of today is of considerable significance in beginning the process of community renovation. Knowledge of the past might include assembling old pictures such as this one, dated 1899, of the main street in town, called Merchants Row. These building still stand.

There is a strong desire by this rural community to remain as a rural agricultural town despite all the economic problems of doing so. Dirt roads become a means of town planning for the community. But do not misunderstand these comments: If a newcomer wants to be a collaborative community member in Fairfield, he or she are very much welcomed and will get as much volunteer work as he or she can handle.

These rural attitudes come from the history of the area's settlement. Such history is an important part of sustainable rural development (see Photo 8.1), and so in this case study the following historical detail is provided: Fairfield, about 60 square miles of hardwood forest, was first settled in 1763 and was almost entirely deforested by 1830.

Zadock Thompson (1842) describes the town as "having an uneven surface, but very little of it so broken as to be unfit for cultivation. The soil is good. There are 15 school districts, each with a comfortable school house; 2 churches, one Episcopal and one Congregational; 3 stores; 4 grist mills; 8 saw mills; 2 fueling mills; 1 carding machine; 2 tanneries; 530 horses; 3,636 cattle; 9,700 sheep; 800 swine; 4,270 bushels of wheat; 35 bushels of barley; 7,071 bushels of oats; 718 bushels of rye; 1,770 bushels of buckwheat; 5,685 bushels of Indian Corn; 76,920 bushels of potatoes; 7,765 tons of hay; 71,765 pounds of maple sugar; 24,663 pounds of wool; and a population of 2,448."

Fairfield's population peaked in 1850 at 2,591, reached its lowest point in 1960 at 1,225, and has slowly increased since then. According to the 1990 U.S. Census, Fairfield had a population of 1,680 and 80 working farms, most of which were dairy farms—some producing corn, but little else. There were about 9,000 cows and 100 sheep. Twenty-two percent of those employed listed farming as their primary source of income—mostly dairy farming, with one intrepid sheep farmer. Many families also make maple syrup in spring (which can come any time between February and May).

Farm-derived income, however, is strongly supplemented by off-farm earnings; 60 percent of the employed worked outside Fairfield in the cities of Burlington, Essex Junction, and St. Albans; 3 percent of Fairfield's population lived below poverty level; many women and children used the town primarily as a bedroom community. The children today have less and less connection to the town, and agriculture is no longer part of anyone's formal education. Indeed, a series of interviews of Vermont farm families found that, of the children raised on the farms, few are interested in going into farming, especially dairy farming (Lansdale 1996). Dairy farming, however, is the primary activity that provides the rural landscapes featured in *Vermont Life* magazine and beloved of many if not most Americans. Indeed, the fall 1997 edition features Fairfield, as does the spring 1999 edition of the national *Yankee* magazine. The articles capture all the glorious aspects of rural life. Here we are reminded that most of the "sugaring" (as it is called) takes place using horse-drawn sleds or wheeled wagons to collect the sap from buckets hanging on the maple trees. The Howrigans, seven generations now in town, justify the use of horses with slow comments such as "Well, it's hard to find a tractor that knows which tree comes next." Like most of the sugarmakers, they combine traditional elements of making the syrup with modern techniques. There are many horse teams still in town. People like draft horses. They are typically out on the pastures all year except for the four to six weeks of sugaring in the spring.

The overall socioeconomic base of the town has, however, changed. Few people are traditional homemakers, and fewer still have time to volunteer. Fairfield may be unique in its retention of some fine rural traditions, but it is a typical example of living conditions in an agricultural rural town that are often masked by the popular misperceptions of Vermont.

EPIC used several integrated approaches to rural community development in Fairfield, working with individuals and ad hoc groups to identify their innovative ideas, encourage their work, and provide technical and human resources where possible. The focus was always on opportunities, not problems. Some examples:

- EPIC provided funding for a business plan to be written in order to establish the first coffee shop/bakery in town, now housed in an old, formerly abandoned building. It serves local produce and employs a group of local women who can now work close to home (Photo 8.2).
- EPIC worked with children (students in the sixth through eighth grades) and the town planning commission and zoning board to guide the new town plan, using graduate students in natural resources planning at the University of Vermont as facilitators, but encouraging the voices of the children to be heard and to guide the town planning process (Photo 8.3).
- EPIC asked local people to nominate present or potential leaders from the community to take an in-depth EPIC leadership course.

Photo 8.2. Several rural development projects found that renovating old, abandoned buildings was an important step in community revitalization. Here, an old post office was turned into a bake shop with a small cafe. Run by local women, with local food, it is the only coffee shop for miles, offering meals to take out on the way home in the evening or just a place to catch up on local news.

Photo 8.3. These sixth graders were involved in providing ideas about how they would like the town to plan for use of its natural resources.

- EPIC persuaded farmers to nominate themselves for awards in a project called Barn Again!, which encourages heritage preservation of working barns.
- EPIC encouraged landowners to take holistic resource management seminars.
- EPIC selected demonstration farms for intensive pasture management and farm economic analysis.
- EPIC worked with landowners to identify a more diverse range of natural resource products available from their land.
- EPIC provided environmental indicators for schoolchildren to work with.
- EPIC provided seed grants to small new businesses.
- EPIC helped provide funds a new community center.
- EPIC shared with landowners possible sources of funding for soil conservation.
- EPIC defrayed costs for volunteers wishing to attend workshops on board development, fund-raising, and how to set up or run a nonprofit organization.

One of the spin-offs from the leadership workshops was in the village of East Fairfield. Here, the efforts of a group of EPIC leadership graduates led to the renovation of an abandoned school building in the center of village and to the establishment of the Fairfield Community Center (Photo 1.4). There had been no community meeting place in the town for decades—possibly not since the mid-nineteenth century (discussed in Chapter One).

It is interesting to note here that the women leading the charge, so to speak, were initially mobilized by the idea of a factory taking over what they saw as community space in the center of their rural village at the east end of town. The group was initially formed to oppose an economic development project that they saw as a good idea but in the wrong place. The proposed use of the building accordingly became a catalyst for ideas for better uses of the building. This changed the group's initial negative and antagonistic focus to a positive set of ideas revolving around the concept of a community center.

Challenged to prove their claim to the site (there were many competing interests for this centrally located, large, open space and the building on it), the group not only restored the building and the site, but also transformed it into a hotspot of activity. In the seven years since its formation, the volunteer group has met local needs by offering the Center as a site for regular programs, each run by interconnected but separate small groups, typically run by women.

An example of the use of a seed grant in Fairfield shows that it only takes a small amount of funding—combined with dedication, community spirit, and hard work—to challenge the world. Sarah Kittell requested an EPIC seed grant for a struggling new business: a coffee shop and a bakery, Chester's Bakery (Photo 8.2). There was no other such coffee shop for 20 miles. The last one had collapsed decades ago. Sarah had quit her job as a school nurse in Burlington, tired of driving 700 miles a week from her family home in Fairfield to the South Burlington High School, and was hoping to work closer to home and the community. The seed grant provided limited technical assistance, which contributed to the successful growth of the business. The bakery and coffee shop, which are located next door to the town clerk's office, has since become an important local meeting place where residents can catch up on community news and pick up supper to take home for the family at the end of a busy day. EPIC funded Mrs. Kittell, who demonstrated qualities of a leader and a good entrepreneur. She uses local organic produce and employs local women and teenagers. Rural, community-based, multipurpose businesses like this need some type of nurturing to increase their chances of long-term survival in the broader competitive economic context. Here was an example of both social and economic development occurring simultaneously.

There's a postscript to this story. About three years later, the town decided that this was a much-needed business (the town Selectmen themselves liked to meet there for coffee and pie before meetings), and so the Selectmen permitted Sarah to buy the building instead of continuing to lease it. This further increased her self-confidence, and she was elected state senator from Franklin County. She was appointed to the Senate Agriculture Committee, serving as its Chair only two years later, and, armed with many EPIC contacts in her network, she has many diverse individuals and groups to call on for ideas and information (because Vermont has a citizen legislature, without staff). However, given the time away doing legislative work, something needed to be done to keep the bakery functioning. So now the local women who work there are setting up the business as a cooperative, meaning that there is a sustainable community base for the business.

There are more operating dairy farms in Fairfield than in any other town in the state, by far, and many of these farms are owned and operated by large families, such as the Howrigans and the Branons. The style of agriculture is quite traditional by and large—meaning they still use confinement dairy farming methods—but several dairy farmers have begun to use intensive pasture management and low-input agriculture methods, taking a lead in conserving farmland for future generations. In order to maintain agriculture in a region, it is essential to retain a viable number of farms and to protect their soils. Conservation of farmland is vital in order to assure the necessary agricultural infrastructure, veterinarians, farm products stores, and so forth. Urban encroachment on farmland is not new and tends to occur incrementally for a long time before it is noticed, making farmland protection all the more difficult.

In Fairfield, agricultural conservation has taken place in several ways, most of it indirectly if not directly connected to the EPIC project.

First, in the face of pressure to develop the town as a bedroom community, the citizens used the town plan and zoning ordinances to effectively constrain building to only the village areas. They also vote annually on the number of building permits for new houses, to keep within the planned agricultural carrying capacity of the town. Farming does not provide a huge tax base, especially when school funding, until last year, was linked directly to property taxes. In the mid-1980s, I substantially rewrote the town planning and zoning documents, with support of the town fathers (at that time, I was a resident and volunteer in Fairfield). The intention of the town plan was that it would include the history of settlement of the town in detail as well as a discussion of the cultural history and the physical landscape. The plan has lots of pictures and was intended for easy use and to stimulate thoughtful decision and the type of growth that would help all sectors of the population within the ecological carrying capacity.

Second, and linked to the first, agricultural conservation was likewise encouraged through the purchase of development rights on local farms. The first of these efforts took place in 1991 by farming couple Sonny and Carolyn Boomhower, who worked with the Vermont Land Trust (Photo 8.4) to conserve their farmland as an agricultural land trust. As discussed in Chapter Six, land trusts have become an important tool in farmland conservation. By 1996, the second farm in Fairfield was conserved, and by 1999, twelve of the eighty farms—or 15 percent—were conserved. In each case, land use must remain agricultural. For most of the farm families, this meant turning an unproduc-

Photo 8.4. Sonny and Carolyn Boomhower were the first family in their town to place their family farm in conservation easements to preserve the farm for the future. Within ten years, about ten more farms in town had sold or given their development rights to the same land trust.

tive asset—development rights—into a productive one that provides money to reduce long-term debt, build a new barn, or purchase more land.

The Boomhowers, dairy farmers in the area since 1957, have seven children, thirteen grandchildren, and one great-grandchild; most of their family still live relatively close by. They are independent-minded, hardworking Americans. Although not elected town officials, they could always be relied upon to run the annual community fund-raiser or the spring dance for the school, or to provide help at haying time or if someone's equipment broke down. They always welcomed newcomers, and, since they could not afford to go out, they invited folks over. Filled with curiosity about the world and interested in hearing about innovative ways to work the land and protect farmland, they would ask questions of those of us visiting: "How do they farm and protect farmland in England or New Zealand?" During the late 1970s, they watched newcomers such as the Flack/Richardson family set up intensive pasture management on sheep farms. As a consequence, by the late 1980s the Boomhowers themselves began to experiment with pasture management on their dairy farm, eventually becoming one of the EPIC demonstration farms in the early 1990s. We learned from them and they learned from us.

But life was not easy economically and the Boomhowers struggled to make ends meet. They experimented with low-input agriculture, including intensive grazing. In their desire to have a farm to pass on to their children, they used an idea we had first discussed fifteen years earlier, and, based on a family decision, sold their development rights to the Vermont Land Trust in 1991. Their action was at first derided by other farmers, but the Boomhower's risk-taking not only paid off for their family, but also for the community, which saw eleven more farms in Fairfield doing the same thing over the next six years. As discussed in Chapter Two, innovation takes about twenty years to become part of commonly accepted practice. With 15 percent of the farms conserved in that one town, there is a core of sustainable farmland for the future. The idea, once alien, has become, essentially, "institutionalized."

Of course, life for the Boomhowers is not easy. Carolyn still works thirty hours a week off the farm. The money from purchase of development rights did not pay off all their debt, although it provided family security for the present and future. The pasture management has definitely increased profit margins, with reduced expenses for purchased forage and harvested forage, and their debt load was reduced. Pasture

The following was written by Carolyn Boomhower, published in part in the annual report of the Vermont Land Trust following its annual meeting, which was held in Fairfield, as a "model" town for agricultural conservation.

In 1957, when Sonny and I came as newlyweds to join Sonny's parents on the farm, we were the exception. All of his siblings had left farming to find a better living after a childhood of hardship and deprivation on the family farm. There were few young couples willing to work so hard for so little return. Our neighborhood had a pattern of one occupied farm and two abandoned. Over the course of the first ten years of our life on the farm, we watched as barns and farmhouses fell into their foundations. It was a lonesome time. Luckily, Sonny and I had seven children, who became each other's friends and playmates, and a wonderful farm landscape for their playground. We did not force them to do chores as sometimes happens, so even today, they always come to help when we need it, and, after twenty years off the farm, our oldest son is back working with us. Actually, we have always had some of the children at home helping in some way or another.

In the forty-one years that Sonny and I have been farming, we have seen changes too great for the public to keep up with. We were raised in the horse-powered age. Every farm had one or more teams. Next came secondhand tractors and basic haying equipment, including a side mower, a dump rake, and a field elevator that fed loose hay onto a flatbed wagon, where someone stood and leveled the load with a pitchfork. The hay was unloaded by an overhead fork that ran on tracks suspended from the peak of the barn, and dropped into a "bay," where someone leveled it by hand. All very labor intensive and dependent on sunny weather to ensure a good crop. Cows were milked by hand on the average farm. Farms required many hired hands or the farm children.

By the late 1950s, our family farm had converted to basic motor-powered balers that made square bales of hay. Stacking a wagonload of bales that had to make the journey over rough fields, up hills, and back down without the bales sliding off the wagon was a skill that many of us took great pride in. Milking was done with stainless steel pails suspended from . . . straps around the cows' bodies. Milk was strained and put into stainless steel milk cans that were submerged in ice coolers, later converted to motor-cooled water. The milkman picked up the cans of milk each day to deliver fresh milk to a creamery a few miles from the farm. The stables were cleaned twice a day by hand.

In the late 1960s, bulk tanks and cement floors changed the course of dairy farming forever. Small farms (20 cows or less) couldn't afford the modern changes and so were forced out of business. Farmers who stayed in business absorbed neighboring farms. Farmers formed cooperatives as a means to get a better share of the milk market.

Up to this point, farmers sold their milk to private milk handlers, who paid as little as possible. By the late 1970s, co-ops began to merge to make

(continues)

a more cost-effective milk-handling system. Farmers were advised by banks to devote all their energies and financial resources to solely producing milk.

But something else happened in the 1970s. Fairfield saw an amazing "back to the land" movement, and we were right in the middle of it. The young people were seeking a more simple life (they thought!), so they sought out local farm families to learn from and share with. We welcomed them. This ended forever our isolation and offered our children a window into a world they would not otherwise have had. Twenty-something years later, we live in a busy rural neighborhood.

From the mid-1970s to the mid-1980s, milk prices were in line with the cost of production, so farmers improved their farms and invested in expansion. An overproduction problem emerged when our government was not successful in securing the world market share it was counting on. The price of milk dropped like a rock, as did the price of land. However, our indebtedness stayed the same, and so did the cost of production. Farmers who could negotiate their financing did so hoping for a quick upturn in milk prices. Those who could not were forced out of business. Farmers who survived the crisis were forced to increase their cow numbers significantly to catch up with their indebtedness and the fast-rising cost of production. This trend of high-cost, low-income persisted long enough to have changed the farming landscape forever.

Big farms are becoming the norm. Keeping costs down has become more important than the actual production per cow. We hope there is a future for small, efficient, low-impact farms working beside the high-tech agribusiness farms. Farming will always be a demanding way of life, no matter how it is modernized, but it is still a wonderful place where you can be with your family and community.

management has freed up more time for community interaction. But, unfortunately, manure management to prevent stream pollution forced Sonny and Carolyn, like most Vermont dairy farmers, to have to cost-share construction of a manure pit in recent years. This not only increased debt but also—worse—led to an imbalance in the nutrient cycle (which the regulators had failed to recognize). One needs to walk in their shoes and in those of others like them to better understand the foundations of the rural dilemma and the true price of food production.

Life is not perfect in Fairfield of course, despite the Boomhowers, seed grants, demonstration farms, school children helping with town planning, Barn Again! awards, the farm-development-rights purchases, the new coffee shop in Fairfield Center, new farmhouse bed-and-breakfast accommodations for tourists, leadership workshops, and the community center in East Fairfield. But there does seem to be a renewed spirit in all age groups, and in both men and women, along with greater confidence in the community's ability to maintain the kind of agricultural community that the citizens want and adaptability to meet the demands of urban visitors, residents, and the global marketplace.

Like the Buschkoetters in Nebraska, the Boomhowers will probably work all their lives to maintain the rural landscapes that all Americans can enjoy, preserving farmland and soils for future generations, producing the food we eat, and taking an active role in their community. The spirit of the individual in each of these people is part of the spirit of the whole community. With encouragement, there will be volunteer leaders in the community who will help weave the whole together.

Lessons Learned about Small Town Renewal

The towns discussed in this chapter, in different regions of the country, of different sizes and economic diversity, each have their own unique story. No two towns will be exactly alike, either in the challenges that face them or in the paths they take toward sustainability. However, there are common elements in these towns that others can adapt and certain lessons that can be shared. All of the indicators presented in the opening section of this chapter are present in the three case histories discussed, and the indicators can be useful guides to stimulate thinking by those both inside and outside a rural community.

The indicators should not, however, be viewed as anything but indicators. A community may have all the stress indicators on the list, suggesting a serious or unresolvable set of problems, yet the residents might see their lives in a much more positive vein.

I hesitate to say that Fairfield is a "sustainable community," because "sustainable" is a fragile concept interpreted differently depending on disciplinary perspective and time in the decade. Fairfield does have a renewed community spirit, however, and appears to be sustainable and able to adapt to future changes. Certainly Fairfield is not self-sufficient—it is closely tied to external market economies. I can say that the EPIC model for stimulating rural, community-based development involving many disciplines and perspectives in an integrative manner seems to have been useful in Fairfield. The system approach meant that all aspects of the entire community were touched over the same period of time, but the work was not planned as a great model, nor were the details and steps written beforehand. Serendipity and chance played a large part, and the five-year EPIC effort in Fairfield was built on many years of prior knowledge. The real work was done by the inhabitants, and the story is ongoing.

When asked what they considered important lessons learned, a group of local leaders provided the following observations:

- An individual can make a huge difference.
- Leadership development is a very worthwhile investment.
- Just because a community has many indicators of stress does not mean that all is lost; the trend can be reversed.
- Change is the one thing of which we can be certain and that must be anticipated in community decisions.
- Women play a role in rural development that is so critical to success that it cannot be overstated.
- Children are an underused community resource, and youth leadership programs are an excellent investment.
- Senior citizens have a lot of experience that is underutilized, and there will be more of them over the next few decades.
- Collaboration with "town fathers" can accelerate community development, building tradition into modern trends.
- A systems approach to community development is more likely to have long-term sustainable results than short-term single-issue efforts.
- Communities do need outside resources as catalysts for change, but they must be left to identify their own needs and to tackle them with minimal outside help.
- New or small community groups need simple and inexpensive assistance in such things as board development, fund-raising, and guidance on how to run meetings, but only when the community asks for help.
- The process of community renewal, in its diverse forms, is as important as the results.
- A catalyst, like EPIC, should be seen as innovative, visionary, and creative, but, above all, compassionate.
- Adversity can mobilize a group, but community sustains the effort.
- Volunteer work is an excellent school for citizenship and the strengthening of democracy leadership development within a community.

Chapter Nine

Rural Communities for the Twenty-First Century: Looking Behind the Economic Strengths in America

Although this book does not focus on rural economic development, some mention must be made of the conflicting realities in the economic strength of the United States. The resilience of the U.S. economy in recent years is remarkable; most economists believe that the country has not seen such a strong economy in many decades. In spite of this, issues still exist in rural America that should concern all Americans, as discussion and examples presented in earlier chapters have shown. Urban and rural regions are more interlinked economically and technologically than ever before, with over 25 percent of the urban/suburban populations living in rural regions. Despite the economic strength of the nation as a whole, rural regions have a host of economic problems and associated social and ecological problems.

For both rural and urban populations, there is a desire for a strong rural America. Small, human-scale communities, preserved historic town and village centers, and strong downtowns in rural service centers must somehow be maintained and strengthened. This needs to occur within the reality that Wal-Mart and Home Depot stores do indeed offer cheap commodities affordable to rich and poor alike. To balance everyone's needs while seeking economic diversity requires that locally owned businesses must be maintained along with the national chains.

Farmland conservation is vital, as are constraints on urban sprawl in viable agricultural lands. There is a need to foster research on low-input agriculture and to support family farms and organic agriculture, and to encourage consumption of locally produced food. This must take place within the reality that many rural poor are malnourished even though the United States has agricultural policies that produce the cheapest food in the world. The economics of this food production system are undoubtedly helping to fuel a depression in rural America with fewer, bigger, and more sophisticated farms. Although the overall economy is flourishing and unemployment is at an all-time low, these positive circumstances are not much felt in rural America. The small farm, and the farmer who wishes to provide food with an emphasis on farming methods that improve the ecosystem and to provide humane living conditions for domestic animals, producing *quality of nutrition* rather than volume of commodity, will be hard-pressed to survive without an educated consumer market demanding these more expensive products. Also, we need forest policies that promote ecologically sustainable forests and forest products and provide much-needed forestry management for the millions of acres of tiny, individually owned parcels of forestland in the East.

No single approach or set of policies will be able to address the serious needs of rural America today. Changes must be comprehensive, and several threads must be followed simultaneously. The metaphor of the threadbare fabric in need of patching provides a useful picture for both rural and urban populations. We cannot wait a generation to see if improved education will have taken place. We cannot wait a generation to see if altruism will replace competition. If we are to change policies, we need to change values and attitudes toward the whole environment in which we live and from which we derive our food and all other means of survival. If we can learn about the whole country and its interconnected systems, and if we can try new ways of changing our rural communities learned through lessons shared by others, then the logic of seeking more comprehensive approaches will become more widespread. From this new perspective, clearly seeing the realities of the present, sustainable rural communities may evolve.

Comprehensive Approaches

The diversity of rural America is remarkable in many ways. The natural resource base and settlement history that resulted in the logging and the sawmills of the Northwest contrast with the farming of the Great Plains. There are towns and cities with heavy industry scattered across the breadth of the rural landscapes. In some rural areas, service industry and tourism are less significant than high-tech computer-based industries. In some regions, small, rural communities are a long way from the nearest service center, while others have small service centers scattered more evenly over the region. Thus, each region of America will differ in its priorities. Most Americans do not know a great deal about their rural hinterlands, except perhaps through an occasional vacation. But the visitor tends to see only the surface culture and environment at that moment in time. It is difficult to look behind the preferred vision of rural landscapes.

If sustainable rural development is to take place, we need to more effectively share knowledge about rural America as a system, or as a series of interlocking systems. Rural communities must also be seen as systems that include both human and natural resources as parts of the whole. Fragmentation in education means that most people cannot understand the ecology, economics, agriculture, forestry, history, culture, and so on that make up the whole. It is difficult to teach these concepts and linkages once the fragmentation of education begins to be established in the first few grades. Teachers are often constrained in their work by a school and government system mandating that schools deliver what are essentially social services in addition to standard curricula. Many schools, at all levels, are also disconnected from their local communities, and little experiential education can be taught in the short blocks of time normally allotted for a specific class subject period. Simple changes in educational delivery could be critical. University curricula are often outmoded, with a system of course requirements established many years ago under different parameters. Overhaul in substance and in delivery is long overdue.

Support for truly integrating research with education in institutions of higher education will also need to be much strengthened. The institutional structure, selection process for leaders, and past history of the institution make universities cumbersome and very slow to change. But, since they are largely responsible for teaching our teachers, the cycle is difficult to break. Those working on education reform can easily get caught up in the same old linear thinking and simply tinker with the present system instead of standing back and perhaps starting again with a different set of concepts. This frustration is certainly reflected in the flurry of charter schools nationwide and the inability of professors to keep students' attention in Friday classes. I contend that the rewards for rural communities and society as a whole will be great if comprehensive change is implemented.

Add to this the enormity of problems faced in urban American schools or in regional rural high schools, where one or two or three thousand children under the age of eighteen are crowded into buildings filled with conflict, frustration, and danger. These schools are often larger than the total population of the towns in which the children live. I contend that children under the age of eighteen should, regardless of rural or urban location, be taught in small schools of never more than 500, and more typically 150, children. This can help build community. Every person will be able to be on the softball team or have a chance at a scholarship. All the rural development work that I have seen, taken part in, or led in several countries has indicated that people like to be praised, meet face to face, have fun, share food together, learn about their home areas, learn how it all works, and develop a sense of belonging. This can only happen in small schools that are connected with the local community.

Children deserve to be taught in schools that are rooted in communities and to learn about their immediate neighborhoods and the region around it, about their ancestors, and about the environment and natural resources that give them life. They need to learn the wisdom of the elders both literally and metaphorically if they are to be able to develop an understanding of the whole of land, air, water, and the role that we play in the use of these resources. Here, one can see a principle of rural development that is respect for the past and respect for others. This is a principle that children need to hear in the classroom and to learn through outdoor experience. In such a community setting, children and youth can undertake projects with town planners, municipal officers, hospitals, and farmers and not be isolated from reality in classroom settings. The several seed grants in communities demonstrated the synergistic benefits for the children, adults, and the community as a system.

Sustaining a Continually Changing Process

Rural areas of the nation are changing. Change is undoubtedly the only thing of which we can be sure. Thus, an adaptable, flexible approach must be taken. Programs must be such that there is continual education of a new cadre of leaders at the most grassroots level, so that as they progress and gain skills and confidence, they can move to higher levels in the system. It takes a generation of training and education to build cohorts of competent leaders, not only the traditional Out-front Leader who has a "take-charge" mode of operating, but also the Servant Leader and the Transformational Leader. The ability to blend humor with humility will be an important characteristic of the modern rural leader.

Here is where the need to encourage more women and senior citizens to take leadership roles is needed, along with leadership by youth in community settings. There must also be a concerted effort to involve the disenfranchised in a collaborative manner. Such continuous investment in leadership development is critical, especially inasmuch as it is easier to run leadership courses than to change a university and the educational system. Understanding and using the community resources of people is absolutely critical for rural communities in the twenty-first century.

Sustaining rural communities demands that more citizens learn about agriculture, farming, natural resource conservation, and forestry and that they become involved. Leadership courses that focus in these areas will help, but again, schools must also be involved.

Sustainability requires a compassion for future generations and the humility to set aside some of our needs in anticipation of theirs. This cannot be done individually. The synergy that comes from community-based and community-driven projects permits a much longer-term effect. Furthermore, although no two rural communities are identical, I have found that there is more similarity between communities than one might imagine. Thus, it is worthwhile to explore what other rural communities have tried, looking at what has worked and what has not.

There needs to be an increased connection between urban and rural societies, and economic development needs to be targeted toward new value-added products, green certification, organic foods, and other market niches not yet fully explored. And rather than competing with each other, communities within a region need to collaborate more.

Conservation, Human Health, and Environment

Merely being a good steward of the land and its resources is not good enough; the steward must endeavor to control the resources. Even where the steward does a fine job of this, there will always be the underlying feeling that we are "managers" of these natural resources. The more we have learned from science, such as ecology and related fields, over the last several decades, the more we find that humans are only a part of the environment—not in charge of it. Our health depends upon our developing a more humble perspective on the conservation of natural resources and environmental protection, because, as we learn about bioaccumulation and biomagnification, the production of healthy food becomes more complex. Closer attention must therefore be paid to toxic pollution, and far more strenuous efforts must be made to provide adequate monitoring of pollutant outputs into our air, land, and water, to identify levels of potentially dangerous chemicals in food, and to assess the human health implications of our actions. Rural development is part of these interconnected systems.

Policy changes to address these broader perspectives on sustainable rural communities are needed nationally, regionally, and at most local levels. It is of paramount importance that we not allow ourselves to become overwhelmed by the magnitude of the problems facing us. "Think globally but act locally" is a wise and useful adage. Local communities can work to identify indicators in their own community and to share their efforts with others. When more people, urban and rural, demand that attention be paid to rural regions, national politicians, in the face of intense pressure, may be willing to take up the task of fully investing in rural communities.

The Role of Foundations, Governments, Universities, and Other Institutions

These policies will require institutions to make them work that are flexible, responsive, and adaptable at local levels. These institutions must also be able to function within the context of comprehensive regional policies in aspects such as trade, transportation, health care, and natural resources.

Institutions have an important role to play in rural development, both directly in terms of the technical and financial assistance that they may supply and also in the tone or the atmosphere that they present to the community. These organizations tend to reflect the present values of society, and their leadership will influence trends in rural communities. Rural community members must have some confidence that they can affect policy changes in the major institutions. For example, foundations, governments, and other institutions should try to better understand what is taking place in rural communities and provide small but sustained amounts of funding to rural areas. These must be sustained over a period of about fifteen to twenty years if the necessary radical changes are to take place and lead to sustainable rural communities in the United States. These institutions must also search more diligently for the local innovators and provide assistance in moving new ideas forward more quickly.

Sustainable Rural Community Development—Synthesis and Conclusions

Rural development is not a new idea, but the addition of the evolving concepts of *sustainability* and *community* is relatively new and not necessarily clearly understood. This book has presented a range of perspectives and lessons learned from a comprehensive approach to rural development that are grounded in ecological principles and sustainable concepts and that engage the community in such a manner that projects became community-based and community-driven. Can the above four words—sustainable, rural, community, and development—be clarified so that they do not merely sound like cute jargon?

Sustainable does not mean self-sufficient. It does not mean a fixed state of harmony. It does not mean a state of homeostasis. Sustainability means that the community as a whole is conserving resources for future generations and adapting to change locally and globally. Rural communities in the United States are part of a global system, and this trend will only intensify in the next millennium. Sustainability is a concept rooted in ecology. Thus the sustainable community will have analyzed its systems of resource use, production, and waste so that it builds rather than destroys or reduces ecological capacity. This in turn will build carrying capacity for more people in future generations.

Rural means not only the wide, open spaces, rolling farmlands, and forestlands with small, often widely dispersed settlements across America (Photo 9.1), but also it includes those urban and suburban communities that exist within regions classified as "rural" and that provide services to the broader rural regions. The links between urban and rural need to be understood more clearly (and strengthened), and the line between urban and rural must be viewed as the ecotone zone that it is. Of significance here is also the acceptance of the fact that while there are some kinds of isolation within rural areas and from surrounding urban areas, there are in reality more connections than ever before. These can be strengths as well—built for mutual benefit.

Community means many things: the physical settlement (town or village), the school, the religious center, the community center, and just that sense you feel when you "belong." All of these aspects of commu-

Photo 9.1. Our preferred vision of a rich rural landscape.

nity should be the hallmark of successful rural development. Rural communities and small towns deserve to be viable entities with full engagement of the people who live there—people committed to providing a balanced and practical legacy for their children and grandchildren, a place where everyone is made to feel welcome and to have a role to play.

Development is much more than only economic development. It includes bettering the lives of people who make their living in rural areas and not just of those who retire or vacation there. Development also includes accommodating the needs of those who live in rural areas but work elsewhere. It must be comprehensive in its processes, addressing traditional economic needs as well as new prospects. It may include decisions not to grow as well as decisions to grow. Development must be undertaken in a manner appropriate to the ecology and to the human culture of the local community and should anticipate the needs of future generations and their ecosystems.

The EPIC model of rural development is built on ten elements that frame a basic approach to such development. The essence of these elements is that the development process begins through a participatory process in the community. The community establishes the vision and sets priorities, drawing around the table a collaborative group that includes women, youth, seniors, and the previously disenfranchised. Systems thinking and innovation are encouraged as goals are set and capacity building begins. Goals are constantly assessed and modified as lessons are learned and shared by all in an open and accessible manner. The EPIC model is transferable in parts and in the whole with adaptation of mechanisms used as culturally and ecologically appropriate.

The EPIC model, informed by the work of others in other rural regions, led to the formulation of its Key Principles of Sustainable Rural Development, outlined in Chapter One and demonstrated through a diverse set of rural development approaches provided throughout the text. These principles must all be present in order for sustainable development to be possible in a community. The principles include community empowerment and a strengthened democracy in which the urban-rural linkages are clearly fostered; innovation is encouraged and supported; systems thinking pervades all community actions as collaborating participants seek leverage points to spur synergistic improvements in many facets of life; youth are involved in community endeavors to assure future sustainability; and the empowerment of women is treated as critical to success.

There are many mechanisms that can be used to attain sustainable rural community development for those who wish to be involved. Those working in development should never lose sight of the inherent complexities of rural communities, nor be overwhelmed by the complexity. There are risks to be taken. The long-term benefits both for rural communities and for society as a whole will be well worth the effort. So let's rededicate ourselves to helping revitalize rural America. And now, back to work!

Sample Forestry Leadership Program

The PRIMARY GOAL of the Forestry Leadership Program is to enhance community leaders' abilities to respond to complex natural resource issues, specifically forestry-related problems, using leadership skills and research and by building on a community network for support.

The curriculum is based on forestry-related rural revitalization issues. It is flexible and can be adapted for use with a variety of adult learners. The model includes the development of a Steering Committee to guide the process and to include the learner in the decision-making process.

The PURPOSE of the Forestry Leadership Program is to expand the pool of community leaders who will become increasingly involved in a broad range of forestry-related issues.

Objectives

Participants will

- Develop an understanding of the social, economic, political, and cultural issues important to public decision making.
- Understand the way various levels of government function and how to affect that process.
- Increase individual and group ability to participate in the resolution of public policy issues.

Modified from Lois M. Frey, VT Extension, FLP, Cycle Two, 1992.

- Understand the various methods of decision making and how to implement those methods.
- Enhance communication, group process, and leadership skills.
- Learn to find, assess, and utilize the extensive resources available.
- Increase understanding of the public policy process.

The PHILOSOPHY of the Forestry Leadership Program is that participants be able integrate personal experience and skill with new information, methods, and techniques.

DELIVERY options include a series of workshops developed by a planning committee using the following basic components:

- *Libertyville* is a creative simulation that allows participants to see how communities work.
- *Creating Personal Power* is designed to assist leaders with a variety of individual leadership skills.
- *Group Development* is designed to show how groups work and how to work effectively in group situations.
- *Community Issues* will offer an "ECO System" approach to show the interrelated nature of public issues: natural, technological, and regulatory.
- *Resource Data* is available for public and private use. Access and appropriate use of these materials can assist decision makers.

These delivery options will be determined by the project's Steering Committee, which includes some of the participants nominated and selected, in order to help reach the needs of the entire group of participants. Note: It is very important for long-term success that the Steering Committee be flexible in adapting the program to the needs of the participants.

Who Will Be Selected to Participate?

The Forestry Leadership Program will use an innovative participatory process, centered on a Project Steering Committee, to identify and recruit people who

- Are committed to resolving rural problems.
- Want to work with others, who want to learn from and share with others.
- Are committed to community approaches to problem solving.

- Are committed to addressing natural resource problems.
- Will commit the time *now* to attend all the sessions required of them and will be actively involved in the program.

The program is similar to the EPIC leadership model and includes multiple training sessions that will cover a variety of leadership competencies, including personal leadership, group process, issue analysis, public policy process, and volunteerism. The program will offer a blend of content, process, and experience aimed at developing leadership skills and enhancing an understanding of forestry-related issues.

Program EVALUATION is an essential part of every leadership workshop series. This is accomplished in several ways, as determined by the Steering Committee, using both written evaluation and oral interviews of individuals and in group meetings.

Community Leadership Program: Stewardship of the Urban Landscape

This program is designed for people who want to

- Gain skills for working effectively within community groups and local government, including public speaking, group dynamics, and using the media.
- Learn how to improve urban landscapes and community forestry resources in their towns.
- Improve their ability to advocate and care for street trees and forests.
- Expand their access to resource information and technical assistance.
- Commit a few hours a week for twelve weeks to learn techniques to improve their community's economic, social, and environmental quality.

Forty hours of training will be offered to 25 people through:

- Weekly meetings in Randolph from 7 to 9:30 p.m. on Thursdays, February 5 through April 23.
- Saturday retreats on February 14 and April 25.

Lois M. Frey, University of Vermont Cooperative Extension

Date & Topic	U & C Forestry Competencies	Possible Lecturers: Names and Expertise
February 5	Introduction	Benefits of trees to communities; Community tree programs
February 14 (Saturday retreat)	Libertyville	Relevant community tree issues integrated into program

(continues)

Date & Topic	U & C Forestry Competencies	Possible Lecturers: Names and Expertise
February 19	Tree Biology	How trees grow; What trees need; Assessing urban conditions, site limitations; Selected tree species for region
February 26	Urban Stress on Trees	Environmental and human factors; Diseases and pests; Construction impacts
March 5	Tree Maintenance	Annual inspections; Water, mulch, control weeds, and fertilize; Pruning for safety, health, and appearance
March 12	Tree Inventories	Defining objectives; Legal issues of ownership; Selecting a method for your town
March 19	Shade Tree Committees	Forming a committee; Building your team; Define mission, goals, and objectives; Types of committees; Fund-raising
March 26	Who Are the Stakeholders?	Start at your town offices: town leaders, tree warden, town employees, and committees; Working with tree professionals; Involving your neighbors and local businesses
April 2	Landscape Design	Plant with a purpose; Dealing with the obstacles: sidewalks, signs, utilities, lighting
April 9	Planting Projects	Time line for spring planting; Selecting quality plants; Native vs. nonnative plants
April 16	Gearing Up for Arbor Day	Basics of proper planting; After the trees are planted
April 25 (Saturday)	Commencement	Hands-on experience; All participants

Sample: Stewardship of the Urban Landscape: Community Leadership Program Final Project

Project

Choose a community forestry project that is meaningful for you and your community from the list below (or propose another project idea). Working individually or with a few other members of the class, implement the project and prepare to describe it for the class at our final retreat on April 25th. In your presentation, consider including descriptions of

- The community forestry problem that you are attempting to address.
- The process of developing your project.
- The resources you used.
- Future outcomes of your work.
- Collaboration and communication you developed with town officers or residents.
- Contacts you made with any of the course presenters to gather information or ideas.

Purpose
- To provide a structured opportunity to develop real experience with a community tree project.
- To integrate concepts and skills from the course.
- To expand your knowledge base for a particular tree issue.

• To practice using techniques of public speaking, including using props and visual aids.

(This project is *not* intended to take excessive amounts of time. Choose something that interests you and is manageable.)

Project Topics

1. Research and prepare a document, public comment, or short speech for a public meeting (e.g., select board/city council, planning commission) with a particular request or outcome in mind (e.g., change in town tree or road maintenance policy, funding for tree care or planting, change in town forest management).
2. Create a checklist for your local planning commission or development review board to use when evaluating a proposed development to ensure there are no adverse effects on town trees.
3. Review current town plans and relevant ordinances to identify gaps in tree protection and opportunities to improve protection of trees (e.g., develop a tree ordinance). Develop a fact sheet to distribute to town officers and others to promote your proposal.
4. Write and submit a letter to the editor of a local newspaper, taking a position or seeking to inform the community about a tree-related issue.
5. Cultivate a relationship with a local newspaper in order to promote a feature story on a tree issue in your community or region. Research the issue, bring in "experts" and technical resources, define key messages, and share with news staff.
6. Plan a panel discussion for a community access television program. Define themes, find panelists, gather visual aids, and identify a moderator.
7. Work with a local radio station to develop a public service announcement about a tree issue or a tree program. Draft a script, develop any necessary audio backup, practice timing, record it, and bring to the station. Follow up to find out if the announcement was played and whether the station received any feedback from listeners.
8. Using the "Trees for Local Communities" grant proposal guidelines (or other relevant grant-maker), write a proposal to fund a community tree project (e.g., inventory, planning, planting, maintenance).

9. Create an exhibit or photo-essay display to be placed at town hall, local schools, or local events.
10. Develop a slide show or presentation to bring to area schools or meetings of local organizations.
11. Develop a "speakers bureau" of local and regional resource people who are knowledgeable about trees and community forestry. Create a listing of speakers and their areas of expertise and set out policies for contacting speakers (i.e., paying for fees or travel, advance notice). Be sure to contact speakers yourself to confirm their willingness to participate. Distribute listing to schools and community groups.
12. Plan and promote a tree-related workshop in your community.
13. Work with a local school to organize an Arbor Day tree-planting event or participate in the Arbor Day poster contest.
14. Survey members of your community about community forestry concerns or projects they would support. Determine information needed and the best data-gathering method.
15. Design and/or implement a tree inventory (village trees, roadside trees, big trees, significant trees) to document the status of your community forest.
16. Plant a tree in your community. Select a species and work out a budget. Solicit the donation of a nursery tree or tree work from local nurseries or landscaping companies. Publicize a tree planting ceremony. Get the tree in the ground and create a maintenance plan.

Sample Goals for Farmers Forming a New Local/Community Organization

The following set of recommendations was developed by a group of farmers and others with expertise in grazing. They identified a set of activities for the continued promotion of grass-based farming and then set priorities. They based their recommendations on their experience and the experience of other farmers worldwide.

Goal 1. Form local farmer discussion groups to share information and ideas on grazing issues.

The committee felt that this was the most important activity. They identified two different kinds of discussion groups, both functioning at a local/community level.

Open Group. This group, called an *open* group, provides informal opportunities for new graziers and others with an interest in grass-based farming practices to attend pasture walks, field days, and other special events several times a year. These larger groups would disseminate general information about grazing without focusing too much on specific management issues. Those with a desire to learn more would be encouraged to join or start a *focused* group.

Focused Group. This group is smaller in size (6 to 12 farmers) and more tightly focused on topics common to the interests of individual farmers. Building trust, friendship, and a sense of community among members is a goal common to each focused group.

Focused groups meet once or twice a month, with meetings moving from farm to farm so that every member has a chance to host a pasture walk at least once a year. New members are admitted to groups through a consensus process. As interest grows and the groups begin to grow beyond their optimum size, experienced members provide the leadership to start new groups.

Although focused groups may be the more powerful tool for promoting change, both open and focused groups have a place in the region. Farmers new to grazing will need an entry point for advice and information. Experienced graziers need a stable forum in which to share their expertise, seek guidance, sharpen management skills, and support one another. Farmer discussion groups can fill all these needs.

To start a *focused* group:

Gather over refreshments at someone's farm. Have a pasture walk before the discussion. Focus on issues important to the host farm. Select two facilitators for the next meeting. Encourage group members to seek facilitator training if they wish.

Goal 2. Develop a systematic approach to understanding economics and profitability.

Profitability is one of the primary reasons that farmers adopt grass-based management practices. Currently, it is difficult for producers to make economic comparisons between individual operations. There is a need for a standardized format that farmers could use to track profitability and compare numbers.

Graziers need to work together to develop a farm accounting format that serves multiple financial needs (i.e., monthly cash-flow statements, annual profit/loss, tax records). Agricultural lenders and others involved in farm finances should also be included in this process.

Goal 3. Establish a series of farm demonstration sites throughout the state.

Because firsthand experience is a good learning tool, an on-farm demonstration program should be started that will allow individual producers to use and experiment with different grass-based management practices. Demonstration sites are an excellent resource to show farmers and others the benefits of grazing. Participatory research and demonstration programs have been used effectively throughout the United States to facilitate cooperation between farmers and university researchers.

Goal 4. Form a new farmer organization to manage and oversee grazing outreach and education programs in the state.

Assistance in coordinating and facilitating communication between groups and individuals was a major need identified by the ad hoc committee. Although most information sharing and educational programming could be done at the local level through open and focused groups, it was felt that there would be an ongoing role for a designated entity to assist in these efforts.

A new, statewide, nonprofit graziers association should be formed to provide leadership training and organizing assistance to local community groups with a staff member hired to carry out these tasks. It was strongly felt that this new group needed to be a stand-alone organization, not part of a university, extension, agency, or other established institution. The new organization should have responsibility for outreach personnel. The organization should be a collaborative model, with program support and participation from other state groups, agencies, and institutions that have an interest in the use and promotion of grass-based farming.

Goal 5. Simplicity and sustainability should be key principles integrated into all programming.

Administration of the new organization should be as uncomplicated as possible and not wholly dependent on outside funding. Programs and technical assistance made available to community groups should be easy to manage and with few strings attached. The focus should always be on grassroots involvement and farmer leadership.

Program Assessment

This appendix provides a template for assessing the effectiveness of a recently completed series of community leadership workshops. Some of the lessons learned that are discussed in the text were developed through collecting information from participants using surveys similar to the generic format following below. This mechanism was not the only means of assessment—individual interviews and focus groups were also conducted to provide added depth and to provide a check on the results of the survey.

The goal here is not to have a perfect research instrument but to have a useful tool that can be easily adapted and used by community members on a regular basis. By conducting regular assessments of the impact of leadership workshops, the facilitators and community leaders are better able to adjust their leadership program to more effectively meet local needs. In addition, the assessment can provide useful, sometimes tangential information for others in the community who are engaged in some related aspects of rural community development. The following template is for communities to modify for local use; no prior permission is required to replicate, modify, and use these generic templates.

EPIC/Forestry Leadership Program

Now that the EPIC/Forestry Leadership Program has reached the end of its first phase, we would like your help in assessing how successful the project has been. Please answer the following questions and send this form to us in the enclosed envelope.

Developed by Lois Frey, University of Vermont Cooperative Extension.

When we refer to "community leadership," we mean any of the ways that you are working to improve the health of your community (as you define it). Feel free to use the "comment" sections to write down any additional information or to express any opinions that the questions don't directly address.

1. When you applied to the EPIC/Forestry Leadership Program, you indicated that you were involved in some aspect of community leadership (e.g., serving on a local board, active in a social service organization, member of an advocacy group). *Since your completion of the Leadership course,* how have the following aspects of your community leadership changed?

   a. The number of ways in which you take on community leadership (e.g., the number of organizations you participate in, the number of positions you hold, the types of leadership activities you engage in)
   __increased   Comments:
   __stayed the same
   __decreased

   b. The amount of time you dedicate to community leadership activities (e.g., the number of hours per week, or days per month)
   __increased   Comments:
   __stayed the same
   __decreased

   c. The number of people in your community with whom you interact through your leadership activities
   __increased   Comments:
   __stayed the same
   __decreased

2. What organizations or groups do you participate in now?

3. Within the organizations or groups that you participate in, how have the following aspects of the group's ability to work together changed since your completion of the Leadership course?

   a. Ease of arriving at decisions
   __improved   Comments:
   __stayed the same
   __diminished

b. Involvement of group members (e.g., the percentage of the people in the group who participate actively in discussions or take on responsibilities)
__improved   Comments:
__stayed the same
__diminished

c. Ability to deal with or minimize confrontation or conflict among group members
__improved   Comments:
__stayed the same
__diminished

d. Your satisfaction with decision outcomes
__improved   Comments:
__stayed the same
__diminished

e. Your satisfaction with how decisions are made
__improved   Comments:
__stayed the same
__diminished

4. What was the most useful concept or skill that you gained from the Leadership course?

5. In your community leadership work, which of the following tools and techniques did you use prior to and since completing the Leadership course? (Check all that apply)

	Used prior to course	Use since course
Public presentations	_____	_____
Participation in public meetings	_____	_____
Radio (e.g., PSAs, interviews)	_____	_____
Newspapers (e.g., press releases, editorials)	_____	_____
Television appearances	_____	_____
Research tools (e.g., surveys, literature searches, public documents)	_____	_____
Networks (i.e., information, services, support, access)	_____	_____
Coalitions (i.e., partnership with other groups)	_____	_____

Nominal Group Process _____ _____

6. How have the following aspects of your community leadership changed since your completion of the Leadership course?

    a. Your effectiveness in creating change in your community
       __increased   Comments:
       __stayed the same
       __decreased

    b. The personal satisfaction you gain from your community leadership work
       __increased   Comments:
       __stayed the same
       __decreased

    c. The ability of the groups you work with to stimulate and sustain the interest and involvement of other community members
       __increased   Comments:
       __stayed the same
       __decreased

    d. Your understanding of the context of your community leadership work
       __improved   Comments:
       __stayed the same
       __diminished

    e. Your impact on local policy making (i.e., through participation in community meetings or influencing the decisions of local officials)
       __increased   Comments:
       __stayed the same
       __decreased

    f. Your ability to understand the perspective and motivations of other community members who disagree with your positions
       __improved   Comments:
       __stayed the same
       __diminished

    g. Your understanding of the goals of your community leadership work
       __improved   Comments:

___stayed the same
___diminished

7. Since your completion of the Leadership course, how has your community leadership work affected the following aspects of your community's health?

	Greatly improved	Somewhat improved	Slightly improved	Not at all improved
Natural environment	1	2	3	4
Agriculture	1	2	3	4
Local government	1	2	3	4
Youth development	1	2	3	4
Family health	1	2	3	4
Business community	1	2	3	4
Community involvement/ sense of community	1	2	3	4

Comments:

8. What are some spin-offs or long-term effects of your participation in the Leadership course?

9. What further types of leadership training do you wish were available to you?

10. Please list any other parts of the EPIC project that you have heard of.

11. In what ways could a second phase of the EPIC project help you to continue and improve your work?

Signature (optional)

Possible Project-Level Evaluation Activities

Preproject

- Assess needs and assets of target population/community.
- Specify goals and objectives of planned service/activities.
- Describe how planned services/activities will lead to goals.
- Identify what community resources will be needed and how they can be obtained.
- Determine the match between project plans and community priorities.
- Obtain input from stakeholders.
- Develop an overall evaluation strategy.

Start-Up

- Determine underlying program assumptions.
- Develop a system for obtaining and presenting information to stakeholders.
- Assess feasibility of procedures given the actual number of staff and amount of funds.
- Assess the data that can be gathered from routine project activities.
- Develop a data-collection system, if doing so will answer desired questions.
- Collect baseline data on key outcome and implementation areas.

W.K. Kellogg Foundation Evaluation Handbook, 1998.

Implementation and Project Modification

- Assess organizational processes or environmental factors that are inhibiting or promoting project success.
- Describe project and assess reasons for changes from original implementation plan.
- Analyze feedback from staff and participants about successes/failures, and use this information to modify the project.
- Provide information on short-term outcomes for stakeholders/decision makers.
- Use short-term outcome data to improve the project.
- Describe how you expect short-term outcomes to affect long-term outcomes.
- Continue to collect data on short- and long-term outcomes.
- Assess assumptions about how and why the program works; modify as needed.

Maintenance and Sustainability

- Share findings with community and with other projects.
- Inform alternative funding sources about accomplishments.
- Continue to use evaluation to improve the project and to monitor outcomes.
- Continue to share information with multiple stakeholders.
- Assess long-term impact and implementation lessons, and describe how and why program works.

Replications and Policy

- Assess project fit with other communities.
- Determine critical elements of the project that are necessary for success.
- Highlight specific contextual factors that inhibited or facilitated project success.
- As appropriate, develop strategies for sharing information with policy makers to make relevant policy changes.

Sample Seed Grant Evaluation
Format for Written Responses

Date:
Town:
Contact person:
Address/Phone:

1. Project title and brief description: *(What did you set out to do? In what ways did the project meet your expectations, and in what ways was it different from what you expected? Please make note of any changes that may have occurred in your budget or expenses.)*
2. Transferable lessons: *(What did you or your group learn from this process? For example, if you were to do it again, what would you do the same, and what would you do differently? What advice would you give to another group about to start a similar project elsewhere?)*
3. Where to from here? *(What are the spin-offs for long-term effects of your project, whether in your group, your community, or your life?)*
4. Documentation or publicity: *(If you wish, please attach photos, letters of support, or any other materials that will help give us a feeling for your project. Be sure to include any newsletter, newspaper, or other media coverage your project may have received.)*
5. Advice for EPIC: *(Do you have any feedback or suggestions for EPIC to help us do our job better?)*

Return this form and attachments to EPIC,
at the address above. Thank you!
Question? Please be in touch! Call Susan Clark,
EPIC Coordinator

Approaches to Interviewing

When assessing rural development efforts to determine outcomes or to make midcourse adjustments, it is often important to conduct an interview. There is no perfect format, but here are four different interviews, each with its own characteristics, strengths, and weaknesses. Communities may choose to use several approaches, depending on the overall intent of the interviews.

Type of Interview	Characteristics	Strengths	Weaknesses
Informal Conversational Interview	Questions emerge from immediate context and are asked in the natural course of things; there are no predetermined questions, topics, or wordings.	Increases the salience and relevance of questions; interviews are built on and emerge from observations; the interview can be matched to individuals and circumstances.	Different information collected from different people with different questions. Less systematic and comprehensive if certain questions do not arise "naturally." Data organization and analysis can be quite difficult.
Interview Guide Approach	Topics and issues to be covered are specified in advance in outline form; interviewer decides sequence and wording of questions in the course of the interview	The outline increases the comprehensiveness of the data and makes data collection somewhat systematic for each respondent. Logical gaps in data can be anticipated and closed. Interviews remain fairly conversational and situational.	Important and salient topics may be inadvertently omitted. Interviewer flexibility in sequencing and wording questions can result in substantially different responses from different perspectives, thus reducing the comparability of responses.

(continues)

Type of Interview	*Characteristics*	*Strengths*	*Weaknesses*
Standardized Open-Ended Interview	The exact wording and sequence are specified in advance. All interviewees are asked the same questions in the course of the interview.	Respondents answer the same questions, thus increasing comparability of responses; data are complete for each person on the topics addressed in the interview. Reduces interviewer effects and bias when several interviewers are used. Permits evaluation users to see and review the instrumentation used in the evaluation. Facilitates organization and analysis of the data.	Little flexibility in relating the interview to particular individuals and circumstances; standardized wording of questions may constrain and limit naturalness and relevance of questions and answers.
Close-Field Response Interview	Questions and response categories are determined in advance. Respondent chooses from among these fixed responses.	Data analysis is simple; responses can be directly compared and easily aggregated; many questions can be asked in a short time.	Respondents must fit their feelings into the experiences and researcher's categories; may be perceived as impersonal, irrelevant, and mechanistic. Can distort what respondents really mean or have experienced by so completely limiting their response choices.

Source: Patton 1990.

Appendix C

Resources and Organizations

The following is a listing of local, regional, and national organizations that may be able to provide data, information, ideas of possible sources for funding local projects and contacts with other organizations or individuals. It is not a complete listing, but it does provide resource information from many different perspectives that affect rural America.

1000 Friends of Oregon
Editor
Publications
300 Williamette Bldg.
534 Third Avenue, SW
Portland, OR 97204
Phone: (503) 223-4396

Abya Yala News
Leticia Valdez
Administrative Coordinator
South and Meso American Indian
Rights Center
1714 Franklin St., 3rd Floor
Oakland, CA 94612
Phone: (510) 834-4263

Action for Better Community/CTWO
David Portillo
Newsletter/Public Information
12019 Santa Fe
Denver, CO 80204
Phone: (303) 893-9710

Alaska Center for the Environment
Kevin Harvin, Executive Director
Newsletter
519 W. 8th, Suite 201
Anchorage, AK 99501
Phone: (907) 272-3621

Alaska Health Project Newsletter
Carl Hild
Executive Director
1818 W. Northern Lights Blvd., #103
Anchorage, AK 99517
Phone: (907) 276-2864

Alliance for Transportation and Research Institute
University of New Mexico
1001 University Boulevard, Suite 10
Albuquerque, NM 87106-4342
Phone: (505) 246-6410
Fax: (505) 246-6001

American Forum for Global Education
120 Wall Street, Suite 2600
New York, NY 10005
Phone: (212) 742-8232
Fax: (212) 742-8752

American Friends Service Community for TX, AR, OK
Luz Guerra
Newsletter/Public Information
227 Congress Ave., Suite 200
Austin, TX 78701
Phone: (512) 474-2399

Appalachia
Editor
Appalachian Regional Commission
1666 Connecticut Ave., NW
Washington, DC 20009

Applied Sustainability Enterprises
formerly Global Tomorrow Coalition
1200 G Street, NW, Suite 800
Washington, DC 20005
Phone: (202) 434-8783
Fax: (202) 532-2862

Arizona Toxics Information
Michael Gregory
Newsletter
P.O. Box 1896
Bisbee, AZ 85603
Phone: (602) 432-5374

Arkansas Public Interest Research Group
Larry Froelich, Director
Newsletter
P.O. Box 441
Johnson, AR 72701
Phone: (501) 521-3939

Asian Immigrant Women Advocates
Newsletter
Helen Kim
310 8th St., #301
Oakland, CA 94607
Phone: (510) 268-0192

Association of Leadership Educators (ALE)
23320 West Peterson Ave., Suite 200
University of Illinois
Chicago, IL 60659
Phone: (773) 761-5099
Fax: (773) 761-6995
e-mail: wilson@idea.ag.uiuc.edu

Association of Vermont Conservation Commissions
HC32 Box 36 Adamant, VT 05640
Phone: (802) 223-5527
e-mail: ilovermont@aol.com

Ban Waste Coalition
Newsletter/Public Information
2760 Golden Gate
San Francisco, CA 94118
Phone: (415) 752-8678

Blueprint for Social Justice
Editor
Twomey Center for Peace through Justice
Loyola University
Box 12, 6363 St. Charles Ave.
New Orleans, LA 70118-6195

California Communities Against Toxics/CCAT
Bill Buck, Coordinator
Newsletter/Public Information
P.O. Box 471990
San Francisco, CA 94147
Phone: (415) 474-7423

Capsules
Editor
Southern Rural Development Center
P.O. Box 5446
Mississippi State, MS 39762-5446

Caring Magazine
Heather Dittbrenner
519 C Street NE
Washington, DC 20002
Phone: (202) 547-7424

Carver Hills Neighborhood Association
Newsletter
Arnold D. Weathersby Sr.
P.O. Box 93947
Atlanta, GA 30377
Phone: (404) 799-5382

Center for Citizen Advocacy
73 Spring Street #206
New York, NY 10012
Phone: (212) 431-3922

Center for Community Advocacy
Vanessa W. Vallerta, Esq.
Executive Director
Newsletter/Public Information
9 W. Gabilan St., #12
Salinas, CA 93901
Phone: (408) 753-2324

Center for Environmental Education
Blueprint for a Green School
400 Columbus Avenue
Valhalla, NY 10595
Phone: (914) 747-4800
Fax: (914) 747-8299

Center for Neighborhood Technology
2125 W. North Avenue
Chicago, IL 60647
Phone: (312) 278-4800
Fax: (312) 278-3840
www.cnt.org/TNW/

Center for Rural Studies
Fred Schmidt, Director
College of Agriculture and Life
Sciences
University of Vermont
207 Morrill Hall
Burlington, VT 05405
www.uvm.edu./~cdae/crs

Center for Sustainable Agriculture
590 Main Street
University of Vermont
Burlington, VT 05405
Phone: (802) 656-0037
Fax: (802) 257-0112
e-mail: kduesterberg@zoo.uvm.edu
www.uvm.edu/~susagctr

Center for Sustainable Living, Inc.
Route 1, Box 107
Shenandoah Junction, WV 25442
Phone: (304) 876-0740
Fax: (304) 876-2783

Center for the New West
Robert Wurmstedt
Communications Director
600 World Trade Center
1625 Broadway
Denver, CO 80202-4706

Centro De Salud Familiar La Fe
Newsletter
Antonio Carrasco
Special Projects Director
700 S. Ochoa
El Paso, TX 79901
Phone: (915) 545-4550

Chicago Academy of Sciences
2060 North Clark Street
Chicago, IL 60614
Phone: (773) 549-0606
Fax: (773) 549-5199
www.chias.org

Children's Environmental Health
Network
Joy E. Carlson
Newsletter/Public Information
5900 Hollis St., Suite E
Emeryville, CA 94608
Phone: (510) 540-3657

Citizens Environmental Coalition
Anne Rabe, Director
Newsletter/Public Information
33 Central Avenue
Albany, NY 12210
Phone: (518) 462-5527

Citizens for a Better Environment
Wendall Chin, Field Organizer
Newsletter/Public Information
500 Howard St., #506
San Francisco, CA 94105
Phone: (415) 243-8373

Citizens Network for Sustainable
Development/U.S. Network for Habitat II
1025 Vermont Avenue, NW, Suite 301
Washington, DC 20001
Phone: (202) 879-4286
Fax: (202) 783-0444
www.9dsnet.com/habitatnetwk

City of Pattonsburg
Town Hall
Pattonsburg, MO 64670
Phone: (816) 367-4412
Fax: (816) 367-2165
see also U.S. Department of Energy,
Center of Excellence for Sustainable
Development

Coastal Enterprises, Inc.
Project Soar
P.O. Box 268 Water Street
Wiscasset, ME 04578
Phone: (207) 882-7552
Fax: (207) 887-7308

Committee for the National Institute
for the Environment
730 11th Street, NW, #300
Washington, DC 20001-4521
Phone: (202) 628-4303
Fax: (202) 628-4311
www.cnie.org/nle

Community Change
Editor
Center for Community Change
1000 Wisconsin Ave., NW
Washington, DC 20007

Community Economics
Book Review Editor
Institute for Community Economics
57 School Street
Springfield, MA 01105-1331
Phone: (413) 746-8660

Community Information Exchange
Amy Olson
1029 Vermont Ave., NW, #710
Washington, DC 20005
Phone: (202) 628-2981 Ext. 10

Community Pollution Scorecard
www.scorecard.org

Council on Environmental Quality
The White House
Executive Office of the President
722 Jackson Place, NW
Washington, DC 20503
Phone: (202) 456-6224
Fax: (202) 456-2710
www.whitehose.goviceq

Desert Citizens Against Pollution
Stormy Williams
Newsletter/Public Information
3813 50th St., W
Rosamond, CA 93560
Phone: (805) 256-2101

Earth Press
705 West Main Street
Carbondale, IL 62901
Phone: (618) 457-3521
Fax: (618) 457-2541

Earthwatch
680 Mt. Auburn Street Box 403
Watertown, MA 02272
Phone: (617) 926-8200
Fax: (617) 926-1973
www.earthwatch.org

Eco Action
Carol Williams, Executive Director
Newsletter/Public Information
250 10th St., NE, Suite 201
Atlanta, GA 30309
Phone: (404) 873-2474

Ecocity Cleveland
David Beach, Editor
2841 Scarborough Road
Cleveland Heights, OH 44118
Phone: (216) 932-3007

Econet
2051 Parton Lane
Arcata, CA 95521
Phone: (707) 822-7947

EE-Link
http://nceet.snre.umich.edu/use.html
see also National Consortium for
Environmental Education and
Training

Eisenhower National Clearinghouse
1929 Kenny Road
Columbus, OH 43210-1063
Phone: (614) 292-7784
Fax: (614) 292-2066
www.enc.org

Environment and Development
Jim Schwab, Editor
American Planning Association
122 South Michigan Avenue
Suite 1600
Chicago, IL 60603-6107
Phone: (312) 431-9100

Environmental Com of Tijuana-
San Diego Region
Kaare S. Kjos, Chairperson
Newsletter/Public Information
2838 Granada Avenue
San Diego, CA 92104
Phone: (619) 285-1725

Environmental Defense Fund
257 Park Ave. S.
New York, N.Y. 10010
Phone: (212) 505-2100
www.edf.org

Environmental Health Center, National
Safety Council
Bud Ward, Editor
Newsletter/Public Information
1019 19th St., NW, #401
Washington, DC 20036
Phone: (202) 293-2270 Ext. 6271

Environmental Health Coalition
Jose T. Bravo
Newsletter/Public Information
1717 Kettner Blvd., #100
San Diego, CA 92101
Phone: (619) 235-0281

Environmental Health Network
Susan Molloy
Newsletter/Public Information
HC 63, Box 7187
Snowflake, AZ 85937
Phone: (602) 536-4625

Environmental Resources Information
Center (ERIC)
Access Eric
1600 Research Blvd., Mail Stop #5F
Rockville, MD 20850
Phone: 800-LET-ERIC
Fax: (301) 309-2084
www.aspen.sys.com/eric

Family Life
Christine Loomis
1290 Avenue of the Americas
New York, NY 10104
Phone: (212) 484-3494

Federation of Southern Coops
Cleo Askew
Land Assistance Fund Newsletter
P.O. Box 95
Epes, AL 35460
Phone: (205) 652-9676

Focus for Research on Poverty (Institute)
Editor
1180 Observatory Drive
3412 Social Science Bldg.
University of Wisconsin
Madison, WI 53706

Food and Allied Service Trades, AFL-CIO
Keith Mestrich
Newsletter/Public Information
815 16th Street, NW
Washington, DC 20006
Phone: (202) 737-7200

Food First News and Views
Andy Cowgill
Book Review Coordinator
Institute for Food and Development
Policy
398 60th St.
Oakland, CA 94618
Phone: (510) 654-4400

Foundation for the Future of Youth
Peace Child International
11426 Rockville Pike, Suite 100
Rockville, MD 20852
Phone: (301) 468-9431
Fax: (301) 468-9612
www.shs.net:8D/rescue/found.htm

Foundation for the Mid-South
Holly Black, Communications Officer
P.O. Box 1640, 4th Floor
Jackson, MS 39201

Four Corners School of Outdoor Education
P.O. Box 1029
Monticello, UT 84536
Phone: (801) 587-2156
Fax: (801) 587-2193

Friends of the Environment
Debbie Buckner
Newsletter/Public Information
Route 1, P.O. Box 76
Junction City, GA 31812
Phone: (706) 269-3630

George Washington University
Institute for the Environment
2121 Eye Street, NW, Suite 603
Washington, DC 20052
Phone: (202) 994-3366
Fax: (202) 994-0723
www.gwu.edu/greenu

Georgia Environmental Organization
Olin M. Ivey, Executive Director
Newsletter/Public Information
6750 Peachtree Industrial Blvd.
Suite 802
Atlanta, GA 30360-2218
Phone: (404) 447-4307

Georgia Institute of Technology
Center for Sustainable Technology
School of Civil Engineering
Atlanta, GA 30332-0355
Phone: (404) 894-1444
Fax: (404) 894-2281

Global Action and Information Network (GAIN)
740 Front Street, Suite 355
Santa Cruz, CA 95060
Phone: (408) 457-0130
Fax: (408) 457-0133
www.gain.org/gain

Global Environment and Technology Foundation (GETF)
7010 Little River Turnpike, Suite 300
Annandale, VA 22003-3241
Phone: (703) 750-6401
Fax: (703) 750-6506
www.gxinet.com
www.gnet.org

Global Research Institute
705 West Main Street
Carbondale, IL 62901
Phone: (618) 457-2485
Fax: (618) 457-2541

Global Rivers Environmental Education Network (GREEN)
721 East Huron Street
Ann Arbor, MI 48104
Phone: (313) 761-8142
Fax: (313) 761-4951

Government Information Locator Service for U.S. EPA
U.S. Environmental Protection Agency
www.epa.gov/gils

Grandparent Times
Margaret M. Clark
1107 S. 20th Street
Arlington, VA 22202
Phone: (703) 979-7170

Grassroots Coalition for Environment and Economic Justice
Newsletter/Public Information
P.O. Box 380
Clarksville, MD 21029
Phone: (410) 964-3574

Great Lakes Natural Resource Center
Newsletter/Public Information
506 E. Liberty, 2nd Floor
Ann Arbor, MI 48104-2210
Phone: (313) 769-3351

Great Lakes Reports
Editor
Council of Great Lakes Governors
35 East Wacker Drive, Ste. 1850
Chicago, IL 60601

Greenbelt Alliance
Jim Sayer, Communications Director
116 New Montgomery St., #640
San Francisco, CA 94105
Phone: (415) 543-4291

Green City Project
Sabrina Merlo, Project Coordinator
Newsletter/Public Information
P.O. Box 31251
San Francisco, CA 94131
Phone: (415) 285-6556

Greenspace Alliance
1211 Chestnut Street, Suite 900
Philadelphia, PA 19107
Phone: (215) 563-0250
e-mail: pecphila@libertynet.org

Greenwire
3129 Mt. Vernon Avenue
Alexandria, VA 22305
Phone: (703) 518-4600
Fax: (703) 518-8702
www.apn.com

Highlander Research and Education Center
Larry Wilson
Newsletter/Public Information
1959 Highlander Way
New Market, TN 37820
Phone: (615) 933-3443

High School for Environmental Studies
444 West 56th Street
New York, NY 10019
Phone: (212) 262-8113
Fax: (212) 262-0702

Home Power
Editor
The Hands-On Journal of
Home-Made Power
P.O. Box 520
Ashland, OR 97520
Phone: (916) 475-3179

HOPE Newsletter
Tubal H. Padilla-Galiano
Director of HOPE Resource Center
Hispanic Office of Planning and
Evaluation
165 Brookside Avenue
Boston, MA 02130
Phone: (617) 524-8888

Human Action Comm Org Newsletter
Eraina B. Dunn
16028 S. Halsted
P.O. Box 1703
Harvey, IL 60426
Phone: (708) 339-7902

Indigenous Women's Network
Newsletter
Marsha Gomez
13621 FM 2769
Austin, TX 78726
Phone: (512) 258-3880

Institute for Forest Analysis, Planning and Policy
Box 44, 15 Bennett Road
Wayland, MA 01778
Phone: (508) 358-2261
e-mail: hagenstein@aol.com

Institute for Southern Studies
Isaiah Madison
Newsletter/Public Information
P.O. Box 531
Durham, NC 27702
Phone: (919) 419-8311

Institute for Sustainable Communities
56 College Street
Montpelier, VT 05602-3115
Phone: (802) 229-2900
Fax: (802) 229-2919
www.isczt.org

Interfaith Impact for Justice and Peace
James M. Bell, Executive Director
Newsletter/Public Information
110 Maryland Ave., NE
Washington, DC 20002
Phone: (202) 543-2800

Intergovernmental Committee in Urban
and Regional Research (ICURR)
150 Eglinton Ave. East, Suite 301
Toronto, Ontario M4P 1E8, Canada
www.icurr.gov.ca

The Island Institute
410 Main Street
Rockland, ME 04841
Phone: (207) 594-9209
Fax: (207) 594-9314

Island Press
1718 Connecticut Ave., NW, Suite 300
Washington, D.C. 20009
Phone: (202) 232-7933
www.islandpress.org

Jacksonville, Florida Indicators Project
Jacksonville Community Council, Inc.
2434 Atlantic Boulevard, Suite 100
Jacksonville, FL 32207
Phone: (904) 396-3052
e-mail: jcci2@jaxnet.com
www.unf.edu/~clifford/jcci

Jupiter Community High School
Environmental Research and Field
Studies Academy
500 N. Military Trail
Jupiter, FL 33458
Phone: (407) 743-6005
Fax: (407) 744-7978

Ka Lahui Hawaii Newsletter
Julie-Ann Cachola, National Secretary
86-062 Hoaha St.
Waianae, HI 96792
Phone: (808) 696-9201

W.K. Kellogg Collection
Rural Development Resources
The Heartland Center for Leadership
Development
Lincoln, Nebraska
www.un.edu/kellogg/index.html

W.K. Kellogg Foundation
One Michigan Ave. East
Battle Creek, MI 49017
Phone: (616) 968-1611
www.wkkf.org

Leadership Initiative Project Newsletter
Angela Brown, Director
Route 1, P.O. Box 119
Kittrell, NC 27554
Phone: (919) 496-7830

Learning Alliance
David Levine
Newsletter/Public Information
324 Lafayette Street, 7th Floor
New York, NY 10012
Phone: (212) 226-7171

Management Institute for Environment
and Business
1101 17th Street, NW, Suite 502
Washington, DC 20036
Phone: (202) 833-6556
Fax: (202) 833-6228

Menominee Sustainable Development
Institute
College of the Menominee Nation
P.O. Box 1179
Keshena, WI 54135
Phone: (715) 799-5614
Fax: (715) 799-5638
www.menominee.com/sdi

Michigan Coalition for Human Rights
Newsletter
Kathryn Savoie, Executive Director
4800 Woodward Ave.
Detroit, MI 48201-1399
Phone: (313) 831-0258

Mid-South Peace and Justice Center
Rita Harris
Newsletter/Public Information
P.O. Box 11428
499 Patterson
Memphis, TN 38111-0428
Phone: (901) 452-6997

Mille Lacs Band of Chippewa Newsletter
Don Wedll, Commissioner of
Natural Resources
HCR 67, P.O. Box 194
Onamia, MN 56359
Phone: (612) 532-4181

Minnesota Advocates for Human Rights
Theresa Gales
The BIAS Project
400 2nd Ave. S., Suite 1050
Minneapolis, MN 55401
Phone: (612) 341-3302

Modcomm
Deb Hoffman, Editor
The Modernization Forum
20501 Ford Road
Dearborn, MI 48128

Monterey County Herald
Judie Telfer, Education/Science
Reporter
P.O. Box 271
Monterey, CA 93942

Mothers and Others
Betsy Lydon
40 W. 20th Street
New York, NY 10011
Phone: (212) 242-0010 Ext. 305

Mountain Association for Community
Economic Development (MACED)
Sustainable Communities Initiative
433 Chestnut Street
Beria, Kentucky, 40403
Phone: (606) 986-2375
e-mail: jgage@maced.org
www.maced.org

Multimedia Development Laboratory
Safety, Health and Environmental
Management Division (mail code:
3207)
Office of Administration

National Association of Black Social
Workers Magazine
Editor
7727 St. Albans
St. Louis, MO 63117
Phone: (314) 645-5105

National Association for Community
Leadership
200 S. Meridian Street, Suite 250
Indianapolis, IN 46225
Phone: (317) 637-7408
www.communityleadership.org

National Association for County
Comm and Economic Development
NACCED Insights
Editor
1101 Connecticut Ave., NW, #700
Washington, DC 20036
Phone: (202) 429-5118

National Association of Physicians for
the Environment
6410 Rockledge Drive, Suite 203
Bethesda, MD 20817
Phone: (301) 571-9791
Fax: (301) 530-8910

National Association State
Development Agencies
NASDA Letter
Editor
750 First Street, NE, Ste. 710
Washington, DC 20002

National Center on Education and the
Economy
700 11th Street, NW
Washington, DC 20001
Phone: (202) 783-3668
Fax: (202) 783-3672

National Coalition Against the Misuse
of Pesticide
Sandra Shubert
Information Coordinator
Newsletter/Public Information
701 E St., SE, Suite 200
Washington, DC 20003
Phone: (202) 543-5450

National Community Reinvestment
Coalition (NCRC)
1875 Connecticut Ave., NW, Ste. 1010
Washington, DC 20009

National Congress for Community
Economic Development
Washington, DC
Phone: (202) 232-0150

National Congress of American Indians
Newsletter
A. Gay Kingman, Executive Director
900 Pennsylvania Ave., SE
Washington, DC 20003
Phone: (202) 546-9404

National Consortium for Environmental
Education and Technology (NCEET)
430 East University,
Dana Building
Ann Arbor, MI 48109-1115
Phone: (313) 998-6726
Fax: (313) 998-6580

National Environmental Education
Advancement Project (NEEAP)
College of Natural Resources
University of Wisconsin–Stevens
Point
Stevens Point, WI 54481
Phone: (715) 346-4179
Fax: (715) 346-3819
www.uwsp.edu/acad/cnr/neeap.htm.

National Environmental Health
Association
Larry Marcum, Manager
Research and Development
Newsletter/Public Information
720 S. Colorado Blvd., South Tower
Suite 970
Denver, CO 80222-1925
Phone: (303) 756-9090

National Environmental Information
Resources Center (NEIRC)
Institute for the Environment
The George Washington University
Washington, DC 20052
Phone: (202) 994-3366
Fax: (202) 994-0723
www.gwu.edu/-greenu/

National 4-H Council
7100 Connecticut Avenue
Chevy Chase, MD 20815
Phone: (301) 961-2800
Fax: (301) 961-2848

National Library for the Environment
1725 K Street, NW
Washington, DC 20006-1401
Phone: (202) 628-4303
Fax: (202) 628-4311
www.cnie.org/nle

National Neighborhood Coalition
NNC Information Report
Toni Breiter, Editor
810 First Street, NW, #300
Washington, DC 20002

National Scenic Byways Clearinghouse
Deidra Goodman
1440 New York Ave., NW, Ste. 202
Washington, DC 20005
Phone: (202) 628-7718

National Science and Technology
Council
Bridge to a Sustainable Future:
National Environmental Technology
Strategy
Office of Science and Technology
Policy, Old Executive Building,
Room 443
17th St. and Pennsylvania Ave., NW
Washington, DC 20500
Phone: (800) 368-6676

National Voter
William Woodwell, Editor
League of Women Voters
1730 M Street, NW, Suite 1000
Washington, DC 20036
Phone: (202) 429-1965

National Wildlife Federation
Conservation Directory (of
Organizations)
1400 16th Street, NW
Washington, DC 20036-2266
Phone: (202) 797-5435
www.nwf.org

Native Action Newsletter
Gail Small, Director
P.O. Box 316
Lame Deer, MT 59043
Phone: (406) 477-6390

The Nature Conservancy
1815 North Lynn Street
Arlington, VA 22209
Phone: (703) 841-5300
Fax: (703) 841-1283
www.tnc.org

Nebraska Indian Intertribal Dev Corp
Newsletter
Daryl La Pointe Sr., HIP/WAP Director
Route 1, P.O. Box 66-A
Winnebago, NE 68071
Phone: (402) 878-2242

Neighborhood Improvement Found of
Toledo Newsletter
Robert F. Burger, Executive Director
1114 Washington Street
Toledo, OH 23624
Phone: (419) 244-1522

New England Environmental Policy
Center (NEEPC)
Hollow Road
North Ferrisburgh, VT 05473
www.neepc.org

New Jersey PIRG
Newsletter/Public Information
11 N. Willow Street
Trenton, NJ 08608
Phone: (609) 394-8155

Newsletter
Craig Bienz, Chief Biologist
Klamath Tribe
P.O. Box 436
Chiloquin, OR 97624
Phone: (503) 783-2219

Newsletter
Curtis Canard, Program Manager
Environmental Services Office,
Cherokee Nation
P.O. Box 948
Tahlequan, OK 74465
Phone: (918) 458-5496

Newsletter
Willis Robedeaux III
Third Member Tribal Council
Otoe-Missoulia Tribe of Oklahoma
Route 1, P.O. Box 62
Red Rock, OK 74651
Phone: (405) 723-4466

New York University
Stern School of Business Management
Global Environmental Program
44 West Fourth Street, Suite 7-73
New York, NY 10012-1126
Phone: (212) 998-0426

Nez Perce Tribe Newsletter
Gwendolyn B. Carter, Coordinator
IHS Management
P.O. Box 365
Lapwai, ID 83540
Phone: (208) 843-2253

Noblesville, Indiana
Center for Urban Policy and the
Environment
342 North Senate Avenue
Indianapolis, IN 46204
Phone: (317) 261-3000

North American Association for
Environmental Education
1255 23rd Street, NW, Suite 400
Washington, DC 20037
Phone: (202) 884-8912
Fax: (202)884-8701

North Carolina Fair Share Newsletter
John Worchek, Director
P.O. Box 12543
Raleigh, NC 27605
Phone: (919) 832-7130

North Carolina Rural Communities
Assistance Project
Stephen J. Dear, Executive Director
Newsletter/Public Information
P.O. Box 941
Pittsboro, NC 27312
Phone: (919) 542-7227

Northeast-Midwest Economic Review
Editor
Northeast-Midwest Institute
218 D Street, SE
Washington, DC 20003
Phone: (202) 544-5200

Northwest Area Foundation
332 Minnesota Street, Suite E 201
St. Paul, MN 55101
Phone: (651) 224-9635
www.nwaf.org

Nuclear Information and Resource Service
Michael Marriotte, Executive Director
Newsletter/Public Information
1424 16th St., NW, #601
Washington, DC 20036
Phone: (202) 328-0002

Office of Science and Technology Policy
*Bridge to a Sustainable Future:
National Environmental Technology
Strategy*
Old Executive Building, Room 443
17th St. and Pennsylvania Ave., NW
Washington, DC 20500
Phone: (800) 368-6676
www.whitehouse.gov

Ohio Environmental Council
Richard Sahli, Executive Director
Newsletter/Public Information
400 Dublin Ave., Suite 120
Columbus, OH 43215
Phone: (614) 224-4900

Oneida Indian Nation of NY Newsletter
Ray Halbritter, Nation Representative
Route 5, P.O. Box 1
Vernon, NY 13476
Phone: (315) 829-3090

Oregon State Public Interest Research Group (OSPIRG)
Quiney Sugarman, Environmental Advocate
Newsletter/Public Information
1536 SE 11th Avenue
Portland, OR 97214
Phone: (503) 231-4181

Pacific Mountain Review/Network News
Richard Dreher, Editor
Rural Comm. Assistance Corp.
2125 19th St., Suite 203
Sacramento, CA 95818

Pacific News Service
News Editor
450 Mission Street, #506
San Francisco, CA 94105

PAHLS Journal
Sue Lynch, Executive Director
PAHLS Alliance for Environmental Justice
102 N. Morgan, Ste. A
Valparaiso, IN 46383
Phone: (219) 465-7466

Partnerships Supporting Education About the Environment
Education for Sustainability: An Agenda for Action
see *U.S. Department of Education*

Physicians for Social Responsibility
Julie Moore, Executive Director
Newsletter/Public Information
1101 14th St., NW, Suite 700
Washington, DC 20007
Phone: (202) 898-0150

Plan LA
Bill Christopher, Coordinator
Newsletter/Public Information
732 N. Gardner St.
Los Angeles, CA 90046
Phone: (310) 247-7987

President's Council on Sustainable Development
730 Jackson Place, NW
Washington, DC 20503
Phone: (202) 408-5296
Fax: (202) 408-6839
www.whitehouse.gov/PCSD

Project Learning Tree
1111 19th Street, NW
Washington, DC 20036
Phone: (202) 463-2472

Project WILD
5430 Grosvenor Lane
Bethesda, MD 20814
Phone: (301) 493-5447

Publications
Glen Miller, Tribal Chairman
Menominee Indian Tribe
P.O. Box 910
Keshena, WI 54135
Phone: (715) 799-5113

Publications
Jim Willis, General Manager
Confederated Tribes of Grand Ronde
P.O. Box 38
Grand Ronde, OR 97347
Phone: (503) 879-5211

Publications-Noonsack Indian Tribe
Ross Cline, Vice-Chair
P.O. Box 157
Deming, WA 98244
Phone: (206) 592-5176

Publications-Red Cliff Band of Lake Superior
Andrew Gokee, Community Planner
P.O. Box 529
Bayfield, WI 54814
Phone: (715) 779-5805

Publications-Yakima Indian Nation
Wendell L. Hannigan
Water Code Administrator
P.O. Box 151
Toppenish, WA 98948
Phone: (509) 865-5121

Publico Newspaper
Tereza Coelho
R Amilcar Cabral Lote 1
Quinta Do Lambert, LISBOA

Public Technology, Inc.
The Urban Consortium
1301 Pennsylvania Avenue, NW
Washington, DC 20004-1793
Phone: (202) 626-2400 or
(800) 852-4936
Fax: (202) 626-2498
www.pti.nw.dc.us

Pueblo Jemez Newsletter
Roger Fragua, Tribal Administrator
P.O. Box 100
Jemez Pueblo, NM 87024
Phone: (505) 834-7359

Renewable Energy Policy Project
University of Maryland
3140 Tydings Hall
College Park, MD 20742
Phone: (301) 403-4165
Fax: (301) 405-4550

River Voices
Rita Haberman, Director
River Clearinghouse
River Network
P.O. Box 8787
Portland, OR 97207
Phone: (503) 241-3506

Rural Development Perspectives
Dennis Roth
Book Review Editor
USDA/ERS Room 932c
1301 New York Avenue, NW
Washington, DC 20005-4788
Phone: (202) 219-0520

Rural Organizing and Culture Ctr Newsletter
Ann Brown, Education Organizer
103 Swinney Lane
Lexington, MS 39095
Phone: (601) 834-3080

Rural Research Report
Editor
Illinois Institute for Rural Affairs
Western Illinois University
518 Stipes Hall
Macomb, IL 61455

Rutgers University
Center for Urban Policy Research
33 Livingston Avenue, Suite 400
New Brunswick, NJ 08901-1982
Phone: (908) 932-3133
Fax: (908) 932-2363
www.policy.rutgers.edu/cupr/

San Francisco Bay Area EcoTeam
Project
1000 Green Street, PH#1
San Francisco, CA 94133
Phone: (415) 567-8657

Santa Clara Ctr for Occup Safety-Health
Flora Chu, Director
Asian Worker Health Project
Newsletter/Public Information
760 N. First St.
San Jose, CA 95112
Phone: (408) 998-4050

Santa Cruz County Sentinel
John Robinson, Staff Writer
207 Church St.
P.O. Box 638
Santa Cruz, CA 95061
Phone: (408) 423-4242

Sarasota County
County Extension Agents
2900 Ringling Boulevard
Sarasota, FL 34237
Phone: (813) 955-4240
Fax: (813) 955-0413

Sault Ste. Marie Tribe of Chippewa
Indians
Don Togorson
Environmental Director
Newsletter
206 Greenough
Sault St. Marie, MI 49783
Phone: (206) 635-6050

Second Nature
44 Bromfield Street, 5th floor
Boston, MA 02108
Phone: (617) 292-7771
Fax: (617) 292-0150
www.2nature.org

Sierra Club National Headquarters
85 Second Street, 2nd floor
San Francisco, CA 94105-3441
Phone: (415) 977-5500
Fax: (415) 977-5799
www.sierraclub.org

Silicon Valley Toxics Coalition
Leslie Byster, Editor
760 N. First Street
San Jose, CA 95112
Phone: (408) 287-6708

Small Flows
Jill Ross, Editor
National Small Flows Clearinghouse
P.O. Box 6064
Morgantown, WV 26506-6064
Phone: 800-624-8301

Small Town
Kenneth Munsell, Director
Small Town Institute
P.O. Box 517
Third Avenue and Popular Street
Ellensburg, WA 98926
Phone: (509) 925-1830

Smithsonian Institution
1100 Jefferson Drive, SW
Washington, DC 20560
Phone: (202) 357-4792

Society of American Foresters, SAF
(has state and regional chapters)
5400 Grosvenor Lane
Bethesda, MD 20814
www.safnet.org/about/links.htm

Sonoma State University
Department of Environmental
Studies and Planning
1801 East Cotati Avenue
Rohnert Park, CA 94928
Phone: (707) 664-2249

South & Meso Amer. Indian Info Ctr
Newsletter
Nilo Cayuqueo, Director
P.O. Box 28703
Oakland, CA 94604
Phone: (510) 834-4263

Southern Empowerment Project
Newsletter
Walter Davis, Recruiter/Trainer
323 Ellis Avenue
Maryville, TN 37801
Phone: (615) 984-6500

Southern Growth Policies Board
Robert Donnan
P.O. Box 12293
Research Triangle Park, NC 27709

Southern Organizing Comm Newsletter
Connie Tucker, Executive Director
P.O. Box 10518
Atlanta, GA 50310
Phone: (404) 755-2855

Southern Rainbow Education Project
Newsletter
Owen Patton, Program/Field
Director
46 E. Patton Avenue
Montgomery, AL 36105
Phone: (205) 288-5754

Southern University
Center for Energy and
Environmental Studies
P.O. Box 9764
Baton Rouge, LA 70813
Phone: (504) 771-4724
Fax: (504) 771-4722

Southwest Network for Environmental
and Economic Justice Newsletter
Richard Moore, Coordinator
P.O. Box 7399
Albuquerque, NM 87194
Phone: (505) 242-0416
Fax: (505) 242-5609

St. Francis of Assisi School
1938 Alfresco Place
Louisville, KY 40205
Phone: (502) 245-7000 or
(502) 459-3088

Student Conservation Association
Box 9867
Arlington, VA 22219
Phone: (703) 524-2441
Fax: (703) 524-2451

Sustainability Project (The)
4 Gavilan Road
Santa Fe, NM 87505
Phone: (505) 466-2052
Fax: (505) 466-2052

Sustainable Community Roundtable
*Creating a Sustainable Community
in South Puget Sound*
2129 Bethel Street, NE
Olympia, WA 98506
Phone: (360) 754-7842

Sustainable Seattle
909 Fourth Avenue
Seattle, WA 98104
Phone: (206) 382-5013

Sustainable Wisconsin
929 North Sixth Street
Milwaukee, WI 53203
Phone: (414) 227-3270
Fax: (414) 227-3168

Syracuse University
Crouse School of Management
Crouse Hinds, Suite 200
Syracuse, NY 10324
Phone: (315) 443-3751
Fax: (315) 443-5389

Texans United Education Fund
Rick Abraham, Executive Director
Newsletter/Public Information
12655 Woodforest, Suite 200
Houston, TX 77015
Phone: (713) 453-0853

The Center for Rural Pennsylvania
Editor
Publications Department
212 Locust Street, Ste. 604
Harrisburg, PA 17101
Phone: (717) 787-9555

The Earth Network
Lorenz Joseph
717 W. Maxwell
Chicago, IL 60607
Phone: (312) 226-3248

The Network Bulletin
Ed Lytwak
Book Review Editor
The Carrying Capacity Network
2000 P St., NW, Ste. 240
Washington, DC 20036
Phone: (202) 296-4548

The Responsive Community
Editor
The Communitarian Network
2020 Pennsylvania Ave., NW, Ste. 282
Washington, DC 20006

The Workbook
Kathy Cone, Editor
P.O. Box 4524
105 Stanford, SE
Albuquerque, NM 87106

Three Circles Center for Multicultural Environmental Education
P.O. Box 1946
Sausalito, CA 94965
Phone: (415) 331-4540
Fax: (415) 331-4540

Tides Foundation Economics Working Group
3407 34th Street, NW
Washington, DC 20016
Phone: (202) 542-4800

Toxic Communications and Assist Project Newsletter
Barbara Sullivan
Program Coordinator
Albany State College
504 College Drive
Albany, GA 31705
Phone: (912) 430-4823

Tri Valley Cares
Marylia Kelley, Coordinator
Newsletter/Public Information
5720 East Ave., #116
Livermore, CA 94550
Phone: (510) 443-7148

Tufts University, Fletcher School of Law and Diplomacy
Global Development and Environment Institute
Cabot Building
Medford, MA 02155
Phone: (617) 627-3700
Fax: (617) 627-3712

Union of Concerned Scientists
Warren Leon
Deputy Director for Programs
Newsletter/ Public Information
1616 P Street, NW, #310
Washington, DC 20036
Phone: (202) 332-0900

United Church of Christ Community Racial Justice Newsletter
Vivian Lucas Wynn
P.O. Box 187
Enfield, NC 27823
Phone: (919) 437-1723

United East Austin Coalition
Sabino Renteria, President
Newsletter/Public Information
1511 Haskell Street
Austin, TX 78702
Phone: (512) 478-6770

United Nations
Department of Public Information
Room S-894
New York, NY 10017
Phone: (212) 963-4556

University of Arizona
Recycling Office
P.O. Box 210049
Tucson, AZ 85721-0049
Phone: (520) 621-1264
Fax: (520) 621-6086

University of California at Berkeley
College of Natural Resources
101 Giannini Hall
Berkeley, CA 94720
Phone: (510) 642-7171
Fax: (510) 642-4612

University of Louisville
Institute for the Environment and Sustainable Development (IESD)
Louisville, KY 40292
Phone: (502) 852-6512
Fax: (502) 852-8361

University of Michigan
School of Natural Resources and the
Environment
430 East University
Ann Arbor, MI 48109-1115
Phone: (313) 764-6453
Fax: (313) 936-2195
www.snre.umich.edu

University of Oregon
Institute for a Sustainable Environment
130 Hendricks Hall
Eugene, OR 97403-1209
Phone: (503) 346-3895
Fax: (503) 346-2040

University of Vermont
Environmental Programs in
Communities (EPIC)
153 South Prospect
Burlington, VT 05401
Phone: (802) 656-4055
Fax: (802) 656-8015

University of Washington
Center for Sustainable Communities
224 Gould Hall, Box 355726
Seattle, WA 98195
Phone: (206) 543-7679

University of Wisconsin, Milwaukee
Center for Urban Community
Development
161 West Wisconsin Avenue
Milwaukee, WI 53217-3985
Phone: (414) 227-3280
Fax: (414) 277-3168

U.S. Agency for International
Development
320 21st Street, NW
Washington, DC 20523
Phone: (202) 647-4000

U.S. Chamber of Commerce
1615 H Street, NW
Washington, DC 20062
Phone: (202) 659-6000
Fax: (202) 463-5836

U.S. Department of Agriculture
(USDA)
14th St. and Independence Ave., SW
Washington, DC 20250
Phone: (202) 720-2791

USDA Forest Service
210 14th St., SW
Auditors Building
Washington, D.C. 20250
Phone: (202) 205-0957
Fax: (202) 205-0885
www.fs.fed.us/

USDA Cooperative State Research,
Education and Extension Services
(CSREES)
Natural Resources and
Environmental Management
(NREM)
Agbox 2210329
*See also State-based Cooperative
Extension Offices*

USDA National Agricultural Statistics
Services
www.usda.gov/nass/aggraphs/
graphics.htm

U.S. Department of Commerce
Bureau of Economic Analysis
14th St. & Constitution Ave., NW
Washington, DC 20230
Phone: (202) 606-9900

U.S. Department of Commerce
National Oceanic and Atmospheric
Administration (NOAA)
Sea Grant Program
#5222 14th St. & Constitution
Avenue, NW
Washington, DC 20230
Phone: (202) 482-2663

U.S. Department of Commerce
Office of Economic Conversion
Information (OECI)
14th St. & Constitution Ave., NW
Washington, DC 20230
Phone: (800) 345-1222

U.S. Department of Education
Office of the Deputy Secretary
600 Independence Avenue, SW
Washington, DC 20202
Phone: (202) 401-1000
Fax: (202) 401-3093
www.ed.gov

U.S. Department of Energy
Center for Excellence for Sustainable
Development
P.O. Box 3048
Merrifield, VA 22116
Phone: (800) 357-7732
www.crest.org/doe/

U.S. Department of Energy
Office of Energy Efficiency and
Renewable Energy
2801 Youngfield Street, Suite 380
Golden, CO 80401
Phone: (303) 231-5750

**U.S. Department of Housing and
Urban Development**
Indicators on Sustainable Cities
Office of Policy Development and
Research
451 Seventh Street, SW
Washington, DC 20410
Phone: (202) 708-3896
Fax: (202) 619-8000
www.hudser.org

U.S. Department of the Interior
Water and Science Branch
1849 C Street, NW, Mail Stop 6640
Washington, DC 20240
Phone: (202) 208-5691
Fax: (202) 371-2815
www.state.gov

U.S. Department of Labor
www.dol.gov

U.S. Department of State
2201 C Street, NW, Room 7250
Washington, DC 20520
Phone: (202) 647-4000
Fax: (202) 647-0753

**U.S. Environmental Protection Agency
(EPA)**
Safety, Health and Environmental
Management Division (mail code:
3207)
Office of Administration
401 M Street, SW
Washington, DC 20460
Phone: (202) 260-1640
Fax: (202) 260-0215
e-mail:jimeno.julius@epamail.epa.gov
www.epa.gov

U.S. Environmental Protection Agency
Office of Communications, Education,
and Public Affairs (mail code: 1707)
Environmental Education Division
401 M Street, SW
Washington, DC 20460
Phone: (202) 260-4965
Fax: (202) 260-4095

U.S. EPA Green Communities
www.epa.gov/region3/green/kit

U.S. Fish and Wildlife Service
National Education and Training
Center
4401 N. Fairfax Drive
MS 304 Webb
Arlington, VA 22203
Phone: (703) 358-2504

U.S. Geological Survey
http://info.er.usgs.gov

**U.S. National Aeronautics and Space
Administration (NASA)**
300 E Street, SW
Washington, DC 20546
Phone: (202) 358-0000
Fax: (202) 358-3251
www.nasa.gov

U.S. Postal Service
Environmental Policy Management
475 L'Enfant Plaza, SW
Washington, DC 20260-2810
Phone: (202) 268-3364
Fax: (202) 268-6016

Vermont Grass Farmers Association
(VGFA)
Center for Sustainable Agriculture
590 Main Street
Burlington, VT 05405
Phone: (802) 656-3834
e-mail: sflack@zoo.uvm.edu

Vermont Lead Safety Project
Lesley Wright
14 Pleasant Street
Bristol, VT 05443
Phone/Fax: 802-453-5617
e-mail: VLSP@Together.net

Vice President Albert Gore
White House
1600 Pennsylvania Avenue, NW
Washington, DC 20016
Phone: (202) 456-1414
www.whitehouse.gov

Voices
David Grant, Executive Director
Rural Southern Voice for Peace/
Listening Project
1898 Hannah Branch Rd.
Burnsville, NC 28714
Phone: (704) 675-5933

Wakeup Newsletter
Lillie C. Webb
P.O. Box 572
107B Broad Street
Sparta, GA 31087
Phone: (706) 444-5896

War on Waste
Mary Tutwiler, Chairperson
Newsletter/Public Information
701 E. Main Street
New Iberia, LA 70560
Phone: (318) 365-2923

Water Information Network
Puerco Valley Navajo Clean Water
Association
P.O. Box 314
Sanders, AZ 86512
Phone: (602) 729-4129

West County Toxics Coalition Newsletter
Henry Clark, Executive Director
1019 MacDonald
Richmond, CA 94801
Phone: (510) 232-3427

West Dallas Coalition of Environmental
Justice Newsletter
Luis D. Sepulveda, President
5105 Goodman Street
Dallas, TX 75211
Phone: (214) 330-7947

White Earth Land Recovery Newsletter
Winona LaDuke
P.O. Box 327
White Earth, MN 56591
Phone: (218) 473-3110

Women's Agricultural Network
590 Main Street
Burlington, VT 05405-0059
Phone: (802) 656-3276
Fax: (802) 656-8874
e-mail: wagn@zoo.uvm.edu
www.uvm.edu/~wagn

Working Notes on Community
Right-to-Know
Paul Orum, Coordinator
Working Group on Community
Right-to-Know
218 D Street, SE
Washington, DC 20003
Phone: (202) 546-9707

World Resource Institute
Environmental Education Project
1709 New York Avenue, NW
Washington, DC 20006
Phone: (202) 638-6300
Fax: (202) 638-0036
www.wri.org

Yale University
School of Forestry and Environmen-
tal Studies
205 Prospect Street
New Haven, CT 06511
Phone: (203) 432-5100
Fax: (203) 432-5942
www.academic programs

Yellow Creek Concerned Citizens
Larry Wilson, President
Newsletter/Public Information
Route 2, P.O. Box 68AA
Middlesboro, KY 40965
Phone: (606) 248-8213

YWCA of the USA
Education for Global Responsibility
726 Broadway, 5th Floor
New York, NY 10003
Phone: (212) 614-2700
Fax: (212) 677-9716

LEADERSHIP AND RURAL DEVELOPMENT PROJECTS THAT FORMED THE W. K. KELLOGG FOUNDATION'S RURAL AMERICA INITIATIVE

Listed alphabetically by organization

Leadership for Economic Development: Developing Leadership in Rural Communities
Auburn University, Auburn, AL.
Cosponsored by the Alabama Cooperative Extension Service and the Economic Development Institute at Auburn.
Contact: Auburn University
104 Duncan Hall
Auburn, AL 38649
Phone: (256) 844-4451

Palmetto Leadership
Clemson University, Clemson, SC.
Sponsored by the Cooperative Extension Service at Clemson University.
Contact: Clemson University
211 Barre Hall
Clemson, SC 29634-0355
Phone: (803) 656-3384

Colorado Rural Revitalization Project
Colorado State University, Fort Collins, CO. A joint effort between the Cooperative Extension Service of Colorado State University; the Colorado Center for Community Development at the University of Colorado, Denver; and the State Department of Local Affairs.
Contact: Colorado State University
234 Aylesworth, NW
Fort Collins, CO 80524
(303) 491-5579

Creating Opportunity for Rural People and Places: A State Rural Economic and Community Development Policy Academy
Council of Governors' Policy Advisors, Washington, DC.
Contact: Council of Governors Policy Advisors
400 N. Capitol St., Suite 390
Washington, DC 20001

Rural Revitalization Initiative
University of Georgia, Athens, GA.
Contact: University of Georgia
Hoke Smith Annex
Fanning Leadership Center
Athens, GA 30602
Phone: (404) 542-6065

Helping Small Towns Survive: A Training Program for Community Development Practitioners
Heartland Center for Leadership Development, Lincoln, NE.
Contact: Heartland Center
941 O. St.
Suite 920
Lincoln, NE 61801
Phone: (402) 474-7667
www.4w.com/heartland

Rural Partners: Helping Rural Communities Prepare for Economic Development
University of Illinois Urbana-Champaign, Urbana, IL. A collaboration between the University of Illinois Cooperative Extension Service and Rural Partners: The Illinois Coalition for Rural Community Development.

Contact: University of Illinois
305 Mumford Hall
1301 West Gregory St.
Urbana, IL 61801
Phone: (217) 333-2792
www.aces.uiuc.edu/~abmas

Tomorrow's Leaders Today
Iowa State University, Ames, IA.
Contact: Iowa State University
303 East Hall
Ames, IA 50011
Phone: (515) 294-8397

Building Community-Based Leadership
for Economic Development
Kansas State University, Manhattan,
KS.
Contact: Kansas State University
51 College Court Bldg.
Manhattan, KS 66506-6001
Phone: (785) 532-6868
www.ksu.edu/kcri

The Appalachian Civic Leadership
Project
University of Kentucky and Berea
College, Lexington, KY.
Contact: University of Kentucky
641 S. Limestone
Lexington, KY 40506-0333
Phone: (606) 257-4852
www.uky.edu/r65/appalcenter

Property Tax Assessment
Computerization Project (PTACP) and
The County Educational Forum (CEF)
Kirtland Community College,
Roscommon, MI. A cooperative
effort between the Department of
Resource Development at Michigan
State University and Kirtland
Community College.
Contact: Michigan State University
312A Natural Resources Bldg.
East Lansing, MI 48824
Phone: (517) 355-6560
www.msu.edu

Community Leadership in Maine:
Insuring a Viable Future for Small
Communities
University of Maine, Orono, ME.
Contact: University of Maine
110 Libby Hall
Orono, ME 04469
Phone: (207) 581-3201
www.umaine.edu

Financial Management for Local Gov-
ernment Officials and Community
Organizations
University of Maryland, College
Park, MD.
Contact: University of Maryland
Suite 2101
Woods Hall
College Park, MD 20742

Leadership and Local Government
Education Project (LLGE)
Michigan State University, East
Lansing, MI.
Contact: Michigan State University
34 Agriculture Hall
East Lansing, MI 48824

Project RECLAIM (Rural Education for
Community Leaders Aimed at
Improved Management of the
Environment)
Midwest Assistance Program, New
Prague, MN.
Contact: P.O. Box 81
New Prague, MN 56071

PRO-MISS Promoting Rural
Opportunity in Mississippi
Mississippi State University.
Contact: P.O. Box 9760
Mississippi State University
Mississippi State, MS 39762
Phone: (601) 325-3048
www.msstate.edu/dept/promiss/

Missouri Rural Innovation Institute
(MRII)
University of Missouri, Columbia,
MO.

Contact: University of Missouri
529 Clark Hall
Columbia, MO 65211

**Training for Local Government
Officials, Local Government Center**
Montana State University, Bozeman,
MT.
Contact: Montana State University
Local Government Center
Bozeman, MT 59717

Montcalm Tomorrow
Montcalm County Board of
Commissioners, Stanton, MI.
Contact: Montcalm County Board
of Commissioners, Box 368
Stanton, MI 48888

Mon Valley Tri-State Leadership Academy
Mon Valley Tri-State Network, Inc.,
at West Virginia University.
Contact: West Virginia University
918 Chestnut Ridge, Suite A8
P.O. Box 6620
Morgantown, WV 26506-6620

**Grassroots Government Educational
Program**
National Association of Towns and
Townships, Washington, DC.
Contact: National Association of
Towns and Townships
1422 K St., NW, Suite 260
Washington, DC 20005

**Leadership Institute for Small
Municipalities (LISM)**
National Forum for Black Public
Administrators (NFBPA)
Contact: National Forum for Black
Administrators
777 N. Capitol St., NE
Washington, DC

**Transformational Leadership Training
(TLT)**
State University of New York at
Binghampton, NY.
Contact: Center for Leadership Studies
LSG 685, P.O. Box 6000
Binghamton, NY 13902-6000

**Community Voices: Leadership
Development for Public Decision
Making: A Multi-State Project for
Limited Resource Audience**
North Carolina Agricultural and
Technical State University,
Greensboro, NC.
Contact: North Carolina A & T
State University
P.O. Box 21928
Greensboro, NC 27420-1928

**Dakota LEADers (Dakota Leadership
Education and Development)**
University of North Dakota, Grand
Forks, ND.
Contact: University of North Dakota
501 Columbia Road
Grand Forks, ND 27420

Training for Rural Officials
Ohio University, Athens, OH.
Contact: ILGARD
67 Bently
Ohio University
Athens, OH 45701

**Program for Local Government
Education**
Washington State University, Pull-
man, WA. A mutual effort between
WSU and the Association of Wash-
ington Cities, the Washington Asso-
ciation of County Officials, and the
Washington State Association of
Counties.
Contact: Cooperative Extension
Washington State University
Pullman, WA 99164-6230

**The Wisconsin Leadership
Development Program.**
University of Wisconsin, Madison, WI.
Contact: University of Wisconsin-
Extension
610 Langdon St., Room 535
Madison, WI 53703-1195

Glossary of Terms

arable land. Land capable of being cultivated, typically by plowing, to grow crops such as wheat or corn.

bioaccumulation. An increase in the concentrations of chemicals in the specific tissues or organs of an organism at higher levels than normal.

biological diversity. The variety of different species, genetic variability with a species, and variety of ecosystems in a given area.

biomagnification. An increase in the concentration of slowly degradable, fat-soluble chemicals in successively higher levels of a food chain.

carrying capacity. The maximum population of a species, or number of individuals or inhabitants, that an environment can support and sustain over time without detrimental effects on basic systems.

community stewardship. See *stewardship.*

conservation. Management of natural resources to provide maximum benefit over a sustained period of time; includes such professional fields as soil and water conservation, forest conservation, and wildlife conservation.

conservation-tillage farming. Crop cultivation systems that minimize soil disturbance to reduce soil erosion, lower costs, and save energy.

conventional-tillage farming. Crop cultivation systems that involve plowing, breaking up the exposed soil, and smoothing the surface.

countryside. A commonly used British term referring to the combination of rural and village landscapes outside obviously urban, densely populated areas. Often used in the United States to describe rural areas.

ecologically sustainable development. Development in which the total human population size and development of the natural resource base in a region are limited to the level that does not exceed the ecological carrying capacity and is therefore sustainable over time.

ecotone. Transitional zone in which one type of ecosystem tends to merge with another.

Environmental Protection Agency (EPA). Federal agency responsible for implementing federal policies—through education, regulation, and environmental research—to control air and water pollution, radiation and pesticide hazards, and hazardous and solid waste disposal.

exponential growth. Growth in which some quantity, such as population or energy consumption, increases by a fixed percentage of the whole over a given period of time. When the increase in quantity is plotted over time, this type of growth produces a J-shaped curve.

extended city. Extended city boundaries that include territory that is essentially rural in character. ("Non-urban portions of an extended city containing one or more areas, each at least 5 square miles in extent and with a population density of less than 100 persons per square mile, which constitute at least 25 percent of the legal city's land area of a total of 25 square miles" [U.S. Census Bureau].)

externality. Social benefits (*external benefits*) and social costs (*negative externalities*) that are not included in the market price of the product or service. Examples in agriculture of *external benefits* to the public from farming are provision of scenic beauty and wildlife habitat; *negative externalities* are the impacts of water or air pollution and destruction of habitat by poor farming practices.

Farm Bureau. The American Farm Bureau Federation, established in 1919, is an independent national organization of farmers and ranchers. There are Farm Bureaus in all 50 states, with 2,800 county Farm Bureaus and a membership of 4.7 million families. According to the Farm Bureau's current statement of purpose adopted in 1920, "The purpose of the Farm Bureau is to make the business of farming more profitable and the community a better place to live."

fee simple. A freehold form of land ownership of virtually infinite duration and of absolute inheritance free of any condition, limitations, or restriction to particular heirs. Fee simple is the most common form of private land ownership in the United States.

Grange. The popular name for The Patrons of Husbandry, a farmers' social organization founded in 1867 and with over 800,000 members in the late nineteenth century. Grangers formed cooperatives and other collective programs, including banks and insurance companies, to help resolve economic problems in agriculture. Today, the Grange is greatly reduced in influence in most rural areas, serving primarily social functions.

homeostasis. Maintenance of favorable internal conditions in a system despite fluctuations in the external conditions affecting the system.

industrial agriculture. Forms of agriculture using large inputs of energy from fossil fuels, water, fertilizers, pesticides, and genetically engineered plants to produce large quantities of crops and livestock products for domestic and export markets.

integrated pest management. The combined use of biological, chemical, and cultivation systems in sequence and timing to reduce pest populations below levels that cause economically unacceptable losses in agriculture and forestry, with minimum environmental impact.

land grant university. The system of state colleges and universities created by the Morrill Act of 1862, which granted lands to the states to provide endowments for the establishment of "agricultural and mechanic colleges." These A&M colleges later became the centers of research in agriculture and technology, with community outreach programs through the cooperative extension service. In some states, the land grant college is a unit within the state university (e.g., University of Minnesota and the University of Vermont); in others, it is a separate state college or university (e.g., Texas A&M and Michigan State University).

limiting factor. The single factor that most limits the growth, abundance, or distribution of the population of a species in an ecosystem. Sometimes used in reference to economic systems.

megalopolis. A region made up of several large cities and their surrounding areas in sufficiently close proximity to be considered a single urban complex. A term often used to describe the continuous urban complex from Boston to Washington, D.C.

metropolitan statistical area (MSA). A city with 50,000 or more inhabitants or an urbanized area of at least 100,000 (75,000 in New England). (See *Statistical Abstract of the United States,* 1995, p. 960.)

Moonies. A popular name for the Unification Church, an international Christian religious sect founded by Rev. Sun Myung Moon in Korea, widespread in the United States, with substantial economic holdings.

Morrill Act. See *land grant university.*

organic farming. A system of agriculture using organic fertilizers (manure, legumes, compost) and natural pest control instead of commercial inorganic fertilizers and synthetic pesticides and herbicides. Certification by regional organic farming associations may also limit use of pharmaceuticals on livestock, genetically manufactured organisms, other chemicals, and types of equipment and packaging that could contaminate food products.

prior appropriation. A legal principle by which the first user of water from a stream establishes a legal right to continued use of the amount originally withdrawn; typically part of the water laws in much of the western United States.

riparian rights. System of water law typical in the eastern United States that guarantees in perpetuity the same quality and quantity of water along the entire length of a stream or river, equally, for all abutting owners.

rural. Geographical areas beyond urban areas of defined size. Sparsely settled hinterland countryside, usually with extensive forests, pasture, and cultivated lands; areas that do not meet definitions of urban or portions of extended cities. See also *extended city, urban area/urban fringe,* and *countryside.*

scientific hypothesis. An educated guess that attempts to explain a scientific law or certain scientific observations, usually based on previous education, research, or extensive study of publications.

sphere of influence. A region over which political and economic influence is wielded by one town or city.

stewardship. The concept of caring for the property of another. Derived from the Anglo-Saxon word *stigweard,* meaning the major domo, caterer, or person in charge of a pigsty. Today used in relation to natural resources conservation; for example, a government forester is the steward of public lands or a private owner is holding his or her lands in stewardship for future generations, with a responsibility to the local community as well.

taking. A legal concept. For example, where a private property owner may lose the full value of his or her property through some change in a regulation.

threshold effect. A harmful or fatal effect of a small change in environmental conditions that exceeds the limit of tolerance of an organism or population of a species.

tragedy of the commons. The depletion or degradation of a resource to which people have free and unregulated access, such as the depletion of fish in ocean areas beyond territorial limits or overgrazing on a common pasture.

urban. Heavily settled and populated areas within major city-suburban complexes.

urban area/urban fringe. As defined by the Census Bureau, an *urban area* is composed of one or more places that together have a minimum of 50,000 persons; *urban fringe* is defined as generally consisting of a contiguous territory having a density of at least 1,000 persons per square mile. Both of these "official" designations include myriad qualifications based on geographical criteria. Note: Complete criteria and definitions are available from the Chief, Geography Division, U.S. Census Bureau, Washington, DC 20233.

urban hinterland. Regional expanses of land relatively distant from major urban areas, but primarily influenced by urban socioeconomic and political systems.

urban population. All persons living in (a) places of 5,000 inhabitants or more, incorporated as cities, villages, boroughs (except Alaska), and towns (except in New England, New York, New Jersey, Pennsylvania and Wisconsin), but excluding those persons living in rural portions of extended cities; (b) unincorporated places of 5,000 inhabitants or more; and (c) other territory, incorporated or unincorporated, included in urbanized areas. See *urban area/urban fringe.*

urban sprawl. Gradual spreading of urban development to relatively unexploited land adjoining the urban area; haphazard growth usually associated with commercial strip development, large shopping mall complexes, and new housing projects beyond existing urban development.

USDA. United States Department of Agriculture. A federal agency responsible for regulating agriculture, promoting domestic and foreign marketing, scientific research, nutrition programs, and management of the national forests and national grasslands. It also includes cooperative programs with the states to provide education and services to farmers through such agencies as the extension system, the Natural Resources Conservation Service, and the U.S. Forest Service.

Bibliography

Adams, John D. 1986. *Transforming leadership: From vision to results.* Alexandria, Va.: Miles River Press.

Alchin, Edmond W., and Pairat Decharin. 1979. An ecosystem approach to community development research. In *Community development research: Concepts, issues, and strategies,* edited by Edward J. Blakley. New York: Human Sciences Press.

American Association of University Women. 1992. *How schools shortchange girls.* Washington, D.C.: The American Association of University Women Educational Foundation.

Auburdene, Patricia, and John Naisbitt. 1992. *Megatrends for women: From liberation to leadership.* New York: Fawcett Columbine.

Ayres, Janet et al. 1990. *Take charge: Economic development in small communities.* Ames, Iowa: North Central Regional Center for Rural Development.

Beattie, Mollie, et al. 1993.*Working with your woodland: A landowner's guide.* Hanover, N.H.: University of New England Press.

Bennis, Warren. 1989. *On becoming a leader.* New York: Addison-Wesley.

Bennis, Warren, and Burt Nanus. 1992. *Leaders: The strategies for taking charge.* New York: Harper and Row.

Bensinger, Nancy, M. Lapping, and E. Blakely. 1994. Rural diversity: Challenge for a century. In *Planning and community equity.* Chicago: Planner's Press.

Berry, Joyce K., and John C. Gordon. 1993. *Environmental leadership: Developing effective skills and styles.* Washington, D.C.: Island Press.

Blacksell, Mark, and Andrew Gilg. 1981. *The countryside: Planning and change.* London: George Allen and Unwin.

Blakley, Edward J., ed. 1979. *Community development research: Concepts, issues, and strategies.* New York: Human Sciences Press.

Bliss, John C., and A. Jeff Martin. 1989. Identifying NIPF management motivations with qualitative methods. *Forest Science* 35 (2): 601–22.

Bohm, David. 1980. *Wholeness and the implicate order.* London: Ark Publications.

Brown, Lyn Mikel, and Carol Gilligan. 1990. *Listening for self and relational voices: A responsive/resisting reader's guide.* Monograph, Cambridge: Harvard Project on Women's Psychology and Girl's Development.

————. 1992. *Meeting at the crossroads: Women's psychology and girl's development*. Cambridge: Harvard University Press.

Brundtland, G. H. 1987. *Our common future: World commission on environment and development*. New York: Oxford University Press.

Bryk, A. S., ed. 1983. *Stakeholder-based evaluation*. San Francisco: Jossey-Bass.

Burns, James McGregor. 1978. *Leadership*. New York: Harper and Row.

Campbell, D. T., and J. C. Stanley. 1966. *Experimental and quasi-experimental designs for research*. Chicago: Rand McNally.

Carson, Rachel L. 1962. *Silent spring*. Boston: Houghton Mifflin.

Chabot, G. 1950. Les conceptions francaises de la science geographique. *Geografisk tidsskrift* 12: 309–21.

Chambers, Robert. 1983. *Rural development: Putting the last first*. London: Longman.

Chen, Huey-tsyh. 1990. *Theory-driven evaluations*. San Francisco: Sage Publications.

Christenson, James A., Kim Fendley, and Jerry W. Robinson Jr. 1989. Community development. In *Community development in perspective,* edited by James A. Christenson and Jerry W. Robinson Jr. Ames: Iowa State University Press.

Clark, Susan. 1996. Citizen participation and personal political power: Case studies of two grassroots environmental groups. Master's thesis, University of Vermont.

Cloke, P. 1977. An index of rurality for England and Wales. *Regional Studies* 11: 31–46.

Clout, Hugh D. 1975. *Regional development in Western Europe*. New York: John Wiley and Sons.

Coles, Robert. 1993. *The call of service: A witness to idealism*. New York: Houghton Mifflin.

Connell, James P., Anne C. Kubisch, Lisbeth B. Schorr, and Carol H. Weiss. 1995. *New approaches to evaluating communities initiatives: Concepts, methods, and contexts*. Washington, D.C.: Aspen Institute.

Covert, R. W. 1977. *Guidelines and criteria for constructing questionnaires*. University of Virginia: Evaluation Research Center.

Covey, Stephen R. 1990. *Principle-centered leadership*. New York: Simon and Schuster.

Cox, Thomas R., Robert S. Marshall, Phillip Drennon Thomas, and Joseph Malone. 1985. *This well-wooded land: Americans and their forests from colonial times to the present*. Lincoln: University of Nebraska Press.

Cronbach, Lee J., and Associates. 1980. *Toward Reform of Program Evaluation*. San Francisco: Jossey-Bass.

Cronon, William. 1983. *Changes in the land: Indians, colonists, and the ecology of New England*. New York: Hill and Wang.

————. 1995. The trouble with wilderness; or, getting back to the wrong nature. In *Uncommon ground: Toward reinventing nature,* edited by William Cronon. New York: Norton.

Daly, Herman E. 1996. *Beyond growth*. Boston: Beacon Press.

Daniels, Thomas L. 1998. *Where city and country collide*. Washington, D.C.: Island Press.

Daniels, Thomas L., John W. Keller, and Mark B. Lapping. 1995. *Small town planning handbook*. Chicago: American Planning Association.

Daniels, Thomas L., and Mark Lapping. 1996. Rural America needs more, not less, planning. *Journal of the American Planning Association* 62 (3): 285–88.

Davidson, O. G. 1990. *Broken heartland: The rise of America's rural ghetto*. New York: Free Press.

Daysh, George H. J. Personal communication. 1963. Daysh was the first Minister of Town and Country Planning in Britain in 1943; later, he was a professor of geography at and then chancellor of the University of Newcastle Upon Tyne in England.

DeVille, Jard. 1984. *The psychology of leadership: Managing resources and relationships*. New York: Mentor Books.

Dubos, Rene. 1972. *A God within*. New York: Charles Scribner.

EPIC. 1993a. *EQI: Vermont environmental quality index*. Burlington: University of Vermont.

———. 1993b. *The EPIC Project*. Burlington: University of Vermont. Videocassette.

———. 1994a. *Clues to the past: Slides and curricular material for teaching community-based local history*. Burlington: University of Vermont.

———. 1994b. *Teaching with architecture: A casebook for classroom and community*. By Kathryn Hatch. Historic Preservation Program, Burlington: University of Vermont.

———. 1994–96. *The EPIC journal*. Burlington: University of Vermont.

———. 1996. *The green guide: Conservation funding opportunities for Vermont landowners*. Burlington: University of Vermont.

Etzioni, Amitai. 1964. *Modern organizations*. Foundations of Modern Sociology Series. Englewood Cliffs, N.J.: Prentice Hall.

Fetterman, David M., Shakeh J. Kaftarian, and Abraham Wandersman, eds. 1996. *Empowerment evaluation: Knowledge and tools for self-assessment and accountability*. Thousand Oaks, Calif.: Sage Publications.

Feuerstein, Marie-Therese. 1986. *Partners in evaluation*. London: Macmillan Publishers.

Fink, A., and J. Kosecoff. 1989. *How to conduct surveys: A step-by-step guide*. Newbury Park, Calif.: Sage Publications.

Fisher, Roger, and William Ury. 1983. *Getting to yes*. Harvard Negotiation Project. New York: Penguin.

Flack, Sarah. 1995. The relationship of light and plant response in a complex pasture sward with particular emphasis on white clover. Master's thesis, Burlington: University of Vermont.

Flader, Susan L., ed. 1983. *The Great Lakes forest: An environmental and social history*. Minneapolis: University of Minnesota Press.

Flora, C., J. Flora, J. Spears, L. Swanson, Mark Lapping, and M. Weinberg. 1992. *Rural communities: Legacy and change*. Boulder: Westview.

Ford, Steve. 1994. Seasonal dairying. *Farm Economics*, Nov./Dec. Penn State Cooperative Extension. Newsletter.

————. 1996. Grazing looks better as dairy profits tighten. *Farm Economics,* Jul./Aug. Penn State Cooperative Extension. Newsletter.

Foster, Rick. 1997. Speaking of leadership: Defining and developing leadership for the twenty-first century. *Proceedings of the Association of Leadership Educators.* 9–12 Jul.

Freeman, H. E., G. D. Sandur, and P. H. Rossi. 1989. *Workbook for evaluation: A systematic approach.* Newbury Park, Calif.: Sage Publications.

French, Hilary. 1998. Investing in the future: Harnessing private capital flows for environmentally sustainable development. *World Watch Paper* 139. Feb. Washington, D.C.: World Watch Institute.

Frey, J. 1983. *Survey research by telephone,* 2nd ed. Newbury Park, Calif.: Sage Publications.

Frey, Lois, and Christine Negra. 1996. Community leadership education in Vermont. *Proceedings of the Annual Conference of the Association of Leadership Educators.* July.

Furano, Kathryn, Linda Z. Jucovy, David P. Racine, and Thomas J. Smith. 1995. *The essential connection: Using evaluation to identify programs worth replicating.* Philadelphia: Replication and Program Strategies.

Galston, William A., and Karen J. Baehler. 1995. *Rural development in the United States: Connecting theory, practice, and possibilities.* Washington, D.C.: Island Press.

Gardner, John W. 1987. *Leadership papers.* Published by author. Sponsored by Independent Sector.

Garkovich, Lorraine E. 1989. Iowa local organizations and leadership in community development. In *Community development in perspective,* edited by James A. Christenson and Jerry W. Robinson Jr. Ames: Iowa State University Press.

Gilligan, Carol. 1987. Women's place in man's life cycle. In *Feminism and methodology,* edited by Sandra Harding. Bloomington: Indiana University Press.

Gilligan, Carol, Lyn Mikel Brown, and Annie Rogers. 1990. Psyche embedded: A place for body, relationships and culture in personality theory. In *Studying persons and lives,* edited by A. Rabin, R. Zucker, R. Emmons, and S. Frank. New York: Springer.

Glacken, C. J. 1967. *Traces on the Rhodian shore: Nature and culture in Western thought from ancient times to the end of the eighteenth century.* Berkeley: University of California Press.

Glesne, Corrine, and Alam Peshkin. 1992. *Becoming qualitative researchers: An introduction.* White Plains, N.Y.: Longman.

Gottman, Jean. 1947. De la methode d'analyse en geographie humaine. *Annales de Geographie* 56: 1–2.

Graham, Hilary, and Jane Jones. 1992. Community development and research. *Community Development Journal* 27 (3): 235–41.

Gray, S. T., and Associates. 1998. *Evaluation with power: A new approach to organizational effectiveness, empowerment, and excellence.* San Francisco: Jossey-Bass.

Greenleaf, Robert K. 1977. *Servant leadership: A journey into the nature of legitimate power and greatness.* New York: Paulist Press.

Guba, E. C., and Y. S. Lincoln. 1981. *Effective evaluation*. San Francisco: Jossey-Bass.

Hagenstein, Perry. 1999. Forest economist, personal communication.

Handy, Charles. 1992. The language of leadership. In *Frontiers of leadership: An essential reader*, edited by Michel Syrett and Clare Hogg. Cambridge, Mass.: Blackwell Publishers.

Hardin, Garrett. 1968. The tragedy of the commons. *Science* 162: 1243–48.

Hartshorne, Richard. 1962. *Perspectives on the nature of geography*. Chicago: Association of American Geographers, Rand McNally.

Heider, John. 1985. *Tao of leadership: Leadership strategies for a new age*. New York: Bantam Books.

Helvarg, David. 1994. *The war against the Greens: The wise use movement, the New Right, and anti-environmental violence*. San Francisco: Sierra Club and Random House.

Henkes, Rollie. 1998. Will your town survive? *The Furrow*. Feb. 30–31.

Henry, G. T. 1990. *Practical sampling*. Newbury Park, Calif.: Sage Publications.

Henry, M., and M. Drabenstoff. 1996. A new microview of the U.S. rural economy. *Economic Review* 81 (2): 53–70.

Herman, J. L. 1987. *Program evaluation kit*, 2nd ed., Newbury Park, Calif.: Sage Publications.

Hocker, Joyce L., and William W. Wilmot. 1985. *Interpersonal conflict*. Dubuque, Iowa: Wm. C. Brown.

Hoskins, W. G. 1970. *The making of the English landscape*. London: Penguin Books.

House, E. R. 1980. *Evaluating with validity*. Beverly Hills, Calif.: Sage Publications.

House, John W., ed. 1966. *Northern geographical essays: In honour of George Henry Daysh*. University of Newcastle upon Tyne, England.

Huey, John. 1994. The new post-heroic leadership. *Fortune Magazine*. 21 Feb., 42–50.

Humboldt, Alexander Von. 1845. *Kosmos: Entwurf Einer Physischen Weltbeschriebung*. Vol. 1. Stuttgart.

Humstone, Beth, and Richard Carbin. 1993. *Report for the countryside institute*. Warren, Vt.: Countryside Institute.

Isaac, S., and W. B. Michael. 1984. *Handbook in research and evaluation*. San Diego: Edits Publishers.

Jacobs, Henry M., ed. 1998. *Who owns rural America: Social conflict over property rights*. Madison: University of Wisconsin Press.

Janvry, Alain de, David Runsten, and Elisabeth Sadoulet. 1987. Toward a rural development program for the United States: A proposal. In *Agriculture and beyond: Rural economic development*, edited by Gene F. Summers, John Bryden, Kenneth Deavers, Howard Newby, and Susan Sechler. Madison: University of Wisconsin Press.

Johnson, Huey D. 1995. *Green plans: Greenprint for sustainability*. Lincoln: University of Nebraska.

Jorling, Thomas. 1982. Alternatives in a time of change. In *New England prospects*, edited by Carl H. Reidel. Hanover N.H.: New England Press.

Kellogg, W. K. Foundation. 1998. *Evaluation handbook*. Battle Creek, Mich.

Keys, J., et al. 1995. *Ecological units of the eastern United States: First approximation*. Atlanta: USDA Forest Service.

Keystone Center. 1996. *The Keystone national policy dialogue on ecosystem management: Final report*. Keystone, Colorado.

Kidder, L. H., C. M. Judd, and E. R. Smith. 1991. *Research methods in social relations*, 6th ed. New York: Holt, Rinehart and Winston.

Kiersey, David, and Marilyn Bates. 1984. *Please understand me: Character and temperament types*. Del Mar, Calif.: Gnosology Books. Distributed by Prometheus Nemesis Book Co.

Kline, Benjamin. 1997. *First along the river: A brief history of the U.S. environmental movement*. San Francisco: Acada Books.

Knight, Richard L., and Sarah F. Bates, eds. 1995. *A new century for natural resources management*. Washington, D.C.: Island Press.

Kosecoff, Jacqueline, and Arlene Fink. 1982. *Evaluation basics: A practitioner's manual*. Newbury Park, Calif.: Sage Publications.

Kroeger, Otto, and Janet M. Thueson. 1988. *Type talk: The sixteen personality types that determine how we live, love, and work*. New York: Dell Publishing.

———. 1992. *Type talk at work: How the sixteen personality types determine your success on the job*. New York: Dell Publishing.

Krueger, R. A. 1988. *Focus groups: A practical guide for applied research*. Newbury Park, Calif.: Sage Publications.

Labaree, Benjamin W. 1982. An historical perspective. In *New England Prospects*. Hanover, N.H.: University Press of New England.

Lake Champlain Basin Program. 1997. *Opportunities for action: An evolving plan for the future of the Lake Champlain Basin*. Grand Isle, Vt.

Lansdale, Sarah. 1996. An analysis of factors contributing to young Vermonter's decisions not to enter dairy farming. Bachelor's thesis, University of Vermont.

Lapping, Mark. 1997. A tradition of rural sustainability: The Amish portrayed. In *Rural sustainability in America*, edited by J. Audirac. New York: John Wiley and Sons. 29–39.

Lapping, Mark, and M. Pfeffes. 1982. Towards a working rural landscape. In *New England Prospects and Choicesc* edited by C. H. Reidel. Hanover, N.H.: University Press of New England. 59–84.

———. 1989. *Rural planning and development in the United States*. New York: Guildford Press.

———. 1997. City and country: New connections, new possibilities. In *Visions of American agriculture*, edited by W. Lockeretz. Ames: Iowa State University Press. 91–104.

Lassey, William R. 1997. *Planning in rural environments*. New York: McGraw-Hill.

Lavrakas, P. J. 1987. *Telephone survey methods: Sampling, selection, and supervision*. Newbury Park, Calif.: Sage Publications.

Leas, Speed B. 1988. *Leadership and conflict*. Nashville, Tenn: Abingdon Press.

Leas, Speed B., and Paul Kittlaus. 1973. *Church fights: Managing conflict in the local church*. Philadelphia: Westminster Press.

Lehnert, Dick. 1996. Grazing raises dairy-farm profits. *Hay and Forage Grower.* March. 53–55.

Leopold, Aldo. 1947. *A Sand County almanac and sketches here and there.* New York: Oxford University Press.

Linney, J. A., and A. Wandersman. 1991. *Prevention plus III: Assessing alcohol and other drug prevention programs at the school and community level.* Rockville, Md.: U.S. Dept. of Health and Human Services.

Linton, David L. 1946. *Discovery education and research.* Inaugural Lecture, University of Sheffield, England.

Littell, J. H. 1986. *Building strong foundations: Evaluation strategies for family resource programs.* Chicago: Family Resource Coalition.

Love, A. J., ed. 1991. *Internal evaluation: Building organizations from within.* Newbury Park, Calif.: Sage Publications.

Lowenthal, David. 1958. *George Perkins Marsh, versatile Vermonter.* New York: Columbia University Press.

Luther, Vicki, and Milan Wall. 1989. *The entrepreneurial community: A strategic leadership approach to community survival.* Lincoln, Neb: Heartland Center for Leadership Development.

———. 1991. *Studying communities in transition: A model for case study research and analysis, featuring a case study of Superior, Nebraska.* Lincoln, Neb.: Heartland Center for Leadership Development.

Mackinder, Halford J. O. 1931. The human habitat. *Scottish Geographical Magazine* 40 (7): 321–35.

MacLeish, William H. 1994. *The day before America: Changing the nature of the continent.* New York: Houghton Mifflin.

Madaus, G., M. Scriven, and D. L. Stufflebeam, eds. 1985. *Evaluation models.* Boston: Kluwer-Nijhoff Publishing.

Maddux, Robert B. 1990. *Delegating for results.* Menlo Park, Calif.: Crisp Publications.

———. 1992. *Team building.* Menlo Park, Calif.: Crisp Publications.

Magdroff, F. 1993. The rise of America's rural ghetto. *Monthly Review* 44 (11): 42.

Margoluis, Richard, and Nick Salafsky. 1998. *Measures of success: Designing, managing, and monitoring conservation and development projects.* Washington, D.C.: Island Press.

Marsh, George Perkins. 1864. *Man and nature: Or physical geography as modified by human action.* New York: Charles Scribner.

Martin, David K. 1996. Confronting change in rural communities: A blueprint for community development in an era of transformation. *Small Town.* Jul./Aug. 26–29.

Matusak, Larraine. 1997. *Finding your voice: Learning to lead anywhere you want and make a difference.* San Francisco: Jossey-Bass.

Maxwell, J. A., and Y. S. Lincoln. 1990. Methodology and epistemology: A dialogue. *Harvard Educational Review* 60 (4): 497–512.

McCullough, Robert. 1995. *The landscape of community: A history of communal forests in New England.* Hanover, N.H.: University Press of New England.

McEvoy, Thom J. 1985a. An educational approach to increase the production benefits from private nonindustrial woodlands in America. In *Technologies to benefit agriculture and wildlife.* Workshop Proceedings. U.S. Congress, Office of Technology Assessment: Washington, D.C. OTA-BP-F-34. May.

———. 1985b. Coverts: Better woodlands through education. *American Forests* 91 (10).

———. 1998. *Legal aspects of owning woodland.* Washington, D.C.: Island Press.

McEvoy, Thom J., J. S. Broderick, and L. Alexander. 1984. A preliminary approach to improve the effectiveness of extension wildlife habitat education: Using demonstration sites and teaching woodland owners how to be extension educators in their communities. *Proceedings of the Fourth National Fish and Wildlife Extension Conference.*

McEvoy, Thom J., J. R. Stewart, and S. Broderick. 1985. *Criteria for evaluating the effectiveness of opinion leaders who promote forest management.* Transactions, N.E. Fish and Wildlife Conference.

McKnight, John L., and John Kretzmann. 1990. *Mapping community capacity.* Chicago: Center for Urban Affairs and Policy Research at Northwestern University.

McNally, David. 1990. *Even eagles need a push: Learning to soar in a changing world.* New York: Delacorte Press.

Miles, M. B., and A. M. Huberman. 1994. *Qualitative data analysis: An expanded sourcebook,* 2nd ed., Thousand Oaks, Calif.: Sage Publications.

Miller, Char. 1997. *American Forests: Nature, Culture, and Politics.* Lawrence: University Press of Kansas.

Moen, Janet Kelly, and Kim Nesvig. 1993. Collaboration and community: How small towns in the Dakotas organized for leadership and economic development. *Small Town* Sept./Oct. 26–29.

Moore, Kathryn M., and Ann M. Salimbene. 1991. The dynamics of the mentor-protégé relationship in developing women as academic leaders. *Journal of Educational Equity and Leadership* 31: 51–64.

Morris, Lynn Lyons, and Carol Taylor Fitz-Gibbon. 1978a. *How to deal with goals and objectives.* Beverly Hills, Calif.: Sage Publications.

———. 1978b. *How to design a program evaluation.* Beverly Hills, Calif.: Sage Publications.

———. 1978c. *How to measure program implementation.* Beverly Hills, Calif.: Sage Publications.

———. 1978d. *How to present an evaluation report.* Beverly Hills, Calif.: Sage Publications.

Morrison, Ann M. 1987. *Breaking the glass ceiling: Can women reach the top of America's largest corporations?* San Francisco: Jossey-Bass.

———. 1993. *The new leaders: Guidelines on leadership diversity in America.* San Francisco: Jossey-Bass.

Muenscher, Walter. 1987.*Weeds.* Albany, N.Y.: Cornell University Press.

Murphy, Bill, Joshua P. Silman, Lisa E. Mccrory, Sarah E. Flack, Abdon L. Schmitt, and Nthoana M. Mzamane. 1994. Greener pastures on your side of the fence: Better farming with Voisin grazing management of permanent pastures. *American Journal of Alternative Agriculture* 1 (4): 147–52.

———. 1997. Management of natural Kentucky bluegrass-white clover pasture. *American Journal of Alternative Agriculture* 12 (3): 140–42.

——. 1998. *Greener pastures on your side of the fence,* 4th ed. Colchester, Vt.: Arriba Publishing.

Murray, Michael, and Larry Dunn. 1996. *Revitalizing rural America: A perspective on collaboration and community.* New York: John Wiley and Sons.

Myers, Isabel Briggs, and Peter B. Myers. 1980. *Gifts differing: Understanding personality type.* Palo Alto, Calif.: CPP Books. Reprinted 1993.

Nanus, Burt. 1992. *Visionary leadership: Creating a compelling sense of direction for your organization.* San Francisco: Jossey-Bass.

Nation, Allan. 1988. *Holistic resource management.* Washington, D.C.: Island Press.

National Center for Clinical Infant Programs. 1987. *Charting change in infants, families, and services: A guide to program evaluation for administrators and practitioners.* Washington, D.C.

Negra, Christine. 1998. *Identifying factors leading to effective local conservation commissions.* Burlington: University of Vermont Extension.

Nielson, Joyce M. 1987. *Evaluating service programs for infants, toddlers, and their families: A guide for policy makers and funders.* Washington, D.C.

——. 1990. Introduction. *Feminist Research Methods,* edited by J. Neilson. Boulder, Colo.: Westview Press.

Nierenberg, Gerald I. 1984. *The art of negotiating.* New York: Simon and Schuster. Reprinted 1968.

O'Brien, David J., Edward W. Hassinger, Ralph B. Brown, and James R. Pinkerton. 1991. The social networks of leaders in more or less viable rural communities. *Rural Sociology* 56 (4): 699–716.

Ogilvie, Alan G. 1938. The relations of geology and geography. *Geography* 22: 75–82.

Patton, Michael Quinn. 1982. *Practical evaluation.* Newbury Park, Calif.: Sage Publications.

——. 1990. *Qualitative evaluation and research methods,* 2nd ed. Newbury Park, Calif.: Sage Publications.

——. 1997. *Utilization-focused evaluation: The new century text,* 3rd ed. Beverly Hills, Calif.: Sage Publications.

Petulla, Joseph M. 1997. *American environmental history.* Columbus, Ohio: Merrill Publishing.

Pierce, Neal, and Curtis Johnson. 1997. *Boundary crossers: Community leadership for a global age.* University of Maryland, College Park: The Academy of Leadership Press.

Power, Thomas M. 1996. *Lost landscapes and failed economies.* Washington, D.C.: Island Press.

Rasch, Virginia J. 1998. *Vermont conservation handbook.* Adamant, Vt.: Association of Vermont Conservation Commissions.

Reason, Peter. 1993. *Human inquiry in action: Developments in new paradigm research.* Newbury Park, Calif.: Sage Publications.

Reidel, Carl. 1982. *New England prospects.* Hanover, N.H.: University Press of New England.

——. 1987. Leadership land. *Journal of Forestry* July. 17–21.

——. 1995. The great green east: Lands everyone wants. *American Forests* 101 (9): 12–15.

Reidel, Carl, and Jean Richardson. 1992. A vision of the future for federal land management: Public and private cooperative paradigm. In *Multiple use and sustained yield: Changing philosophies for federal land management?* Washington, D.C.: Congressional Research Service, Library of Congress, Dec. 143–68.

———. 1995. *Strategic environmental leadership in a time of change.* Monograph, William J. Donlon Visiting Professorship in Environmental Science. Syracuse, N.Y.: SUNY College of Environmental Science and Forestry.

Reinharz, Shulamit. 1983. Experimental analysis: A contribution to feminist research. In *Theories of Women's Studies,* edited by G. Bowles and R. Klien. Boston: Routeledge and Kegan Paul.

Richardson, Jean. 1970. Domestication of the pecan *(Carya illinoensis)* in North America. Ph.D diss., University of Wisconsin. Chicago: University of Chicago Microfilms.

———. 1988. New landscapes for old: Are we asking the right questions? In *Proceedings of a conference on planning for the changing landscape of rural New England: Blending theory and practice.* Durham, N.H.: New England Center.

———. 1990. Comparative trends in integrated land use planning. In *Proceedings of the twentieth symposium of the European Association of Agricultural Economists,* edited by M. C. Whitby and P. J. Dawson. Newcastle upon Tyne, England: University of Newcastle upon Tyne.

———. 1994. Leadership in public policy and environmental affairs. In *Leadership in science,* edited by Wilbur W. Everett. Arkadelphia, Ark.: Ouachita Baptist University.

———. 1996. Building community in rural areas. *Proceedings of the Annual Conference of the Association of Leadership Educators.* July 1–7.

———. 1997. Strategic leadership: From fragmented thinking to interdisciplinary perspectives. In *A Leadership Journal: Women in Leadership—Sharing the Vision* 1 (2): 91–100.

———. 1998. Re-weaving the fabric of rural Vermont: The EPIC project. *Small Town.* Jan./Feb. 4–15.

Riso, Don Richard. 1987. *Personality types: Using the enneagram for self-discovery.* Boston: Houghton Mifflin.

Robert, Henry M. 1990. *Robert's rules of order.* Glenview, Ill.: Foresman.

Rogers, Everett M. 1983. *Diffusion of innovations,* 4th ed. New York: Free Press.

Rossi, Peter H., and Howard E. Freeman. 1993. *Evaluation: A systematic approach.* Newbury Park, Calif.: Sage Publications.

Salant, Priscilla, and Anita J. Waller. 1995. *Guide to rural data.* Washington, D.C.: Island Press.

Sanders, James R. 1994. *The program evaluation standards: How to assess evaluations of educational programs,* 2nd ed. Thousand Oaks, Calif.: Sage Publications.

Sauer, Carl Ortwin. 1925. *The morphology of the landscape.* Berkeley: University of California Publications in Geography, 2: 19–53.

———. 1967. *Man and life: A selection for the writings of Carl Ortwin Sauer,* edited by John Leighly. Berkeley: University of California Press.

Savitt, Ronald, and Pauline Sullivan. 1995. Developing marketing plans for redeveloping small rural communities. Paper presented at Eighth International Conference on Research in Distributive Trades, hosted by CESCOM, 1–2 Sept. at Universita Bocconi, Milan.

Savory, Allan. 1998. *Holistic resource management.* Washington, D.C.: Island Press.

Saxe, L., and M. Fine. 1981. *Social experiments: Methods for design and evaluation.* Beverly Hills, Calif.: Sage Publications.

Schalock, Robert L., and Craig V. D. Thornton. 1988. *Program evaluation: A field guide for administrators.* New York: Plenum Press.

Schorr, Lisbeth B., and Anne C. Kubisch. 1995. New approaches to evaluation: Helping Sister Mary Paul, Geoff Canada, and Otis Johnson while convincing Pat Moynihan, Newt Gingrich, and the American public. Presentation to the Annie E. Casey Foundation Annual Research/ Evaluation Conference: Using Research and Evaluation Information to Improve Programs and Policies. Sept.

Scriven, Michael. 1991. *Evaluation thesaurus,* 4th ed., Newbury Park, Calif.: Sage Publications.

Shadish, William R., Jr., Thomas D. Cook, and Laura C. Leviton. 1991. *Foundations of program evaluation: Theories of practice.* Newbury Park, Calif.: Sage Publications.

Silva, Karen E. 1994. *Meetings that work.* New York: Business One, Irwin/Mirror Press.

Sitarz, Daniel, ed. 1998. *Sustainable America: America's environment, economy, and society in the twenty-first century.* Carbondale, Ill.: Earth Press.

Smith, M. F. 1989. *Evaluability assessment: A practical approach.* Boston: Kluwer Academic Publishers.

Smith, Perry M. 1993. *Taking charge: Making the right choices.* Garden City Park, N.Y.: Avery Publishing Group.

Solberg, Dustin. 1999. The disappearing farm. *High Country News.* 21 June. 31 (12).

Sonnerup, Kerstin, Ronald Savitt, and Pauline Sullivan. 1997. Universities working with communities to foster entrepreneurship: A case study in Vermont. *Economic Development Review* Summer. 36–42.

Speizer, Jeanne J. 1981. Role models, mentors, and sponsors: The elusive concepts. *Signs: Journal of Women Culture and Society* 6: 692–712.

Spiegel, Hans B. C. 1979. Theoretical research and community development practice. In *Community development research: Concepts, issues, and strategies,* edited by Edward J. Blakley. New York: Human Sciences Press.

Stainback, W., and S. Stainback. 1988. *Understanding and conducting qualitative research.* Dubuque, Iowa: Kendall/Hunt Publishing Company.

Starrels, M., S. Bould, and L. Nichols. 1994. The feminization of poverty in the United States: Gender, race, ethnicity, and family factors. *Journal of Family Issues* Dec. 15 (4) 590–607.

Stockdill, Stacey Hueftle. 1993. *How to evaluate foundation programs.* St. Paul, Minn.: The Saint Paul Foundation.

Stohr, Walter B. 1987. Local initiatives in rural areas. In *Agriculture and beyond: Rural economic development,* edited by Gene F. Summers, John

Bryden, Kenneth Deavers, Howard Newby, and Susan Sechler. Madison: University of Wisconsin Press.

Sullivan, Pauline, and Ronald Savitt. 1997. Store patronage and lifestyle factors: Implications for rural grocery retailers. *International Journal of Retail Distribution Management* 25 (11): 351–64.

Suzuki, David, and Peter Knudtson. 1992. *Wisdom of the elders: Sacred native stories of nature.* New York: Bantam Books.

Swan, William S. 1991. *How to do a superior performance appraisal.* New York: Wiley and Sons.

Swanson, Bert E., Richard A. Cohen, and Edith P. Swanson. 1979. *Small towns and small towners: A framework for survival and growth.* London: Sage Publications.

Swanson, Louis E. 1989. The rural development dilemma. *Resources for the Future.* Summer. 96: 14–16.

Syrett, Michel, and Clare Hogg. 1992. *Frontiers of leadership: An essential reader.* Cambridge: Blackwell Publishers.

Tannen, Deborah. 1990. *You just don't understand: Women and men in conversation.* New York: Ballentine.

Thompson, Zadock. 1842. *Thompson's Vermont: History of Vermont, rural, civil, and statistical.* Burlington, Vt.: Chancy Goodrich.

Thorburn, Thomas L. 1996. W.K. Kellogg Foundation, personal communication.

Tjosvold, Dean, and Mary M. Tjosvold. 1993. *The emerging leader: Ways to a stronger team.* New York: Lexington/Macmillan.

Tracy, Diane. 1990. *Ten steps to empowerment: A common sense guide to managing people.* New York: Quill, William Morrow.

Travers, J. R., and R. J. Light. 1982. *Learning from experience: Evaluating early childhood demonstration programs.* Washington, D.C.: National Academy Press.

Tregoe, Benjamin B., et al. 1989. *Vision in action: Putting a winning strategy to work.* New York: Simon and Schuster.

Uhlig, Harald. 1956. Die Kulturalandscaft: Methoden der Forschung und das Beispiel Nordostengland. *Kolner Geographishe Arbeiten* 1–98.

United Way of America. 1995. *Current United Way approaches to measuring program outcomes and community change.* Alexandria, Va.: United Way of America.

Ury, William. 1993. *Getting past no: Negotiating your way from confrontation to cooperation.* New York: Bantam Books.

USDA. 1937. *Yearbook of agriculture.* Washington, D.C.: U.S. Government Printing Office.

———. 1995. *Understanding rural America.* Economic Research Service, Agricultural Information Bulletin Number 710.

Van der Eyken, W. 1992. *Introducing evaluation.* The Hague: Bernard van Leer Foundation.

Vidal de la Blache, Paul. 1896. Les principes de la geographie generale. *Annales de Geographie* 5: 129–42.

———. 1925. *Principes de geographie humaine.* Paris.

Vermont State Agency of Human Services. 1998. *The social well-being of Vermonters, 1997 and 1998.* Montpelier, Vt.

Voison, A. 1988. *Grass productivity*. Washington, D.C: Island Press. (Originally published 1959.)

Voth, Donald E. 1979a. Problems in the evaluation of community development efforts. In *Community development research: Concepts, issues, and strategies*, edited by Edward J. Blakley. New York: Human Sciences Press.

———. 1979b. Social action research in community development. In *Community development research: Concepts, issues, and strategies*, edited by Edward J. Blakley. New York: Human Sciences Press.

———. 1989. Evaluation for community development. In *Community development in perspective*, edited by James A. Christenson and Jerry W. Robinson Jr. Ames: Iowa State University Press.

Wallerstein, Nina. 1993. Empowerment and health: The theory and practice of community change. *Community Development Journal* 2 (3): 218–27.

Weiss, Carol H. 1995. Nothing as practical as good theory: Exploring theory-based evaluation for comprehensive community initiatives for children and families. In *New approaches to evaluating community initiatives: Concepts, methods and contexts*, edited by James Connell et al. Washington, D.C.: Aspen Institute.

Weiss, H. B., and R. Halpern. 1989. *The challenges of evaluating state family support and education initiatives: An evaluation framework*. Cambridge, Mass.: Harvard Family Research Project.

Weiss, H. B., and F. H. Jacobs, eds. 1988. *Evaluating family programs*. New York: Aldine de Gruyter.

Welch, Mary Scott. 1981. *Networking: The great new way for women to get ahead*. New York: Harcourt Brace.

Wheatley, Margaret. 1992. *Leadership and the new science: Learning about organization from an orderly universe*. San Francisco: Berrett-Koehler.

Whorley, Joseph S., Harry P. Hatry, and Kathryn E. Newcomer, eds. 1994. *Handbook of practical program evaluation*. San Francisco: Jossey-Bass.

Wibberly, G. P. 1954. Some aspects of problem rural areas in Britain. *Geographical Journal* Mar. 43–61.

Wilkin, David, Leslie Hallam, and Marie-Anne Doggett. 1992. *Measures of need and outcome for primary health care*. Oxford: Oxford University Press.

Williams, Harold S., Arthur Y. Webb, and William J. Phillips. 1993. *Outcome funding: A new approach to targeted grantmaking*, 2nd ed. Rensselaerville, N.Y.: The Rensselaerville Institute.

Witten, Michele. 1996. Factors affecting farmer participation in federal cost-sharing programs for soil and water conservation. Master's thesis, Burlington: University of Vermont.

Worthen, Blaine, James R. Sanders, and Jody L. Fitzpatrick. 1997. *Program evaluation: Alternative approaches and practical guidelines*, 2nd ed. White Plains, N.Y.: Longman.

Yavorsky, D. K. 1984. *Discrepancy evaluation: A practitioner's guide*. Charlottesville: University of Virginia, Evaluation Research Center.

Yin, R. K. 1989. *Case study research: Design and methods*, rev. ed. Newbury Park, Calif.: Sage Publications.

About the Author

Jean Richardson is an associate professor of environmental studies, natural resources, and geography (in three different academic units) at the University of Vermont, where she was director of EPIC, a rural community-development project, as well as president of the Faculty Senate. She is an adjunct faculty member at the Vermont Law School and president of a small nonprofit environmental-policy organization. She has served on many boards and commissions, from chair of her hometown planning and zoning board, to the State Environmental (Appeals) Board, to a presidential appointment to the trilateral Commission for Environmental Cooperation as part of the North American Free Trade Agreement. A native of rural Northumberland, England, on the border with Scotland, Jean has lived and traveled extensively in Old World Europe and the New World, as well as in New Zealand, East Africa, China, and Siberia. She ran a family sheep farm in Vermont with her first husband and her children and is skilled in many traditional rural activities, such as gardening, home canning, bread and cheese making, spinning and knitting, and making maple syrup. She holds a Ph.D. in biogeography from the University of Wisconsin, Madison, and completed a law clerkship in Vermont. She is the author and coauthor of numerous articles and reports, including recent work on dioxin contamination of dairy products. Today she and her second husband live on Lewis Creek in Vermont, and her daughters live and work close by. One of her daughters, now married, runs the family farm.

About the Cover Artist

Sabra Field was born in Tulsa, Oklahoma, and she grew up in the metropolitan New York area, graduating from the Bronxville High School in 1953. She earned a B.A. with honors in the arts from Middlebury

College in Vermont and an honorary doctorate of arts in 1991. She holds the M.A.T. degree from Wesleyan. Sabra has lived and worked in Vermont since 1969 as a printmaker. Her prints and books are widely acclaimed, and she has numerous national and international awards. She designed the 1991 Bicentennial postage stamp. Her favorite commissions remain landscape designs for hot air balloons. Her Web site is <www.sabrafield.com>.

Index